I0889595

Praise for *Repoliticizing the Word Through Poetry and Preaching*

"*Repoliticizing the Word Through Poetry and Preaching* imaginatively reconfigures the religious language in the world and words of Black women, from their first publications in the eighteenth century to their rapped, sung, and written texts today. Whether in the elegies of Phillis Wheatley or the lyrics of Lauryn Hill, Professor Langley has you pondering the texts of Black women's writing."

—Rafia Zafar, professor emerita, Washington University in St. Louis

"April Langley's beautifully written study exceeds her aim of bringing the African Sankofa bird and contemporary Afrofuturism to bear on centuries of U.S. Black women's spiritual narratives. More than 'a work of remembrance and re-membering,' *Repoliticizing the Word Through Poetry and Preaching* celebrates ways Black holy women proclaim political power with integrity, insight, and splendor."

—Joycelyn K. Moody, Sue E. Denman Distinguished Chair in American Literature, University of Texas at San Antonio

"April C. E. Langley offers a brilliant argument that Sankofism and Afrofuturism are braided together in the earliest Black women's writing and in modern Black women's cultural productions. From Phillis Wheatley through Maria Stewart and Jarena Lee to our present moment, Black women have, like the symbol of the Sankofa bird, returned to origins to reclaim the forgotten—for instance, liberatory meanings of scripture as well as racist acts of politicization—while, at the same time, defining a future in which Black women's lives matter. Indeed, Langley herself does both in *Repoliticizing the Word Through Poetry and Preaching*. This wide-ranging book should claim the attention of anyone wishing to understand the way responses to our current crises can be seen first outlined in Black women's works."

—John Saillant, professor of English and history, Western Michigan University

"Langley not only traces the religio-political work of Phillis Wheatley Peters, Maria Stewart, and Jarena Lee through what she calls their WordsWork—the repoliticizing of Christianity in both secular and religious realms—but also becomes a profound WordsWorker herself, bringing forward urgent wisdom from the past. Langley shows that Black women's spiritual writing in early America is a crucial site for imagining Black futures that in the current moment of regressive racial politics provides a particularly poignant road map forward."

—Wendy Raphael Roberts, author of *Awakening Verse: The Poetics of Early American Evangelicalism*

REPOLITICIZING THE WORD THROUGH POETRY AND PREACHING

African American Life Series

A complete listing of the books in this series can be found online at wsupress.wayne.edu.

REPOLITICIZING THE WORD THROUGH POETRY AND PREACHING

Early Black Christian Women's Lives Matter

April C. E. Langley

WAYNE STATE UNIVERSITY PRESS
DETROIT

ISBN 9780814349892 (paperback)
ISBN 9780814349908 (hardcover)
ISBN 9780814349915 (ebook)

Library of Congress Control Number: 2025932089

Cover illustration and design by Kristle Marshall.

Published with support from the Arthur L. Johnson Fund for African American Studies.

Wayne State University Press rests on Waawiyaataanong, also referred to as Detroit, the ancestral and contemporary homeland of the Three Fires Confederacy. These sovereign lands were granted by the Ojibwe, Odawa, Potawatomi, and Wyandot Nations, in 1807, through the Treaty of Detroit. Wayne State University Press affirms Indigenous sovereignty and honors all tribes with a connection to Detroit. With our Native neighbors, the press works to advance educational equity and promote a better future for the earth and all people.

Wayne State University Press
Leonard N. Simons Building
4809 Woodward Avenue
Detroit, Michigan 48201-1309

Visit us online at wsupress.wayne.edu.

In loving memory of my mother, Alga Faye Brown,

August 16, 1929–April 13, 2023,

whose faith in God and commitment to living a life that matters inspired me.

Long before the hashtags,

you insisted on the truth that our lives matter.

"Don't let anyone tell you who you are. You belong to God."

I love you, Mommy.

Contents

Preface

Why My Life Matters

It was 2020, with the pandemic in full force, and I had just begun to serve as interim chair of English in addition to my duties as chair of the Black Studies Department. As a longtime associate professor who had all but given up on ever making full professor, I decided to polish off some teaching and research notes with ideas that I'd been wanting to write about for some time, to try my hand at integrating research into my very busy administrative academic schedule. With all that I was juggling, it seems counterintuitive that I would have chosen this particular time to write a scholarly article, but it felt like something was calling me, urging me toward fleshing out this idea I couldn't shake—words that just would not cease. It was as if my ancestors were calling out to me across time with reminders that "this too shall pass." Their herstories were urging me on, and I had lived so long with them in my memory that their lives started taking on new dimensions in my present. They survived smallpox, yellow fever, high infant mortality rates, slavery, indentured servitude and, of course, racism and sexism. How did they survive? I knew well how, because after decades of teaching hundreds of students in various disciplines—literature, Black studies, religious studies, and women's and gender studies—much of what I taught in nearly every single course had encompassed some element or aspect of lives that included attention to Black women's secular and spiritual selves. Their lives mattered not only for the rich cultural, historical, and literary knowledge they supplied, but also for the way their wisdom validated my own experiences—my choices to embrace intellect with faith. Their lives made my life matter. So during those challenging times, with all that was happening, I kept my faith intact. I prayed and meditated daily, with a fervent devotion to maintaining my connection to a life beyond the daily hashtags of Black lives that had ceased to matter—of those who were being lost every day.

There was a tickertape of COVID deaths, a rise in anti-Black violence, and a cultural climate in which death and race- and gender-based divisiveness was normalized, at least from my perspective. Attending my church online, I noticed an unmistakable rise in attendance. Not only had these crises driven many in my communities back to church, or perhaps to a first-time declaration of faith, but in those spaces, I began to notice a coming together of people who were seeing their own humanity in a different light, perhaps for the very first time. Beyond the spiritual aspects, there seemed to be a rising awareness of the need to address the political climate that had, in the worst of times, fueled a resurgence of the myth of white supremacy. Black women seemed especially at risk—from a loss of employment to domestic violence and the elevated stress levels of those already overstressed that was (then) exacerbated by underlying health conditions, especially for those who were primary caregivers of children and the elderly. COVID opened the floodgates of existing disparities: the overcrowding of shelters, lack of access to medical care, loss of income, and death—way too many deaths. Not surprisingly, it was during this time that Black women—as they have always done throughout history—pivoted: they started their own businesses, they created collectives for wellness: physical, political, and economic. Black women fought back against the triple pandemics of COVID, racism, and sexism by establishing their own ways of resisting and rising in the worst of times. I was among the many who were lifted by the power, presence, perseverance, and prayers of my sistahs. And I recalled: this is what we have always done. I remember my mother taking in typing, cleaning at a bakery at night after leaving her pink-collar job, walking miles to work during a massive bus strike, and always praying that God would stretch that last bit of bread until the next payday, making sure her daughter earned high marks in school and fighting off the ravages of poverty and prejudice that tried to take us out.

It was prayer I kept coming back to, time and time again. I reflected on those long prayers—at home, in church, at gatherings of family and/or friends (large or small), which always seemed to be followed by strategies and conversations about how to best navigate the hard times. As their prayers revealed, literally called out, the burdens and needs of each person prayed for, folks would come together to figure out how best to be of service, with God's help, of course. Sometimes, when I reflect on Phillis Wheatley's poems, Jarena Lee's sermons, and Maria Stewart's speeches, they all feel like long prayers—offering us a way out of no way—calling us to come back to retrieve what has always sustained us—community, humanity, and yes, our faith in times of crises. Most important, it was not a blind faith, but rather one that called us to use every bit of everything with which we had been blessed, including our mind power—the kind of wisdom and intellect that empowers us with strategies for resisting and overcoming. As I navigated my own burdens during this time, most pressing was my aging mother, who had Alzheimer's and lived in a nursing home. My spouse and I had been primary caretakers and supporters for her for so long, long before she entered long-term care. For me, each day was filled with stress. Waking up and wondering if this would be the day I would get the call, as so many other people had, that COVID had taken my parent. I look back and I'm grateful that she survived COVID more than once, as well as several hospital stays for non-COVID-related illnesses, and that I was able—thanks to the amazing staff at her care facility—to make window visits, have FaceTime calls, and receive frequent health updates. Managing two academic units, teaching online, serving on multiple university task forces and committees, participating in faculty mid-career programs, all while working remotely from a rural location with limited reliable internet service—cellular phone and jetpacks—during which time we lost power and water due to an ice storm that lasted almost two weeks, I kept writing and praying. I mostly wrote poetry and nonfiction prose with some meditations; I just could not seem to pull my words together to write a scholarly article. Indeed, it seemed I could write anything but what I was determined needed to be said.

Perhaps this was the problem. What needed to be said, that is, written, could not be done within a "scholarly" frame; or so I thought. If you've been with me up until now, it won't be difficult to imagine some possible sources of my academic writer's block. Taking a reflective step back to gain some perspective on my own mindset, I realized that writing was not the problem. Neither, surprisingly, were some of the challenges created by the COVID pandemic. Mine is not a COVID narrative—well, not entirely. Yes, the difficulties and obstacles were most certainly and vividly revealed and exacerbated by the health pandemic; however, it was the race-gender pandemics that created the most serious troubling of my writerly spirit. In Tsitsi Dangarembga's words, it was "writing while Black and female" that triggered the existing difficulty.[1] I was experiencing a "wound" (23) that was a symptom of being a Black woman writer. How else could I explain such trepidation after already publishing one book and having been the author of several articles? So I prayed and did what so many women and others had done and were doing. I went back to look for what was most valuable. What I found, and what I decided was most valuable to bring forward, was in the maps that Wheatley, Stewart, Lee, and other foremothers left. Drawing upon the perseverance and power of words—in this case my own words—I retrieved the lessons that I had taught others.

That is, I did what I'd learned and what I'd taught my students who struggled with writing for years. I took my own advice and started free-writing from my many teaching and research notes—especially those research notes that I had all but shredded (digitally speaking). Once I completed this "dirty" draft, I took the advice of a wise scholarly mentor or two to get another pair of eyes on it to see if it was worth moving forward. To my surprise, two extremely busy people agreed to read what at the time I felt was a complete "mess," and to tell the truth, it was. Nonetheless, they took time to read and offer notes, with the most encouraging comments about the substance of the essay but with many suggestions about the format. The most prominent, and I now realize most promising, feedback was that this essay really seemed more like a draft of a book. There was simply too much to be contained in one essay. At the time I tried diligently to revise the essay, believing that if I could only get an article published this year, as it had been a couple of years since I'd published a peer-reviewed essay, I might feel more like I mattered in the Academy as a scholar and a thinker, not merely as a Black woman willing to do a lot of extra service labor. I would begin to see myself as more than the way I'd heard others like me described: just a "long in the tooth" associate who was "stuck in the middle" and whose research was no longer relevant. Thousands of words later, when I had far exceeded any reasonable article length and there was no turning back, I answered the call to write this book. It would matter because the lives of the women I was writing about mattered.

The lives of Black, Christian, and politically engaged artivists, writers whose words, languages, and lives I had lived with for many decades mattered significantly not only to me but also to countless others whose lives matter—regardless of any constructs—then and now. This was the birth of #EarlyBlackChristianWomensLivesMatter, a book that matters because I matter.

Repoliticize

By Dr. April Langley

You politicize, you politicize,
As we rehearse the meaning of your lies

You politicize, you politicize,
And our lives no longer matter

You politicize, you politicize,
And we endure as you rewrite our history

You politicize, you politicize,
Carnivorously feasting on our fears of the other

You politicize, you politicize,
Clinging desperately to the fragile walls of hate

And We RE-politicize, We RE-politicize
With the Truth of our creation and the Gospel of our being

We RE-politicize, We RE-politicize
Taking back the bones you stole, moving forward with our ancestors

And We RE-politicize, We RE-politicize
Recovering what was never really lost

And We RE-politicize, We RE-politicize
With Fortitude and Bravery, the everlasting connectedness of our humanity

And We are Not Afraid,
Not of lies, not of separation, not of grief, not of loss, not of others
Nor of the frail, decaying walls of hate you hastily built out of fear

And we are Truth moving forward . . .
Crushing barricades, breaking chains
RE-Politicizing the Word and Worlds through Poetry, Preaching,
And WE who Matter

Prologue

The Akan proverb Sankofa (*san* [return], *ko* [go], *fa* [look, seek, take]) reminds us that "it is not taboo to go back and fetch that which you have forgotten." This invitation that I have enthusiastically accepted, this call to which I have responded to re-member that which has been and continues to be dismembered (and dis-remembered) raises several questions as I engage the connections between Black women across four centuries through a Sankofic lens: why do the eighteenth- and nineteenth-century activist women writers I look at in this study matter? What purpose does a consideration of how they used religion to set a political agenda for Black women specifically—and Black people as a whole—to challenge dominant discourses that attempted to oppress and silence their voices serve? To whom, for whom, and to what end are their voices relevant to a generation for whom the evidence of widespread violence against Black women, children, and men is easily accessible through social, conventional, and personal media?[1] Can this snapshot of early Black women's use of strategies that appear to deploy the "master's tools" be useful at a time when White privilege and nationalism seem to operate with impunity?[2] That is, what impact can those words and strategies of early social justice activists or freedom strategists and warriors have on the conscience, ethics, or morality of a rapidly filling swamp of deplorable actors who are unapologetically unaccountable to, or for, any sense of rules and fairness? Moreover, what possible value could such methods, grounded in biblical texts and contexts, as those employed by women like Phillis Wheatley, Maria Stewart, and Jarena Lee bequeath to a generation of survivors so far from their foremothers' faith?[3] The idea of faith that I invoke here is meant to signify the notion of "we've come this far by faith" and its civil rights roots/routes in the Christian faith, which today seems further from any Black experience in the United States than in all previous generations. Indeed, "the Black church" is nothing more than an idiom that many argue holds little in the way of reality as a center of spiritual and political renewal and strategy. Shouldn't we be moving forward, not looking back? Shouldn't we be speaking truth to power through an Afrofuturistic lens rather than a Sankofic one? The short answer: we should use both, and it is most assuredly what this book intends. We cannot move forward without looking back and retrieving what is of most value to us from the past, bringing it into our present and future.

In "The Emergence of *Sankofa* Practice in the United States: A Modern History," Christel N. Temple articulates popular African Diaspora practices in the use of Sankofa as a means of "retrieving what was lost" (126–127). My consideration of Sankofic lenses is meant to signify "several orientations toward African consciousness," including but not limited to "cultural behaviors documented in its early usage by enslaved Africans who came to the Americas" (128). Important is their "later usage . . . as resistance . . . rejecting Eurocentric . . . world views and insisting on the relevance of African conceptual possibilities . . . and symbolic gestures of Diasporan Africans interested in general forms of 'returning to the source'" (128). I am most interested in how we might "profit in the present from experiences of the past to prosper in the future" (Anne Mette Jørgensen, qtd. in Temple 136). In Wole Soyinka's terms, I am looking at how early Black women's lives matter in the context of a "past [that must] address its present." Of course, connections between Sankofic and Afrofuturistic lenses hinge on an understanding of the forward-moving aspects of Sankofa. The symbol and meaning of Sankofa as the Akan bird that goes back to retrieve must necessarily bring forward what is most valuable for the future. As such, the journey to our past, as we observe in the women of this study, is ultimately about securing through imagining a more viable future. Mark Dery, whose 1994 "Black to Future" engages the question of "why . . . so few African Americans write science fiction, a genre whose close encounters with the other . . . seem uniquely suited to the concerns of African-American novelists," coined the term *Afrofuturism* as a concept to describe "African-American signification that appropriates images of technology and a prosthetically enhanced future" (180). Therefore, what I want to suggest by raising this somewhat hypophoric question is to challenge any assumptions about an adversarial relationship between Afrofuturism and Sankofa, and to underscore my argument about the value of early Black women's spiritual writing as a plausible point of return and retrieval, one of those "unlikely places" (182) of departure to "imagine possible futures" (180).

Scholars have already begun to make connections between Wheatley and Afrofuturism, and it's not at all a stretch. In fact, if any artist could be seen as imagining a future by appropriating technology (for example, the Bible and Judeo-Christian rhetoric, the neoclassical, and myths), it would be Wheatley—and Stewart and Lee are also among this group for whom the kaleidoscopic range of Afrofuturism matters. In her 2019 master's thesis, "The Mammy, the Breeder and the Race Woman: Storytelling as Subversion in Selected Novels by Contemporary Black Women Writers," OlaOmi M. Amoloku argues (based on Ytasha Womack's definition of Afrofuturism, and echoing Audre Lorde's bio mythography) that "Black female artists . . . [t]hrough [the] radical act of self-definition . . . can be categorized as Afrofuturist" (9). Richard J. Douglass-Chin offers some interesting insights into the connections between "black expressivity . . . submerged in the writings" of early Black women like Lee and that "in later fictional writers such as Zora Neal Hurston, Toni Morrison, Toni Cade Bambara and Alice Walker" (97). Specifically, Douglass-Chin points to the "different circumstances" under which they "operated" (97). Elisabeth McClanahan Harris uses the term *counter-memory* (following Michel Foucault and George Lipsitz) to describe a "process that uses elements of both myth and history" and that "looks to the past for the hidden histories excluded from dominant narratives" to describe how African American women's narratives, "rejecting any theology that would denigrate them[,] . . . looked to the Bible as a site of theological counter-memory" (97). She argues that "counter-memory offers a useful theoretical framework for reading the theological nuances of African American women's conversion narratives" (98).

In his 2004 essay "American Slavery in History and Memory and the Search for Social Justice," Ira Berlin maintains that the "intense engagement over the issue of slavery signals—as it did in the 1830s and the 1960s—a crisis in American race relations that necessarily elevates the significance of the *study of the past in the search for social justice*" (1251; my emphasis). Ironically, however, this current climate of anti-Black violence and internal (and international) racial conflict reminiscent of a not too distant past has left us with a somewhat hazy view of our present. At a time when understanding the causes and conditions of this climate, and creating viable strategies for attaining stable social justice and progressive movements for Black human rights are essential, clarity of purpose grounded in a serviceable history is critical. Yet some of the issues that Berlin addressed, such as apologies for slavery by U.S. presidents from the "safe" distance of the "coast of Africa [rather than] the heartland of the United States" (1254); popular depictions of slavery in literature (fiction, nonfiction, and scholarly) and film (blockbuster commercial and documentary); and the public attribution of significance and homage paid to the formerly enslaved African Americans at monuments, historic sites, and academia, all markers of America's "renewed interest in slavery" (1253), seem distant memories from centuries past. This renewed interest has of course taken many turns—for better or worse—depending on where one stands on issues related to recent major controversies: Critical Race Theory (CRT) and the 1619 Project (see Strout et al.).

In fact, they are reminders of a somewhat more recent history from less than two decades ago. Indeed, one of the many lessons to be gained from the post-Obama era racial backlash, which ushered in yet another echo of post–civil rights reconstruction, is that our nation's return to regressive politics may signal it is time to bring up strategies from the past that worked—hence the Sankofic lens. Put another way, as we consider "new technologies for hacking white supremacy," it is important to analyze what we've done right in the past—what has worked and what has not (Greene-Hayes and James 68). If, as James and Greene-Hayes suggest, "'Black Power' is love talk" because "internal dialogues/monologues offer insights into our fears and desires" (70), then deliberation on historical strategies and mechanisms of empowering Black women's self-talk (albeit through heteropatriarchal lenses) from our past might serve as useful bridges, links, and perhaps lenses for grappling with the complicated and awkward "twists and turns" of speech and actions.[4] The questions I have posed here are not rhetorical.

I want to join conversations already in progress, to extend and employ tools of analysis and theories—especially those that became more firmly established in the past three to four decades, and those that have shifted our knowledge center as it applies to religion, social justice, and literature—located at the interstices of race and gender. Reading through a framework of what Vincent L. Wimbush has termed scripturalization, I am employing a theory and critical model from Katherine Clay Bassard to analyze these women's scriptural sampling (implicit and explicit) across several genres.[5] Scriptural sampling goes beyond, as Bassard argues, simple biblical allusion or paraphrase as it engages with deeper employment of the technique of "literary" sampling (*Transforming Scriptures* 51). I am aligning myself with Bassard here. That is, this type of engagement "is deeply embedded in African American culture, particularly musical performance. By extension, the intertextual dimension of 'sampling' informs African American religious culture-sermons, spirituals, hymns, and so forth—and the genre of performative prayer . . . [which signifies] those prayers 'composed' for public performance in African American worship and/or written for publication, and that are thus connected to a different ethos of community, ownership, and language than privatized utterance" (51–52). Throughout, I thus deploy elements of literary or biblical sampling (used interchangeably) to analyze early Black Christian women writers Phillis Wheatley, Jarena Lee, and Maria Stewart, with a few connections to their secular cousin Frances Harper and others, continuing through to current uses, forms, and genres, musical and literary, by such contemporary artivists as Beyoncé, Lauryn Hill, and others.[6] Relatedly and necessarily, this study takes full advantage of spaces that the scholarship of Joycelyn Moody cleared in appreciation of the permission, if you will, to read religion, gender, race, and early Black feminist aesthetics as accepted rather than excepted. Moreover, I follow the indications of and deliberately acknowledge the powerful arsenal that scholars from Carla Peterson to Chanta M. Haywood, Regis M. Fox, and others far too numerous to cite here have provided. Building upon their inaugural and enduring work, *Repoliticizing the Word Through Poetry and Preaching* samples, mixes genres, and more fully appreciates the power of early Black women's words with the aim of probing and perhaps recovering significant useful linkages between centuries of "prophesying daughters" like Wheatley, Stewart, and Lee and their WordsWork that propels us forward.[7] As such, my analyses extend "beyond mere quotation to the echo and reverberation, the *creative re-use* of selective phrases of scripture" (Bassard, *Transforming Scriptures* 55; my emphasis). This creative reuse, a "bold re-voicing of scripture" (58), marks early Black Christian women's artistic laboring with scripture (WordsWork) in such a way that they are able to "go back and fetch" (Sankofa) knowledge that has been lost through the politicization of the Word (biblical scripture) for political aims of oppressing and enslaving Black people, through a reappropriation of holy writ to imagine a future (Afrofuturistically) and create a countermemory in which #BlackChristianWomensLivesMatter in perpetuity. *WordsWork* is a term I use to signify the interconnected secular "words" and sacred Word in the "works" of these early Black Christian writers. Their aesthetic is spiritual, political, and creative in many dimensions and modes—both spoken and written—addressed to diverse audiences. Their works perform work through their linkages to the Word.

Significantly, "to preach [or write through the lens of] the spiritual is not to sacrifice the political [which was *already*] *highly* politicized" (Zackodnik 19; my emphasis).[8] Thus, these early Black Christian women writers engage in creative, spiritual, political, and aesthetic work of *repoliticizing* the Word. My use of this term is with the understanding of the basic meaning of "repoliticize": to politicize again that which was already politicized. More precisely, it both connotes resistance, reactive and proactive response to seemingly innocuous aspects of society and culture that normalize oppressive actions, and denotes deliberative strategies for replacing previously politicized frames of reference, especially those that permit and enable oppression at multiple levels of race, gender, class, caste, and status. In the context of the early Black women writers examined in this text, their repoliticization of the Word actively resists and exchanges secular myths that undermine spiritual truths. They engage, in short, in a process of recovering the Word for the people it was intended to serve, "the least of [their] brethren" (Matthew 25:40, KJV). In doing so, they can be seen to be doing the work of God by revealing, challenging, and adopting approaches that reframe and recover their spirituality by reversing the politicization and polarization of Christianity intended to subvert divine Truth. Thus, this study is a work of remembrance and remembering, one that attends to the intensely powerful and authoritative meaning as well as the brilliant and imaginative thoughts, promises, and strategies employed then that are deployable now, albeit in distinctly unique ways, to authorize and repoliticize expressions of writing and speaking faith toward disarticulating oppressive powers from divine ones, wherever and whenever they exist.

Acknowledgments

Deepest gratitude to my ancestors whose presence I felt throughout this process as well as to Alexandra Socarides and Theresa Gaul, who read the very messy "article" that was the seed of this study and saw it as a full manuscript before I even imagined it as such. Theresa later read the first full manuscript draft during the summer of 2023 and provided notes despite her busy schedule. Thank you to Rafia Zafar for reviewing my book proposal and asking essential questions (really hard ones) that I had overlooked in the framing of this study's contexts that matter significantly. Indeed, she remains a mentor and scholar whose words, work, actions, and support of others inspires—a living ancestor. She watered and nourished the seeds planted, providing passages and maps throughout my academic career. I also thank Joy A. J. Howard, who joined this village as my developmental editor during a time when I was struggling to complete a chapter that had all but brought the project to a complete halt. She reminded me of the power of my own words and gently walked me through a rediscovery of my authorial voice. Chapter by chapter through the final draft copyediting, Joy's confidence in my project allowed me to see my work's value despite many challenges—personal and professional. I am grateful to Pascale Perraudin, my writing and thinking buddy (our scholarly interventions were mostly virtual but for a couple of glorious coffee/brunch visits when I was able to be in town), with whom I met biweekly for several years as we powered through hard conversations, diligently affirming and supporting each another through some rough times—I'm still encouraged by your postcard theory, and can't wait to read the book (slowly, of course, if it is not translated from French).

To Roxanne Donovan: it would take an entire book to thank you for what you have given and how you have enriched my life, my perspective, and reinforced the power of community. Completing this project, as you know, has been more than just a scholarly endeavor. The process of writing and researching this book and seeing it through to completion has been about a return to an authentic self I'm so grateful to embrace. It's been a journey to myself—on the mountain and in the Focus Friday sessions with my besties (too numerous to name here, so if I missed you please forgive me—charge it to my head, not my heart): Ching-In "Chingy" Chen, Andrea Harris, Lisa Jennings, Jacqueline Koonce, Sonja L. Lanehart, Joycelyn Moody (mentor, dear friend, motivator, and the inspiration for my continued love of teaching and research on early Black women's religious writing and thinking), Marisol "Mari" Negron, and Jessica Retis. Through obstacles, micro-aggressions, challenges, losses, so many frustrations, COVID, and something new nearly every time we met, we held each other up and shared our wins, near wins, feelings, and fears. We refused to give up on ourselves or each other. Each time one of us made it to the finish line we were there to cheer them on, to celebrate, always reminding ourselves that it was our humanity not the work we produced, that mattered most. When Roxanne and Joycelyn Moody cofounded Well-Academic in 2015, they opened the floodgates for so many of us in the academy who have been marginalized, and nearly a decade later we continue to keep moving forward in wholeness, courage, and community.

Thank you to Faculty Women of Color in the Academy (FWCA), with special appreciation to its founder, Dr. Menah Pratt-Clarke. I'm grateful for the annual conferences that also gave me an opportunity to attend Michelle Boyd's InkWell Academic Post-Conference Writing Retreats. The past two years' workshops have yielded substantial progress at stages of my writing when I needed it most, and the many women scholars, writers, and activists with whom I had conversations have nourished my creative spirit as well. Of course, the Wayne State University Press editors (Annie Martin, Marie Sweetman, Sandra Korn) and Director Stephanie L. Williams invested time and resources, as did their selection of excellent readers who forensically examined drafts and whose feedback strengthened the quality of the work—with special thanks to Robin DuBlanc for her equally forensic editing of the nooks and crannies that might have been missed. Any errors or omissions are mine, and for the quality of the manuscript, it is to this fine group of readers and editors that I owe thanks.

Because life happens even, and especially, in the midst of trying to meet publication deadlines, I want to thank my squad—an amazing community of caring "family" who are always there to remind me that it's alright to ask for help. And they are the first to offer and step up when I need it most: Todd Shaw—one of the best colleagues a new faculty member could have and an amazing vice chair. Thanks for sharing your time, expertise, and experience to support me as I navigated the administrative waters as a new chair of a new department of African American studies. Lindsay Arave (an amazing business manager) always made sure I was able to work remotely while doing research and always ensured that my research materials and books arrived "freaky fast." If there is a more efficient staff member of the University of South Carolina I haven't met them. Thanks for your support and positive attitude—you're the best! Thanks to both the University of Missouri and the University of South Carolina (Colleges of Arts and Science) for the research support and funding that helped me complete this project.

Dean Stephanie Shonekan, you are my sister, my friend, my inspiration, and example of what it means to be human while leading and blazing paths for others. You lifted me from the sunken place, and I am forever in your debt, one that I gladly pay forward, because it's what we do. I remember when we sat down at the Kaldi's and I shared the news about the Wayne State University Press book contract, and you said with so much enthusiasm: "This is a game-changer." You were right, because writing this book and having it published has reminded me of what I love about my work and the words I use to express that love—and, as always, that I matter. Thanks for validating me when others did not see me. Watching you shine as you lift others has been an honor and a gift. To my two best friends and sisters in spirit, Peaches Henry and Jennifer King: thanks for being here with me from the beginning through all the ups and downs—Mommy loved you both. I could not end these acknowledgments without thanking my big sister Phyllis Kendrick-Hale (whom I cherish) and our mom, who gave us each other. Wanda Langley-Hardy and Bettye Langley-Lyles, my precious sisters-in-law and sisters in love, you continue to lift me.

Eternal gratitude to Jimi (James Edward Langley), my partner for life, for your encouragement and consistent reinforcement and validation of my authentic and whole self. Your forty-one years of *agape* love have always given me the courage to fly when I only half suspected I could crawl. This year I'm proud to call you an author of your first book, one that you wrote even as you were caring for me—through it all.

Acknowledging the village of ancestors, elders, kith and kin, institutions, organizations, colleagues, and societies that have been part of this journey has been bittersweet. My dear mother—to whom this book is dedicated—transitioned on April 13, 2023, after enduring Alzheimer's for the final five years of her life. Thank you, Mommy. #YourLifeMatters

Introduction

Black women in the twenty-first century no longer need to justify their humanity, intellect, spirituality, and worthiness. Black women are neither expected, as were their ancestors, to speak in veiled language now referred to as code-switching, nor expected to raise their voices for others while silently enduring the violence of inequities and oppressions that for so long sent them to their prayer closets—turning only to God for justice, compassion, and comfort—for an acknowledgment of their enoughness, their internal and external beauty, their brilliance, and especially their authority to assert equitable being among all humanity. "For [eighteenth-century women like] Wheatley, desire, at times, is both an admission of a physical need (see, for example, her requests for the profits from the sale of her poetry) and a religious imperative that seeks its satisfaction in the pleasure of godly salvation" (Bynum 51).

Or do contemporary reports of inequities, oppression, violence, and unremunerated labors—in nearly every area of Black women's lives from preacher, parent, teacher, doctor, lawyer, engineer, artist, athlete, actor, and politician, to name only a few—suggest that there is still a need to claim and restate what is hardly obvious: that Black Women's Lives Matter? Have we reached a moment when we need, once again, to repoliticize institutions like religion to reclaim what has been regressing, being carefully stripped away: our humanity? If indeed Christianity, for example, had already been "heavily politicized" (Zackodnik 19) in ways that intended to strip the human and civil rights of Black women and men, then what would it look like to engage in the work of recovering spiritual truths from and through the power and authority of the Word in order to counter destructive myths and reclaim sacred covenants and secular rights—without sacrificing either? Is it time to revisit some elements from lessons of the past and consider how some of those former strategies might be retooled in this present era? The words of the twenty-two-year-old Black woman poet Amanda Gorman, spoken at the inauguration of President Joe Biden, reflects on the progress made in her poem "The Hill We Climb," invoking a sense of the urgency facing our nation—and evoking a voice of spirituality:

Scripture tells us to envision
that everyone shall sit under their own vine and fig tree
And no one shall make them afraid
If we're to live up to our own time
Then victory won't lie in the blade
But in all the bridges we've made
That is the promised glade
The hill we climb
If only we dare (43–51)

We will not march back to what was
but move to what shall be.
A country that is bruised but whole. (76–78)[1]

This contemporary clarion call reaches back to Wheatley's own appeals for freedom and justice—joining the poetic ministry across centuries, as Gorman reminds us that "being American is more than a pride we inherit, / it's the *past we step into* / and how we *repair* it" (52–54; my emphasis). This "past" into which we "step" enables a Sankofic lens through which we might not only "repair" what has presumably been broken, but "to turn back to appreciate the significant roles African women play politically, economically, spiritually, and socio-culturally. This can only enhance the full inclusion and participation of women in the society" (Amenyedzi 24). As I have written before, "In the spirit of Sankofa, it is the messages, lessons and information to be passed on that are most important. For in such words are survival mechanisms and codes for reconnecting with one's community and one's self" (Langley 59).

For early Afro-British American writers, religion was politics, and their retooling of Christian rhetoric to "write themselves into existence" is well established. For Black women in particular, the link between faith and fairness was neither fixed nor absolute. As Joycelyn Moody reminds us: "Clearly, for black holy women both the personal and the *spiritual* are political" (17). Three women in particular stand out as early examples and foremothers of our modern Black women's social justice movements, though perhaps not in the ways we might imagine: Phillis Wheatley, Maria W. Stewart, and Jarena Lee. They used Christian rhetoric to meet their respective political agendas that challenged slavery, sexism, and social inequality, as well as to develop healing strategies for their internalized trauma. Significantly, theirs are not the only marginalized voices of repoliticizing, however. Alongside them stands a fervent aesthetic powerhouse whose words evince a leading definer of Sankofic Afrofuturistic artivism: Frances Harper. Notably, in many ways her works and life foreshadow those of women like Amanda Gorman—those twenty-first century artivists who offer some linkages to Wheatley, Stewart, and Lee. Early Black women's writing exploited religion to expose "threadbare lies" that bolstered oppressive institutions of slavery, racism, and sexism for what they were—symbols of social death for Black women, against whom such violent and brutal expressions of power on their psychic, physical, and spiritual bodies demanded resistance by any means necessary. In so doing, they repoliticized the contexts within which the Word had been used to construct the proper places and spaces for Black women in early America—manipulating sacred texts for social justice at the forefront of political movements and intersectionality. To be sure, the political was not only personal, it was spiritual as well.[2] Consequently, I will consider how elements of their respective works manifested resistance, using a repoliticization of the Word through expressed concern for the most oppressed ones—those who experienced physical, psychological, and sometimes spiritual bondage. These writers provide maps for the symbolic and literal recovery of Black women and girls in the distinct ways they challenged oppressive and violent actions against their bodies, and the methods through which they wielded religious hammers to tear down political walls of sexism, bigotry, class, and caste prejudice, using their words to challenge misinterpretations of Christianity to construct and validate societal views of the Black woman's place, rewriting scripts for meeting social injustice with the power of the Word, in their own words—thus effecting a repoliticization of their faith.[3]

Several elements connect Wheatley, Stewart, and Lee. Each has a "first": respectively, first published American Black author, first woman to speak publicly before a mixed audience of men and women, first woman authorized to preach in the African Methodist Episcopal church.[4] I consider all three as the first published political Black women writers of their respective literary genres/sub-genres: poetry and epistle, speech and essay, narrative nonfiction (autobiography) and sermon.[5] In addition to their shared devotion to and focus on Christianity in their personal, political, and spiritual lives, each woman can be said to have delivered words intended to "create a new future for their peoples."[6] In this way, all three can be claimed as foundational voices ushering in an early Black women's preaching tradition—not only in the narration of the itinerant ministry of Lee, but also in the letters, poems, speeches, and political writings of Wheatley and Stewart. Notably, Wheatley's poetry "assumes a deliberately contrived ministerial persona setting forth a highly conventional sermon . . . [that] echoes two centuries of American Puritan preaching" (Richards, "Phillis Wheatley and Literary Americanization" 170). And, as Valerie C. Cooper argues, the "only difference between Stewart's speeches and, say, the sermons of itinerant preachers . . . is their context, not their content. . . . Lee . . . preached in churches and in homes; Stewart spoke in lecture halls. Nevertheless, their message was often very much the same" (9). Similarly, Wendy Roberts argues for the importance of the political within the religious as she observes the "political significance of Wheatley's choice to embrace revivalism and its role of the *woman poet-minister* . . . she dramatically re-schematized the default relationship between the nature of black people and evangelical harmony to instead align Africans with culture and intellect" (130).[7]

Each author used her social justice platform to extend the artificial boundaries of religion in ways that challenged historical and contemporary framings of it as a static "opiate of the masses."[8] Their works extend beyond simple, albeit well-articulated, understandings of religion as a tool of oppression to instructive remedies with precedent-setting paradigms for empowerment and social justice.[9] The historical, social, and political contexts, and the class/caste positions and conditions under which Wheatley, Stewart, and Lee blazed new trails created roads, bridges within each woman's unique geographical space, exposing the difference place made in their ability to speak, write, and advocate for social justice in ways that #SayTheirNames: Wheatley, Stewart, Lee, Alicia Garza, Patrisse Khan-Cullors, Ayọ Tometi (formerly known as Opal Tometi), Tarana Burke, and unnamed others, and let us know #EarlyBlackChristianWomensLivesMatter. Reclaiming their time is absolutely necessary for "*a time such as this.*" These words, for which I provide emphasis, reflect and reverberate religio-political-spiritual meanings over time and space as well as a multiplicity of contexts within which they are meant to signify on several fronts. First, there is the biblical reference from the book of Esther: "For if thou altogether holdest thy peace at this time, then shall there enlargement and deliverance arise to the Jews from another place; but thou and thy father's house shall be destroyed: and who knoweth whether thou art come to the kingdom for such a time as this?" (Esther 4:14, KJV). Second, there is the reference to each woman's positioning herself as the one who speaks truth to power precisely at the most crucial time and with regard to the most critical issues facing her people: Wheatley's instructive reminder in "To the University of Cambridge in New-England" when she emphasizes her position as Black instructor to White privileged men—"An *Ethiop* tells you 'tis your greatest foe" (line 28); Lee's questioning of patriarchal authority: "If the man may preach, because the Saviour died for him, why not the woman? seeing he died for her also" (11); and Stewart's "Who shall go forward and take off the reproach that is cast upon the people of color? Shall it be a woman?" ("Why Sit Ye Here and Die?"). Third, and finally, the title of the short autobiographical sketch by the Reverend Debora K. Blanks, African Methodist Episcopal Church (AME) minister and chaplain, whose sermon "Tell God Where It Hurts" connects words that absolutely matter and reframe political contexts from nineteenth- to twentieth- and twenty-first-century oppressive injustices (Larue 56–57). Connecting the nearly silenced voice of the woman with the issue of blood from the New Testament narrative in Luke to contemporary traumatized and disregarded needs of God's othered peoples, Blanks's sermon extends and demonstrates the powerful meaning and purpose of the work by Black women who continue to question, interrogate, and intervene in ways that matter as they continue to repoliticize the Word.[10] Women, then and now, have continued to "press through" attempts to "confine . . . paralyze . . . pulverize . . . suppress . . . [and] render [them] invisible" (Larue 58).

That their writing was political, and that they used eighteenth- and nineteenth-century Christian rhetoric as well as dominant (read "White") Euro-American literary forms to signify gender, race, and caste/class has been soundly established. Moreover, their figurative and literal spaces of liminality have provided critical understandings of their strategic employment and deployment of Black womanity in eras of heightened racism and sexism.[11] What remains is a consideration of why their work matters in an era of unapologetically secular social justice movements that simultaneously draw from and resist historically narrow and exclusionary religious paradigms. Wheatley, Stewart, and Lee were progressive artists, activists, (artivists) and political and spiritual leaders who fashioned inclusive models of resistance to uproot oppression at its core, in all its manifestations, and they stand as precursors to intersectional modern social justice movements from civil rights to Black Lives Matter to #SayHerName and #MeToo.[12]

If, as Patricia Hill Collins and Sirma Bilge argue, "People use intersectionality as an analytical tool in many different ways to address a range of issues and social problems" (4), then Wheatley, Stewart, and Lee provide ample evidence of religion as one significant point of entry through intersectionality. Interestingly, Hari Zyad's "My Gender Is Black" connects the concept of "gender" with "race" in ways that both untangle and further complicate any simplistic notions of gender in a context that provides a critical thread and perhaps a more specific linguistic turn or a language to sift through nineteenth-century Black women's war with connotative Black womanity. Zyad argues, "Blackness ruptures the laws of gender just like the laws of the state seem intent on rupturing Black life. [Moreover], Black gender and anyone who embraces its margins were never supposed to exist comfortably in this world in the first place." Relatedly, the 2015 African American Policy Report (AAPR) "Say Her Name: Resisting Police Brutality Against Black Women" (Crenshaw et al.) underscores the continued and necessary focus on the seemingly invisible violence against Black women's lives, lives that are underserved and "under-protected."[13] This requires the kind of consistent reminders that extend from eighteenth- and nineteenth-century Black women who not only spoke truth to power but also expressed intimate and spiritual truths to the relative power that #BlackWomensLivesMatterToo.

A significant anchoring term in my articulation of these women's use of the spiritual to effect social change in the political arena is the concept of social death.[14] Orlando Patterson uses the phrase "social death" to articulate the position of Black people from the slavery era to post-emancipation, Jim Crow, Reconstruction, and civil rights to the post–civil rights era of the early 1980s. For the most part, this way of understanding the impact of slavery, colonization, and racism that resulted in what Patterson terms "natal alienation" poses some particularly critical entry points for the discussion of Black women's exploitation of the very texts and contexts that reinforced and conspired to alienate them from their natal ties "in both ascending and descending generations . . . from all formal, legal enforceable ties of 'blood,' and from any attachment to groups or localities other than those chosen for [them] by the master" (7). Equally relevant is Vincent Brown's alternative perspective and contestation of Patterson's definition of social death. Brown asserts that "people who have been pronounced socially dead, that is utterly alienated with no social ties recognized as legitimate or binding, have often made a social world out of death itself" (1232).[15] Taken together, both views of social death enable analyses of social justice work in early Black women's writing that might otherwise remain unearthed or underexamined: Wheatley's retooling of the Puritan funeral elegy, Stewart's invocation of secular and sacred martyrdom in her early Black nationalist voicings and meditations, and Lee's celebration and reconciliation with death and dying in her call to preach.

In this study, I draw on some of the groundbreaking methodologies in Katherine Clay Bassard's *Transforming Scriptures: African American Women Writers and the Bible* liberally and flexibly, employing her theories of "turning cursing into blessing" (17) and "literary [scriptural] sampling" (51) as key tools of analyses of the Word in the works of these early Black Christian women writers. Following her, I too, "intentionally gesture toward . . . [the] contemporary" (3). While Bassard's studies point to "twentieth-century and contemporary writers" (3) in particular, I wish to extend her gestures to signal some connections between these early writers and contemporary Black women's "social justice" moves and movements as equally worthy historical links for "further research." If, as Bassard suggests, "black women became responsible for the 'social death' of their children" (16), then women like Wheatley, Stewart, and Lee might have necessarily forged a path through religion as a means to simultaneously deconstruct and reconstruct early American Christian values to meet their political needs.[16] They struck back against a government and a religion that conspired to monetize the Black woman in perpetuity. They used words that worked as a means to reinterpret value and humanity, and to record paths to reparative atonement, spiritual and secular. Of significance is the way the respective statuses—of Wheatley, Stewart, and Lee—as free(d) or freer women permitted them a range of expressive force through religion.[17] Wheatley's devout piety, Stewart's African-centered biblically based politically grounded oratory and literary prowess, and Lee's preaching power gave them access to unique audiences and exposed them to significant opportunities for challenging the status quo that they might not otherwise have experienced as enslaved women. Equally important, as women who possessed the intellect and the moral grounds upon which to speak and write, they used their words as liberatory weapons—expressed on behalf of those who remained in bondage.[18]

In so doing, their writing, speeches, and reimagining of American religion erect bridges (albeit ones that are somewhat unsteady at times) between those eighteenth- and nineteenth-century political debates and issues that remain relevant in the twenty-first century. Afrofuturistically speaking, this means reading early Black women as imagining—vis-à-vis the technology of religion (Christianity and the Bible specifically)—a future in which they have power over their own narratives, bodies, and psyches. In "The M(n)stry: Phillis Wheatley and Fugitive Imagination," Afrofuturist scholar Sherese Francis locates evidence of the poet's Afrofuturistic strain in "On Imagination." Francis asks us to consider "what happens when an enslaved person is given the tools to express her desire for freedom after being captured." And she observes that "an enslaved black woman . . . imagining traveling in a spaceship" is nothing if it "isn't Afrofuturistic and the mind of a Black speculative writer."[19]

We are well aware of such prominent historical figures as Harriet Tubman, Sojourner Truth, and Ida B. Wells and their historical legacy in the continuum of Black women freedom strategists and warriors.[20] Indeed, the 1974 intersectional Black women's lesbian feminist Combahee River Collective deliberately invokes the military action of Harriet Tubman's 1863 Combahee River raid that freed more than 750 enslaved people.[21] However, we are perhaps not as likely to connect the seemingly less overtly militant actions from such predecessors as Wheatley, Stewart, and Lee to contemporary social justice movements. And even when we are inclined to make such connections, viewing their works as links between historical and contemporary activism, at best we tread trepidatiously as we analyze their words through the lens of Judeo-Christian rhetoric and its concomitant values. This apprehension is true for a variety of reasons related to decreased general knowledge of, and a healthy suspicion for, religious language and practices based in the rise of religious nationalism (see Perry and Whitehead), the increase in atheism, and the way that the internet and social media have changed how we communicate.[22] Despite such distinct differences between the eighteenth and twenty-first centuries, some important similarities remain and point toward the viability and necessity of exploring such a continuum.

Expressly, "the experience of systemic oppression has led numerous Black American authors and scholars to excoriate America's ostensibly 'Christian' heritage as hypocrisy and deception, viewing America as essentially anti-Christian" (Perry and Whitehead 5).[23] Not surprisingly, contemporary denouncements echo, if not mirror, similar (perhaps exact) sentiments that motivated the works of Wheatley, Stewart, and Lee. For example: Wheatley highlights the hypocrisy of Christians who, in one breath, "Cry for Liberty," and yet, in another, insist on the "exercise of oppressive Power over others" ("Letter to Reverend Samson Occom").[24] Stewart cautions that "God . . . will [neither] regard the prayers of those who hold religion in one hand, and prejudice, sin, and pollution in the other . . . [nor those] of self-righteousness and hypocrisy" ("An Address: Delivered at the African Masonic Hall"). Lee exposes a Black minister who was so opposed to a woman preacher that "he could not unite in fellowship with [her] even to shaking hands as Christians ought" (*Religious Experience and Journal* 24). Wheatley, Stewart, and Lee invite us to focus on our ongoing failure to adequately #SayHerName as they strategically deploy perhaps one of the most problematic ISAs (ideological state apparatuses) to combat an equally nefarious RSA (repressive state apparatus).[25] One need only consider the driving mission and movement of the 2013 Black woman–founded Black Lives Matter to see the echoes from the eighteenth century to the present: "Black Lives Matter is an ideological and political intervention in a world where Black lives are systematically and intentionally targeted for demise. It is an affirmation of Black folks' humanity, our contributions to this society, and our resilience in the face of deadly oppression" (Black Lives Matter, "Herstory"). Westenley Alcenat underscores this connection: "Black Lives Matter (BLM) activists have placed women front and center in the new activism of the twenty-first century. They have taken up the mantle of Stewart's charge to address gender equality in leadership. Just as Stewart had done in the nineteenth century, BLM has enriched not only the visibility of Black women's leadership, but it has expanded the capacity of the Black social struggle to capitalize on the creative energies of an entire half of the population whose work has always been historically vital" (Alcenat).

Chapter 1, "Wheatley's WordsWorking: #GodsWordsMatter Now and Then," demonstrates how Wheatley's use of the Word in her literary works (occasional, neoclassical, elegiac poetry/verse, and epistle) enables a repoliticizing of religion to make a case for anti-slavery and the rights of women and the poorer classes. Returning to fetch what was lost from ancient works, especially but not only the Bible, this poetess of power also reconstructs the potency of language and recaptures words in the service of humanity—especially that which was seized from enslaved Africans—bringing enabling truths into and through time and space. While Wheatley cannot be seen as an activist in the same way as Maria Stewart or as a Christian proselytizer in the same way as Jarena Lee, her unique forms of literary protests parallel contemporary artivism through religion. Religion for Wheatley was far from merely a tool of her time used to pacify the masses through some opiatic vision of a hereafter in which women and enslaved, indentured, and marginalized others might achieve or secure a life not possible on earth. This poet-preacher-teacher used her highly spiritualized imagination grounded in real-world problematizing of issues and concerns addressed by her Christian God to bring forward narratives that map a way to true freedom for all. This was the work her use of the Word not only invoked but authorized. Her relationship with her dear friend the Reverend Samson Occom, through the teachings of the Reverend Whitefield, only enabled and further informed her WordsWork. In her close attention to the meaning of life and death, she narrativized her elegies, brilliantly manipulating the exegetical forms of protest that framed her poetic ministry. Her works thus serve as witnesses that lives—like Elizabeth "Mum Bett" Freeman's and Lucy Terry's—matter as a preamble to early Black women's rights.

Chapter 2, "Maria Stewart: Repoliticizing, Biblical Sampling, and Her World(s)," demonstrates Stewart's use of her texts for social justice aims, highlighting the significance of political speech and spiritual meditations as a form of prayer and biblical sampling to repoliticize religion. The focus here is not only on how the political informs the spiritual, or how the spiritual informs the political. Rather, I give attention to how the two strengthen and extend one another. Stewart buttresses the force of her voice by drawing on key scriptures from the Bible, and by looping in secular knowledge created and disseminated by both oppressed people and their oppressors. In so doing, she engages in a relayering of the palimpsest, bringing together traces of enslaved, freed, and free Black people's wisdom to more truthfully contextualize their experiences. Stewart thus reveals divisive deceptions by taking back the truth through her conception and enabling of new narratives of hope and strategies for defeating multiple forms of oppression. She thus brings forward existing words from many worlds—women, men, African, American, European, freed, free, enslaved, enslaver, indentured, and disadvantaged—creating a new song. Both her heart and soul were squarely with her people, for whom she demanded a quality and standard of living worthy of human beings, rather than one consigned to enslavement, indenture, or the drudgery of subhuman existence. Stewart's political stance, personal experiences and, above all, her yearning for the complete liberation of all her countrymen and women were emboldened through spiritual meditations—reflected in the words she spoke and wrote and her unwavering dedication to Black women, for whom she fervently advocated. She stands as a model for resistance in a genealogy from Phillis Wheatley Peters to Vice President Kamala Harris.

Chapter 3, "Jarena Lee: Calling the Call," transitions from a focus on how the Word works on the page or is presented on the political stump to consider the ways in which Lee's religious calling extends a physical presence seen first in Stewart's secular and more overtly political speeches. The discussion focuses on the interplay of Lee's application of a kind of secular and indirect sermonizing with a consideration of what and how evangelical itinerancy might be read as political activism. Significantly, of the three Black women authors studied, most readers would regard only Stewart as an *activist*; however, Lee's "religious experiences" enable us to reflect on overt and covert encounters with the political milieu of early American society. Extending theories of Bassard, Haywood, Teresa Zackodnik, and others, this chapter dissects how Lee "[re]politicized the soul" and the implications of this for contemporary Black women's religio-political agendas through the call to preach. I contend that in committing herself to this work, Lee privileges the divine within her and the Word, designing the terms as well as identifying the tools and the power through which her labors will be carried out. I draw attention to the ways that the "religious experiences" that Lee's journal represents a kind of subterfuge through which she imbeds the politics at work in a nineteenth-century Black woman's world, despite the author's stated intentions to "give an account of her call." Likening herself to "Saul of Tarsus," her "heaviest cross" (Lee 17–18) is revealed in her interactions with the slave masters, deists, sexists, and racists she encounters in answering her call from God. She shouts loudly, using evidence from the Word, clapping back at those who would doubt that she is indeed authorized and called by God to preach.

Chapter 4, "Binding Up Together: Addressing Our Past to Face This Present," builds on my analysis of early Black women's words from chapters 1–3, offering detailed analyses of intertextual sampling across time and physical spaces—through eighteenth- and nineteenth-century antebellum and postbellum voices of enslaved and free Black holy women—Wheatley, Stewart, and Lee. Drawing on Frances Harper's poignant utterances, I further contextualize and introduce the interconnected braiding of the WordsWork of this ancestral sisterhood. In so doing, the chapter establishes aesthetic "middle" passages that mark these authors' prescient existential progress into a future that is our present—thus enabling a necessary inter-genre, intra-gender, intercultural re-recovery of early Black women's spiritual writing. Their stories are not only always about the oppressive conditions they endure. While early Black Christian women like Wheatley, Stewart, and Lee shared similar and interconnected discontent, they used their words to hold accountable those who would attempt to steal their joy on this earth and impact their place in heaven. Understanding the interconnected struggles and joys—personal, political, and most definitely spiritual—this chapter considers the context and perspectives within which Black women can and do have it all—while simultaneously calling for those with the most privilege to unite in holding oppressive powers accountable. Specifically, I address the complicated nature of the intersections of gender, race, and age, and the contradictory nature of seemingly incompatible literary and cultural forms of expression through which these women are connected. Their respective battles with the continuum of oppression reveal multiple and overlapping navigations of spirituality. This chapter focuses on comparative analyses of WordsWork, demonstrating these women's early attention to intersectionality—their nuancing and binding together of our words. I address the primary ways that Black women have operated in relationship with—and often troubled—the politics of religion and how they embraced and reframed any stagnant or static view of Christianity (in particular).

Chapter 5, "Black Women's Lives and What Really Matters," shifts from an examination of intertextual moves that matter among Wheatley, Stewart, and Lee to a comparative analysis of contemporary Black women's repoliticization of the spiritual and their intergenerational histotextual use of the Word. This chapter focuses on thinking, doing, and actively working toward what matters most in the WordsWork, repoliticization, and literary sampling of new words. Consequently, I connect threads between contemporary activists, scholars, politicians, community leaders, and artists for whom the personal, political, and spiritual matter: Dr. Monica Coleman (ordained minister, author and activist, Harvard graduate), Congresswoman Cori Bush of St. Louis (ordained minister, registered nurse, BLM activist), Audre Lorde, Maya Angelou, Tarana Burke, Lauryn Hill, Beyoncé Knowles, and others. The throughline from mid-eighteenth-century and nineteenth-century figures like Wheatley, Stewart, and Lee to those who are working today—especially (but not only) to those who are explicitly coming from a Christian, Protestant place is relevant to understanding "hidden figures" that helped to reframe and repoliticize contemporary politics, religion, and artivism—both then and now. This chapter challenges the reader to reconnect with the past, to consider how the spiritual is still being engaged to navigate the extremely critical need for empathy, equity, and humanity found in the Word and the words of our ancestors—like Wheatley, Stewart, and Lee, among others—to be recovered. It is a Sankofic call to bring forward what is most valued from the past—not simply words but of equal importance the maps and strategies and blueprints we made, a way of making words work for rather than against us. It is a Sankofic call to remix, sample, and repoliticize terms for our future—reminders that we matter.

1
Wheatley's WordsWorking

#GodsWordsMatter Now and Then

Phillis Wheatley's eighteenth-century work demonstrates and opens paths to a consideration of how, when, and to what extent the enslaved, freed, marginalized, and celebrated lives of Black people mattered. Wheatley's legacy extends into and through several centuries—nineteenth, twentieth, and twenty-first.[1] The work of Black Christian women like Wheatley mattered to a world that was lost in hatred and oppression, one that had failed to suppress its desire for a power that depended on usurping divine authority, a society that denied the value of one part of humanity in the service of the gain and wealth of another. For Wheatley the attempt to exterminate the humanity of African people through enslavement and violence was not only human genocide—it was an annihilation of Word, and the "Word was God" (John 1:1, KJV). As such, if Black lives were not to matter, if Black lives were not considered lives at all, then neither was God. To deny the humanity and value of Black life was to deny the creator of all life—to heretically and profanely proclaim that God did not matter. For Wheatley it was clear that her work must go back and fetch, must retrieve that value of God's Word for those lives, one of which was her own. If Wheatley could not retrieve her own physical humanity and the concomitant cultural legacy that had been stolen from her, she could repossess and reclaim the souls to which the institution of slavery attempted to lay claim. Given the impassioned attention that the young poet gave to elegies, it is clear that life mattered. All lives were of importance and significance not only to those who loved them here on earth and but also, and more important, they mattered, both on earth and beyond, to a God who had created them. The lives that mattered included Black people's, as she pronounces with her poignant and powerful reminder that "Negroes" were unmistakably part of the Christian God's plan for the salvation of all people, especially those of the "sable race," who were looked at with a "scornful eye" because of "their color" ("On Being Brought from Africa to America").[2] Wheatley's words work to remind her audience of one who had not only been abducted as a child, quite literally "snatched" from her African homeland and her parents' arms, but also of one for whom the "soft captivity" of imagination guided her devout attention to the Word of God in her works. The poet thus deploys an aesthetic that shows how the spiritual and political elements of her use of the Word mattered significantly.[3]

Wheatley's is most emphatically an inaugural and haunting voice that speaks to the resilience of Black humanity, both echoing survivorship and refusing the status of victimhood.[4] "Connotations of survivorship—black bodies, African cultures, and black texts—converge in the figure and poetics of Phillis Wheatley" (Bassard, *Spiritual Interrogations* 36). Expressly, her mediation of the institutions of higher education, religion, and slavery are fluid throughout her writing, with particular resonances in her 1773 poem "To the Right Honourable William, Earl of Dartmouth." In it she exposes the academic institution as an incubator for social inequality and admonishes privileged young White men to divest themselves of the "baneful evil" (line 24) that appears as "transient sweetness" (line 27) but that in reality is sin. Thus, she strongly encourages them to "suppress the deadly serpent in its egg" (line 26).[5] Specific words, here and in many other poems, have been so thoroughly dissected for their indirect references to slavery that they cease to be elusive in the way scholars once imagined and at this point are rarely challenged, but rather tested from a variety of perspectives.[6]

What follows is my deliberation from the vantage point of Wheatley as an antecedent to contemporary Black women's social justice movements. Such an assertion is framed within contemporary contexts and theoretical models that have enabled a more transgressive and progressive view of the poet and her use of religion, not only to expose the tripartite oppression of Black women but also to reveal ways in which she goes beyond a seemingly simple deployment of the "master's tools" to a critical fashioning her own. Deploying what he terms an "Afrosensitive reading," Curtis Anthony Woods maintains that "Wheatley modeled

African diasporic evangelical activism by cementing the gospel and social justice together. [Exemplifying] right theology and right sociology [African diasporic evangelicals in early America] . . . had no other recourse but to speak prophetically into a demonic political system. . . . They believed transformational love would produce, rather than contradict, a political economic system designed to advance global human flourishing for all peoples" (135–136). Wheatley exposes flawed institutionalized oppressions for their brandishing of Christianity as a broadsword against its own people. Her words resultantly performed the work of neutralizing and disarming that powerful weapon through her repoliticized lays and letters—challenging a politicized Christian rhetoric that had already tarnished the purity of a spirituality she devoutly and scrupulously upheld and embraced. Moreover, "Wheatley's missives facilitate the discursive development of a smaller yet growing faithful community, in which she can and does worship together with friends and acquaintances. Wheatley actively participates in the making and revision of those boundaries that make her communities real" (Bynum 63). Bynum's point is relevant to my own argument. Such revision of boundaries includes what I term "repoliticization"—revising the limitations of religion and rewriting its political discourse in service of her artivistic aims. To thus repoliticize is to recover in the most resounding terms possible, with the full authority of the Word, that Black lives matter.

Wheatley's lexicon manifests her resistance against slavery and oppression in her sermonizing that speaks truth to power. She directly challenges the inhumanity of slaveholders while simultaneously conjuring images of Black lives that matter: "Steel'd was that soul and by no misery mov'd / That from a father seiz'd his babe belov'd" ("To the Right Honourable William, Earl of Dartmouth" lines 28–29). For Wheatley, the trafficking in Black bodies, accompanied by the further consignment of children and their parents as inherently moveable, inheritable property (chattel) in perpetuity is unconscionable. Indeed, one can almost hear the anguish evoked in the long "e" sounds in "steel'd" and "seiz'd," emphasized by the contrasting empathy in the alliterative "babe belov'd." Alongside her rebuke of the cold-hearted indifference of White slaveholding Christians who give tacit approval to the cruelty of the heinous and systematic removal of children from their families, she posits enslaved Africans as people who are possessed of "feeling hearts" who "understood" (line 23), because they experienced, "pangs excruciating" (line 26) and "sorrow" due to the ravages of the transatlantic slave trade. There is "no misery" that is appalling enough to induce society to cease the theft of and "trade" in human flesh and the destruction of familial connections. The devout Christian poet and artivist punctuates the position that Black families matter—they are, after all, part of the family of Christ.

Wheatley is rooted in a universal selfhood that links slavery-era politics to the vital and hopeful harvests of modern human rights movements. The poet's moral suasion is not only heard from one voice, effective from one stance, or always about speaking (the speech act), though it is most certainly about intentional hearing, listening, and comprehending with purpose. Wheatley reveals a relationship between knowing and acting upon the knowledge of the strength of one's voice and critical faculties, despite tremendous opposition. Her words make clear the relevance of history—drawing upon the past, confronting challenges and opportunities for progress in the present, and simultaneously grappling with uncertainty while vigorously inseminating future fruitage. Beyond the ongoing contest to legitimize African-descended humanity signified therein is a subtler waging of war against the limitations placed on Black life. Pivoting between many genres and her intersecting roles as poet, preacher, politician, prophet, activist, and African woman Christian, Wheatley's approach to social justice enables gain, even when loss is perceived. Just as one tactic appears destined to be vanquished, another counterbalancing cover emerges, refreshed for the next "leg" of the race.

While it would be another three decades before the American cessation of the slave trade and nearly another century before chattel slavery ended in the United States, Wheatley's "To the University of Cambridge in New-England" offers a striking version of the "audacity of hope" articulated by the first Black president Barack Obama more than two centuries later.[7] As Joel Pace asserts, "In the tradition of Wheatley, many black Atlantic artists have created spiritual utopias with words to express their hopes, but these artists have also used syncopated poetry in the form of hip hop lyrics to create dystopias that give vent to the persistence of racism in the wake of colonialism and slavery" (120). That is, Wheatley's "love of *Freedom* . . . [and] wishes for the common good" (lines 21–22), as well as her reminder of the spiritual redemption gifted to the "*whole human race* [that] by sin had fall'n" (line 17; my emphasis) issues a clarion call to justice by impressing upon us the shared and invaluable humanity of African people: #BlackLivesMatter. The lays she places before us transcend time because the images she captures of redemption, blood, and sin, as well as tropes of lightness and darkness, are metaphors as powerful and meaningful in her generation as they are in ours. Perhaps one of the most evocative images of simultaneous hope and despair, power and disempowerment, life and death, enslavement and freedom, secular and sacred, persona and political, is that of Niobe.[8]

In Wheatley's reimagination and repoliticization of Ovid's neoclassical myth we find a historical mapping of motherhood devalued and marginalized, children murdered in plain sight, with each death functioning as a badge or emblem of political power, reinforced through state-sanctioned violence. Her work creates a context in which the artivist can claim emphatically and graphically that Black mothers matter. In the epyllion "Niobe in Distress for Her Children Slain by Apollo" Wheatley first offers images that may appear to a contemporary reader as strikingly familiar to many—far too many—postmortem photos memorializing Black youth whose lives are cut short by anti-Black police violence.[9] Seven sprightly sons . . . / Seven daughters, beauteous / . . . / bright eyes the living splendors play, / Nor can beholders bear the flashing ray (lines 23–38). Niobe's soon-to-be-murdered fourteen children are described in glowing terms. Disconcertingly, in an August 13, 2019, *USA Today* article by Vandana Ravikumar, comparable imagery is evoked by a family photograph and description with nearly identical language: "19-year-old De'Von Bailey was fatally shot by police in Colorado Springs on August 3. Bailey's family said that they remember him as having '*bright eyes*' and a '*bright future*.'" Tragically, the siblings in Wheatley's poem lose their lives while at play, enjoying each other's company: "Where Thebes' young princes passed in sport the day" (line 110); each brother struck down by a "fatal shaft" (line 127). Comparably, a real boy, seventeen-year-old Trayvon Martin, whose boyish image has been captured nationwide, was murdered: caught off guard as he was walking home from a 7-Eleven store after purchasing candy and fruit juice. He was shot, not in a battle or in the commission of any crime, but while he was simply walking through his neighborhood on the way home from the store. Since Martin's tragic death, there have been many more—far too many—untimely deaths of young Black men and women, boys and girls.

Equally distressing are the gruesome impressions left on our collective memory. Wheatley's depiction of the mythic Niobe provides the following conditions and images through which to consider the children's deaths: the first killed with an arrow shot "through the neck" (line 128), with the remaining six sons meeting a similarly "cruel fate" (line 133) as "together, too, the unbodied spirits fled" (line 135). And, as one after another brother meets his death, we are presented with a gory image of young "Alphenor [who] fails in his fraternal deed" (line 141) and we see his "entrails smoked upon the ground" (line 144). A contemporary vision of such horror might be seen in the photos of the open casket of Emmet Till or even more recently in the photos of the bloodied concrete upon which the body of eighteen-year-old Michael Brown lay face down for hours in the middle of the street. Our social media, television, and other news outlets are now inundated with photos, videos, and words that replay, remix, and sample a refrain that Black children's lives are expendable. They are not in fact throwaway children, at least not to Wheatley, nor, I would argue, to many contemporary readers and thinkers. Wheatley gives attention to loss: Black and White, enslaved and free, at war and at play, disenfranchised, impoverished, striving to survive, and especially those young enslaved boys and girls whose lives (not unlike the teenaged poet who creates these word images) might be cut short in their prime due to violence that makes them collateral damage in wars for which they bear no responsibility. Indeed, Black children's lives matter.

Perhaps even more poignantly connected to what's at stake for contemporary Black women's social justice work and the words that usher in their resistance is how Niobe serves as a reminder of the heavy physical, spiritual, psychological, maternal, generational, and gendered toll of racism and anti-Black violence (see Julion; Smith, "Facing the Dragon"). Christen A. Smith underscores the significance of gender, arguing that "[the] spectacular killing of Black people by the state, either in the shadows of secrecy or in front of loved ones, is a gendered racial performance that includes the explicit targeting of bodies and people (shooting bullets, immediate death), and the residual impact of killing—the effective and affective death that state violence produces slowly . . . and as such it reveals a necropolitical logic at the heart of the nation-state apparatus in the Americas: gendered anti-Blackness" (Christen A. Smith 32). Such is echoed across centuries through the reminders of lost humanity in Abel

Meeropol's lyrics captured in Billie Holiday's haunting voice: "Southern trees [that] bear a strange fruit, / Blood on the leaves and blood at the root" (lines 1–2).[10] We are not only invited to remember the dead, bloody, mangled, hanged, drowned, disfigured bodies of our boys and men: fourteen-year-old Emmet Till, whose open casket revealed the barbaric lynching of this boy in 1955 in Money, Mississippi; eighteen-year-old Michael Brown, whose body lay on a Ferguson, Missouri street for four hours, blood pouring out, in 2014; and of course the May 2020 murder of forty-six-year-old George Floyd in Minneapolis, who was handcuffed, pinned to the ground, and endured the pressure of a knee on his neck for more than nine minutes, the breath of life snuffed out by police officer Derek Chauvin. Then there are pictures, though far less visible, providing evidence of the gruesome murder of our girls and women: twenty-eight-year-old Sandra Bland hanging in a holding cell after having been jailed for a routine traffic stop in July 2015 in Waller Country, Texas; and the bullet-riddled body of Breonna Taylor, who in March 2020 was killed by police in her home in Louisville, Kentucky—the victim of botched no-knock warrant. Beside them lie countless unnamed others—the "thousands gone" (see Berlin, *Many Thousands Gone*; Berlin, "American Slavery"), who died during the Middle Passage as well as the survivors and their descendants who endured all manner of spiritual, social, psychological, and physical trauma.[11] Imagine Wheatley's frail and nearly naked seven-year-old body, traumatized mind, and fretful spirit being readied for purchase in Boston, labeled, in further demonstration of the barbaric enterprise, as a "refuse slave," essentially a throwaway as part of the horrific transgenerational homicidal acts perpetrated against Black women (see Ritchie).[12] The symbolic power of the images of these figures is heightened by the knowledge of the extensive work that remains to be done to unravel such a broken and dysfunctional system of inhumanity.

It is neither ironic nor inconsequential that Wheatley was both a revolutionary poet and a prolific elegist. However, it was the genre of letter writing that enabled her the medium of expression best suited to what might arguably be characterized as her radical or rebellious strain.[13] It enabled a strategy of measured and deliberate continual progress, operating in concert with accelerated activation and agitation—not one overtaking the other, but rather each (slow and swift) moving along the same axes toward overall gains in shared and purposeful goals. Alicia Garza, one of the founding leaders of the Black Lives Matter movement, underscores the significance of continual progress: "There's no way I could've started this by myself. You know why? Because Black people have been struggling since 1619" (Fessler).[14] Another founding member, Patrisse Cullors, "a self-described wife of Harriet Tubman" (https://www.patrissecullors.com/), prison abolitionist, student, professor, artist, and author, complicates even our conceptions of what it means to claim "activist" as an identifying category: "I identify as an organizer versus an activist because I believe organizer is the smallest unit that you build your team around . . . the person who helps to build and launch campaigns, and . . . decides . . . how we're going to change this world."[15] Wheatley's strategic management and coordination of genres and mediums—perhaps using words as her "smallest unit" from which to build and organize—certainly place her squarely within this transhistorical company of national and transnational change agents and human rights activists like co-founder Ayọ Tometi, "a Nigerian-American writer, strategist and community organizer" (*Ted*).[16] Not unlike Wheatley, but expressed in contemporary terms and contexts, "Opal believes that one's spiritual practice and aspirations for dignity and self-actualization is what a rich faith life is about and that it must be further sharpened by engaging in deliberate action for social justice and human rights."[17] Hence, Black Christian women's lives and especially their work and attention to the power of the Word matter.

Wheatley not only eulogized her relationship to a Christian God and his son's redeeming grace with hopeful strains based on her spiritual musings, she also celebrated those who traveled on the earthly plain. It was no mere "pie in the sky" God of whom she spoke. In many ways, Wheatley's elegiac verses provide a map through which she repoliticized perhaps one of the most sacred and spiritual spaces of all, that belonging to mourners, especially those who lost children.[18] Wheatley celebrated those who "helped themselves," those who used their own agency to ensure the wholeness of an abundant and healthy life. For example, she celebrates the subject of "Lady on Coming to North America with Her Son for the Recovery of Her Health," who travels from "*Jamaica's* fervid [and] . . . malignant shores" (lines 3–10), leaving her "spouse bereft of wife and son," who "in dark recesses pours his moan" (lines 15–16).

This woman, who makes a journey that reverses a route taken in one leg of the more treacherous locations of the Middle Passage, in the West Indies, where conditions were indeed "malignant" for enslaved Africans, moves north to recover her health, through Philadelphia and then Boston, enjoys the privilege of a welcoming reception, and finally experiences a joyous homecoming to Jamaica, where her son returns "to his father's ever dear embrace" (line 32)—a far cry from the "babe belov'd" that "from a father [was] seiz'd" ("To the Right Honourable William, Earl of Dartmouth" line 29).[19]

In yet another salute to the survival of women, Wheatley echoes a familial strain in "A Lady on Her Remarkable Perseveration in a Hurricane in North-Carolina." Once again a woman (in this case a widow) journeys through the "horrors of the wat'ry war / . . . / tumultuous roar / . . . [and] thund'ring terrors" (lines 4–14) and is "reliev'd" (line 28) to "embrace" her infant "daughter" (line 30). The fear, terror, and extreme dangers experienced by the widow to whom the poet offers such compassionate expressions in her eulogy are likely re-membered through a lens of her own traversing of the Middle Passage as young child who survived similarly horrific travel—albeit absent the "embrace" of her own mother. This poetic narration becomes yet another opportunity to articulate a familial connection that Christians celebrate and simultaneously deny to enslaved African people. Bassard has addressed Wheatley's use of the elegy to speak for women who lost children and their lives in childbirth to associate a nation's loss of citizens with the many women who died for the cause of national identity.[20]

The constant reiteration of emotions, which scholars attribute to pre-Romantic and sentimental strains, is also a cleverly veiled proof that Black people not only know misery, as in the emotions she emphasizes in her elegiac mode, but also that sadness and pain are associated with natural human affections like love which, Thomas Jefferson maintains, "is ardent, [in Black people] but kindles the senses only, not the imagination."[21] Such is disputed in Wheatley's lines: "In death the friend, the kind companion lies, / And in one death what various comfort dies!" ("To a Lady and Her Children, on the Death of Her Son and Their Brother" [lines 9–10]). Here in the elegiac space between the earthly absence and heavenly presence, the enslaved poet conceives of a world in which a mother and her children are free to mourn the loss of their family member. To be at liberty to mourn is to experience the fullness of "overwhelming sorrow" (line 2), "flowing tears" (line 3), and "sighs on sighs" (line 4), confirmation of the life of those cherished relations who remain. Wheatley's "song" (line 1) is also a reminder of the felt needs that his family are without due to his death. It is this "overwhelming sorrow" (line 1), this empathy for those lost, that "demands [Wheatley's] song" (line 1). It is a song that the poet recognizes as futile, in terms of its ability to bring back a lost loved one, recognizing that the "celestial joys [of which she] sing[s] [are] in vain" (line 21).

On the one hand, Wheatley's words work; that is, they act as salve for hopelessness and despair, not only for the despondent mourner but also for the enslaved African child. "In light of the violence and oppression that she suffered, it should come as no surprise that the poet found solace in death and its promise of freedom and reunion" (Bly 335). What may be less obvious, however, is that "solace" is but one of the central ways that death functions in the poet's words. Scholar Joanna Brooks argues that Wheatley's elegies also serve to "perform the emotional labor of condolence and sympathy [through] participation in [a] transactional, sentimental culture of mourning" (8). In other words, as Brooks sees it, this "sentimental scene-stealing . . . [of] white female audiences blocked the richer, more powerful story Wheatley might have been able to tell" (21).[22] Brooks's troubling of the impact of genre in ways that resist over-celebratory and simplified readings of her elegies posits a version of Wheatley as an astute artivist who was able to control and direct the terms of media from a seemingly disadvantaged locus, one who promoted her works through careful navigation of existing networking systems and nurtured relationships to enhance her audiences' sponsorship. This is an important contribution to the herstory of this early poet, along with its necessary critique of the "failures of [interracial] female solidarity" (18).[23] However, I would add that Wheatley's words also work to simultaneously "unblock" far richer and more powerful stories: eighteenth-century Black women's unity.[24] Such exposes more overtly a historical continuum of intra-gender racism that Wheatley's own words and her embodiment thereof attempted to repeatedly re-center, despite attempts by White men and women to center their own narratives. That is, "Wheatley's very (Black female) body" signifies "a truncated part of a whole community and kin network" (Bassard, *Spiritual Interrogations* 37).

What this suggests, then, is that Wheatley's most powerful stories have yet to be written, as her WordsWork continues to flow through a Black woman's intertextual transhistorical cypher. That is, herstories punctuate critical points of power through the young poet's assuaging of death and loss, stories that ring especially poignantly for her descendants. "The mothers of those killed by police or vigilante violence embody every black mother's deepest fears: that we will not be able to adequately protect our children from or prepare them for a world that has to be convinced of their worth." However, "black women especially know fear—how to live despite it and how to metabolize it for our children so that they're not consumed by it" (McClain).[25]

Wheatley's sampling of scripture laced throughout her elegies highlights a heavenly reward, displacing or functioning as a "stand-in" for the pain the young poet could not freely speak. Consider Moody's reading of Jarena Lee's words through "M. Shawn Copeland['s] . . . *theology of suffering*" (52) as opening a narrative that enables yet another lens through which we might consider death and mourning. Specifically, Lee's words, like Wheatley's elegies, "reconstruct not only [her] own physical suffering, but the suffering of others, including . . . relations and friends," using "the image of her own body to develop an *incarnational* theology" (52). In more secular and contemporary terms, Wheatley's words work to necessarily engage with what scholar Brittney Cooper calls a "Black female experience of embodiment" (*Beyond Respectability* 6). Consequently, if Wheatley's herstory was less seemingly overtly impactful for progressive political movements in the antebellum Black Atlantic, her works nevertheless work as maps to release and guide her twenty-first-century descendants toward #TakingBackHerNarrative. Wheatley's working of the "theme of achievement in the face of marginalization and racial oppression constitutes a continuous thread in the fashioning, appropriation and employment of Wheatley and her legacy" (Sesay 3). Ultimately, a prevailing image of the poet's radical repoliticization of the spiritual is grounded in a devout but not naïve comprehension of power, whose meanings are made visible in her scriptural sampling. Throughout, the poet's mournful strains are echoed in the words of activist Tarana Burke: "You can't do this kind of work without being grounded in a faith that showed possibilities. Christianity is, really, when you take away all the pomp and circumstance, it's about hope and possibility" (qtd. in Segura 1).

Wheatley's words are echoed across centuries, in the silence of the words that Tarana Burke could not utter when a young Black girl attempts to share her story of sexual abuse by her stepfather. Burke poignantly reveals the moment at which the girl recalls the horror too awful to allow her to say, "Me too." Wheatley's elegiac responses are also remembrances, as scholars like Bassard and Moody foreground in their scholarship. Bassard argues that "the issue of ancestors and remembrance will become crucial to an understanding of Wheatley's embracing of the elegiac genre" (*Spiritual Interrogations* 36). Moody makes a similar case about the importance of "remembrance" in early Black women's spiritual writing. She observes that nineteenth-century preacher Zilpha Elaw's narrative "occasioned" a "deftly deploy[ed] sentimentalism to elicit the reader's meditation on the deleterious and tragic consequences of chattel slavery" (65). Remembrances that invoke "the trope of death, especially a woman's or an infant's death . . . integral, [and] endemic to American sentimental literature," serve dual purposes of reinforcing the "significance [of death] for the living" and "establish[ing] ecclesiastical authority" (*Sentimental Confessions* 72). Wheatley's hope as a Christian for a better world beyond the temporal one is mitigated by her empathy for the ones left behind and her desire for a more abundant and equitable life on earth. A similar refrain is echoed in a poem written by a twenty-first century poet, Mercedes. In it, Mercedes both laments the death of Black lives lost and seeks to redirect the grief to social action answering state-sanctioned violence and legislation that seeks to oppress and control women's bodies and reproductive rights. The poet asks us to "focus on / the blood / that's painting / our streets red" (lines 2–5) rather than "the blood that / [she] can't help / but shed" (lines 7–9), inviting us to realize the "unnatural" nature of the former rather than the "natural" type that constitutes the latter. Both the historical and contemporary imagery insist upon rendering that which is invisible visible—Black women and children and their families and communities—evocatively washed in maternal and paternal blood: #RemembranceStillMatters #GodsWordsWorkMatters.

Wheatley was hardly invisible, and yet she was not a "political leader" or social justice activist in the sense of some of the eighteenth- and nineteenth-century Black men and women we have come to associate with early Black nationalism and women's rights: David Walker, Sojourner Truth, Nat Turner, Harriet Tubman, or even Maria Stewart.[26]

In both her own generation and even much later during the Black Arts/ Black Power era of the mid-1960s to 1970s, Wheatley has been painted as an alien, an outsider, even within a supposedly symbiotic chain of signifiers that depends on a view of woman, Negro, African, Christian, pagan, civilized, barbaric, rational, emotional, gentile, aggressive, vengeful, forgiving, White, Black as inherently disconnected. However, this "genius in bondage" was freer than we might imagine, as her voice was both liberated and liberating well before she was legally manumitted. Wheatley enters such spaces already a symbol of dysfunction and foreignness, marked by her contradictions, and this is why her repoliticization of ancient texts, religious and secular, provides such a critical model for articulating and disrupting the politics of religion in our current era.[27]

If we allow ourselves to sit with the reality of what scholars have deemed the paradoxical nature of Wheatley's works, we will find that she has given much indeed to our contemporary #SayHerName and #BlackLivesMatter legacy of social activism.[28] Initially Wheatley's works appear in the form of a "subtle protest" (see O'Neale) drawing upon the only available languages for an eighteenth-century colonial American poet: Judeo-Christian, revolutionary, neoclassical myth, biblical paraphrase, elegy, and epistle. If, as Reginald Wilburn maintains, "the grounds of African American literature reflects *demonic* terrain, a landscape where presumptions of black unrepresentability are rendered false through performances of black literacy" (5; my emphasis), then it becomes evident that the measures taken and the extent to which Wheatley subverted those languages are almost unfathomable.[29] Her choice of "media" is not at all uncommon based on the conventions of the period, but she extended conventional genre and cultural boundaries through her use of diverse tones, textures, rhythms, and forms in ways that could hardly go unnoticed. Her writing was also, more importantly, a part of the growing trend of literary "civil disobedience."[30] She begins this legacy for American women in general and Black women in particular of what I've come to see as strategically managing and manipulating visible invisibility—and perhaps, one might argue, releasing in measured doses the intellectual and poetic arm of the "angry Black woman." It's not simply her letters to the Reverend Occom and Obour Tanner in which she is unapologetically anti-slavery and repulsed by this Christian's nation's hypocrisy—especially regarding her enslaved African brethren and their denied humanity.[31] For Wheatley, all life (especially of African people) and lives matter, and that is all too clear in her works—from cogent arguments against White male privilege that articulate masterfully the impact of toxic masculinity on the world and their own moral degradation to the comforting words she offers to grieving parents, many of whom are women.[32]

Much is made, and rightly so, of the power of the press, especially how the media is a tool both of oppression and empowerment in our current era. Consider the unlimited outlets (from social media formats such as TikTok, X, Instagram, and Facebook to mainstream networks such as CNN, MSNBC, Fox, and even the seemingly insignificant but potent personal text or email message) through which an idea can be captured, held hostage, regurgitated, and reinforced with swift and sometimes reckless and destructive dissemination. Similarly, the power of a tweet or video recording captured on a cell phone, or even a Facebook post, could make or break a political candidate or career, or incur judicial repercussions, and as such could provide necessary evidence to spark demands for justice and accountability—from law enforcement, government officials, and teachers to restaurants and commercial business.[33] So what could an eighteenth-century Afro-British American poet possibly offer to our sophisticated and ever-evolving technological culture?

Words and images, as well as the modes and methods of propagandizing them, are no less dehumanizing and silencing now than they were three centuries ago—they may be starkly different but they can have similar consequences. Audiences still matter. Ironically, we are not always aware of the breadth and depth of the reception of words and images, and the way in which a single voice can sometimes be heard (for better or worse). We require reminders that words and symbols—such as the hashtag—carry (bestow and disseminate) truths and untruths that have critical implications for our movements toward equity inclusion and against injustices. Jefferson's dismissive response to Wheatley's art and Margaretta Odell's manipulation of biographical "facts" regarding the poet's life, to say nothing of the ways in which others following Odell mischaracterized the post-Wheatley prodigious adult life of Phillis Peters seemed to undermine any history of an autonomous free Black poet.[34] B. B. Thatcher's *Memoir of Phillis Wheatley* imagines her in ways that construct her as small and insignificant, that threaten to undermine the power of her words and the meaning of her life for posterity and contemporary colonial American society. Such diminutive and condescending descriptors as "our *little* African" (9), "the *little* slave" (10), and even "African orphan" (26) point to the latter's less than critical understanding of the implications of such phrases. If nothing else, his work provides evidence of a legacy of owning the narratives of Black women.[35] In perhaps one of the most critical pieces of mainstream scholarship written about Wheatley in the past two decades, *Phillis Wheatley and the Romantics* (2010), John Charles Shields introduces us to the connection between this early Black woman bard and her literary influence on "the shaping of what we have come to call the several romanticisms" (ix). What is most significant for my consideration of Wheatley here is Shields's tracing of the history, response, and impact of imagination and its relationship to religion and politics.

Expressly, Wheatley's poetry demonstrates the power of imagination as an important tool in social justice activism, with poems such as "On Imagination," "To S.M., a Young African Painter . . . ," and "Thoughts on Providence," among others providing ample evidence. Consider her invocation of the sacred and otherworldly muses, who not only inspire but simultaneously authorize the freedom of her "faithful tongue" / and "triumph[ant] song" ("On Imagination," lines 6–7) in admiration of a Black artist—an African painter—who is a "muse [that can] inspire each future song" ("To S.M." line 20), and the "Infinite *Love* / . . . / ev'ry creature's want supplies / . . . / to nourish all, to serve one gen'ral end" ("Thoughts on Providence" lines 122–127) and thereby links universal justice and social inequality. S.M.'s painting arouses aesthetic impulses to truth and beauty shared by Wheatley and every human. Wheatley's rendering of sight, sound, speech, thought, smell, and movement as she links the "painter's and the poet's fire" ("To S.M." line 9) ultimately imagines a euphoria of the mind that can be most intensely experienced through her affinity with another African artist. Interestingly, while "Damon's tender sighs" (line 29) is plainly understood as Wheatley's subversion of the pastoral, which "signal[s] her own debt to Vergil's eclogues . . . Damon, a disappointed lover in Vergil's eight eclogue" (Shields, "Phillis Wheatley's Subversion," 263), her reference to Damon here works equally well to punctuate an alternative version and level of filial love signified by the Greek myth of Damon and Pythias. This version of the myth highlights friendship and self-sacrifice as the ultimate examples of Christian love. In what might also be read as an act of biblical sampling in the verse "Greater love hath no man than this, that a man lay down his life for his friends" (John 15:13), the poet's elegiac strain evokes a particular relationship among enslaved African artisans.

They conspire as shared muses to "capture the captivity" through enthralling images of flight and freedom.[36] Wheatley's rapturous language of ascension flows: "on what seraphic pinions shall we move" ("To S.M." 25). While it is tempting to hear only the escapist "pie in the sky" freedom in the hereafter or, equally limiting, to read for only the subversion of the "master's" religion, Wheatley's words work as a link to the nuanced renderings of hope in the face of seemingly unconquerable oppressive forms. Such is shared in the late Maya Angelou's "Still I Rise": "Just like moons and like suns, / With the certainty of tides, / Just like hopes springing high, / Still I'll rise" (lines 9–12). Like Wheatley and Scipio Moorhead, the young Black painter whom the enslaved poet eulogizes, Angelou is "bringing the gifts" of her "ancestors" (line 39). Those "gifts" in written and visual artistry remain critical and galvanizing forces for social justice and for inducing a liberating spirit of self-love. Put another way, "poets promote political engagement and mobilization" through a variety of ways, one of which is "embarking on a journey of self-healing and self-love. The idea is that change happens when people are healthy, self-fulfilled individuals who have access to expressive, supportive outlets" (Chepp 46). Wheatley campaigns throughout her works with words that imagine the kind of radical and transgressive love that unearths connections between the sacred and the profane, eliminating artificial boundaries between religious and political agendas, which can be used to both bind and unfetter.

Another critical concept in Wheatley's repoliticized poetic religious sermonic corpus is her use of "mercy" to challenge oppression by demanding that empathetic actions extend beyond divine intervention or providential acts to actual human actions that respond to institutionalized oppression, such as those by anti-slavery activists, abolitionists, indigent impoverished peoples, and children's and women's rights advocates. Likewise, her use of "mercy" also attends to the kind of personal responsibility that extends from the religious to the secular view, which encourages a change of heart and an openness to others—what we might term inclusiveness or diversity, enabling conscious understanding of the deeper meanings beyond tolerance to embracing acceptance and love—a mirror of God's mercy through human action and interaction. Hence, "Wheatley's poetic energies . . . are brought into the service of attaining freedom, here and now" (Shields, *Phillis Wheatley and the Romantics* 9). Shields points to several passages that enable us to more clearly articulate this legacy and link her with contemporary activism. For example, Wheatley's use of words like *view*, *grasp*, *amaze*, *unbounded*, and *soul* (28) in her poem "On Imagination" enables a consideration of the powerful model or mode of thinking that offers a link between late eighteenth-century Afro-British America and twenty-first-century #BlackWomensLivesMatter and #SayHerName. If, as Shields argues, "Wheatley's work" engages with "the power of imagination . . . in her construction of a poetic world" (28), then such power surely enables her to construct within that "poetic" world a parallel model of the political worlds and moves that matter.[37] Put simply, the poet's imagination is not limited, and as such, she can construct and reconstruct the realities that best serve her purposes. Given her position as an enslaved African, Wheatley's freedom is expressed through her imagination of worlds in which her humanity matters as much as that of her enslavers. To imagine that her life matters alongside that of the rest of humanity is indeed a political act of resistance. Clearly the statement "Black Lives Matter" remains heavily contested and politicized, and to assert her humanity during an era of enslavement was clearly a move that mattered—in figurative poetic spaces and the accompanying physical spaces of the Wheatleys of the world. Her works are intensely sublime and palpably evoke the power of imagination to shift and change streams of power through art. Shields asks us to acknowledge that "Wheatley's conception of the experience of first light becomes synesthetic: that is, the senses of sight and sound are both evoked" (39). That her poetry, especially the invocation of the sublime, muses, and imagination, permitted the reader/hearer to transcend or rise above the physical and psychological pain of slavery, racism, and other forms of oppression is a critical step in the political model. However, what is perhaps more vital is how such seeming transcendence (too often misread as avoidance or passivity) provides an example of self-care, paths to rest and recuperation needed to endure the trials and tediousness of movements well beyond the initial moments. Rising above to observe oneself, to sift through what can and will be internally retained, and to eliminate or discard poisons (such as self-doubt and fear) that threaten to further embalm, suffocate, or silence oppressed people is essential. And this is part of the work that Wheatley's model of imagination establishes as a building block—the poet's world, words, and images construct and deconstruct, frame by frame, leaving necessary shards and "breadcrumbs" for us to follow. Note the movement in Wheatley's words from powerless to empowered through her poetics of ascent (see Shields, *Phillis Wheatley's Poetics of Ascent*).

Beyond the delicately refined lyrical lay is the power of direct language in her epistolary strains. Wheatley's 1774 letter to the Reverend Sam Occom has been accepted as evidence of the young poet's biting criticism of race and slavery in eighteenth-century colonial America, as she exposes Christian hypocrisy and underscores the capricious relationship between religion and politics. Addressing the "thread bare lie" (Barnett 1) of the Christian mission to save pagan Africans by bringing them into a divine light of God's grace, she concurs with Occom's critique of those who would deprive Black people of their natural rights: "Those that invade them cannot be insensible . . . [of] the glorious dispensation of civil and religious liberty, which are so inseparably united, that there is little or no enjoyment of one without the other" ("Letter to Reverend Samson Occom").[38] The body must be freed if people are to possess and exercise the free will promised by God—an argument that pricks the conscience of Christians and exposes the hypocrisy of the nation.

In a contemporary context, economically disenfranchised and underrepresented people cannot fully partake of the advantages of the pursuit of happiness even if they are legally freed, because they lack true liberty. Wheatley's observations here are rife with the language of fulfillment and gratification. "Enjoyment" suggests more than simply the possession and exercise of political and spiritual entitlement, one's birthright, or one's protection from infringement on such claims. Her language also signifies a rising emotion connoting the distribution of splendid lights and lightness that emits pleasure and delight at its release. Moreover, those who have "invaded" and "deprived" the liberties, freedoms, and God-given rights of others might enjoy a similarly liberatory experience, as they are freed from their oppressive work and free to enjoy the spiritual liberty that the "glorious dispensation" of a divinely ordered world allows.

Similarly, her 1776 letter to her close friend Obour Tanner fuses Christian duty with civic responsibility. Wheatley shares her disdain for those who possess a violent and unquenchable desire for power. An "ambition & thirst of Dominion" that is deliberate in its abuse of human and civil rights is "design'd as the punishment of the national views of others." The actions of a supposedly civilized (European) part of the world "[bear] the appearance of greater Barbarity than that of the uncivilz'd [African] part of mankind," exposing the inhumanity of the institution of slavery and the concomitant threadbare lies about the continent of Africa and its people. Such untruths enable otherwise "civilized" people to support the unbridled cruelty and conditions of chattel slavery. However, lest we misread her Christian tone as either passive or insincere, Wheatley challenges secular rule and embraces spiritual authority as the shrewdest political weapon against oppression in her comparison of two unequal forms power: "Let us leave the Event to him whose wisdom alone can bring good out of Evil & he is infinitely superior to all the Craftiness of the enemies of this *seemingly devoted* Country."

Wheatley's words reveal a more expansive and intersectional view of secular and sacred understandings of freedom. She understood religious liberty was not fully enjoyed even by free White citizens. Indeed, early laws requiring mandatory church attendance combined with obligatory taxes did not sit well with all people. Hence, Wheatley's repoliticization of this oppressive faith in both her letters and poems such as "To the Right Honourable William, Earl of Dartmouth" as well as the most often cited but misunderstood "On Being Brought from Africa to America" protests the deleterious effects of slavery and social inequality on women and children. She keenly celebrated the successes and appeared cautiously optimistic about a future she hoped would be realized. As such, her works demonstrate a force of the Word that seems to almost "will" freedom into existence. Her elegies simultaneously celebrated, mourned, and memorialized women and children—making them visible in a cultural context that rendered them invisible. In nearly every word, there is an image of a deific spirit, a power that intervenes on behalf of humanity, with an expressed concern for African-descended women, especially those in bondage. Religion may receive partial credit as it is yet another muse that imbued the poet's verses with such fervor and force.

Both religion and poetry have indeed "made" a Wheatley! No longer consigned to the outermost realm of the "whitewashed" "mockingbird" school of African American literature, this eighteenth-century poet, elegist, political letter writer, and extraordinary philosopher and wordsmith has been validated in a great many contemporary spaces—feminist, womanist, literary, intellectual, religious, and slave writing. Even though she died at such an early age, her works demonstrate a keen and prescient awareness of the world around her, and how the environment impacted women, especially Black women, for better or worse. Her letters to Obour Tanner reveal her devout piety and her wish to mesh her Christian duty with a civic responsibility—to care for the world and to guard against its frailties. Wheatley's "letters direct those *private* readers—a friend, political dignitaries, or an acquaintance—to what matters, and what matters demands that Wheatley share in the experience of faithful living. They privilege not only Christian conversion and the literatures of slavery and sentimentalism, but more specifically . . . ecstatic, charismatic, 'enthusiastic' *religious expression and power*" (Bynum 63; my emphasis).[39] At the same time, her more public poetic tributes were meant to reach out to statesmen and powerful women who had the influence necessary to impact laws and societal views and reshape perceptions of women, people of color, and others (African-descended people, both slave and free, Native Americans, Catholics, non-English, poor Whites, indentured servants, and the like).

Her political stance was in line with eighteenth-century ideas about abolition, women's rights, and the ever-widening disparities in the allocation of resources, as well as the more deeply imbedded hierarchies of race, class, and gender that exacerbated the worst conditions for Black women in a shifting post-revolutionary independent nation. Predating Black women activists like Sojourner Truth, Wheatley recognized the need to keep pressing the issues of social justice and equality for all while the climate of freedom was in the air. While the colonized were demanding their liberty, the enslaved, oppressed, and disenfranchised—especially African women like Wheatley—should continue their resistance. Truth's 1869 words from her "Address to the Equal Rights Association" strike a chord similar to Wheatley's: "So I am for keeping the thing going while things are stirring; because if we wait till it is still, it will take a great while to get it going again" (1).[40] Wheatley's words convey her discernment of the urgency of their import at the forefront of the national imagery.[41] Strategically, she used immutable "truths" based on the Word to advocate in ironically unapologetically resistant and political terms. In Phillip Richards's terms, "Wheatley's literary Americanization . . . show how . . . in the process of *rewriting* the *religious and political* languages of late eighteenth-century New England" she was engaged in a "politicizing experience" ("Phillis Wheatley and Literary Americanization," 186–187; my emphasis). From my perspective, this process was in fact a repoliticization of a religious discourse that had already been rendered heavily politicized.[42] Importantly, "the motivations of this generation of activists," while "much less likely to be religiously affiliated . . . [are] not necessarily irreligious" (Lizza)

Consequently, contemporary activism, by "explicitly rejecting this hetero-patriarchal model of Black male preachers leading the charge and everyone filing in behind them" (Lizza) follows maps from earlier models of protest like Wheatley's. It focuses on underlying collaboration among intersecting systems of oppressions, with religion as a major player. Much has been made over the years of the eighteenth-century poet's "humble" and "demure" affectation and her subtle demeanor as seemingly antithetical to Black resistance.[43] However, when considered along a continuum of Black women who redirected the aim of institutions like religion, patriarchy, and racism toward progressive moves that matter for Black people, Wheatley's words serve as blueprints that sketch pivotal shifts in "technologies" for resistance and a future map wherein religion operates as an intersectional heuristic that confronts social structures of power through the lenses of real and imagined experiences of human trauma, which speaks to universal oppressions and particular manifestations of oppressive structures of power for Black women. Wheatley's scripturalization elides neither the politics of identity—#EarlyBlackChristianWomensLivesMatter—nor the Christian hegemony that worked to create and sustain circumstances under which intersecting institutionalized powers reproduced and fostered social inequality. Indeed, her works both "identify and challenge structures as well as symbols of racism" (Angela Davis 85) and oppression. When we "peruse [her] song," and "wonder from whence" (Wheatley, "To the Right Honourable William, Earl of Dartmouth" lines 20–21), her twenty-first-century descendants might trace a line and plot their courses, emboldened, encouraged, and motivated to action, the eighteenth-century enslaved Black woman poet's words presciently resound the intersectional and inextricable truths captured in #MeToo and #TimesUp.[44] In Wheatley's words: "*No more*, America . . . *No longer* . . . wanton Tyranny . . . meant t'enslave the land" ("To the Right Honourable William, Earl of Dartmouth" 15–19; my emphasis). #WheatleyMatters #WheatleysWordsWorkMatters #EarlyBlackChrisitanWomensLivesMatter

2
Maria Stewart

Repoliticizing, Biblical Sampling, and Her World(s)

> All the nations of the earth are crying out for Liberty and Equality. *Away, away* with tyranny and oppression!
>
> —Maria W. Stewart

Nearly two decades after Phillis Wheatley's passing, from the late eighteenth century to the early and mid-nineteenth century, Maria Stewart responds to her predecessor's call with corresponding connotation that reinforces the urgency of both women's petitions for social justice. Echoing Wheatley's plaintive call, which implores with subtle urgency, "*No more*, America . . . *No longer* . . . wanton Tyranny . . . meant t'enslave the land" ("To the Right Honourable William, Earl of Dartmouth" lines 15–19), Stewart remixes and repoliticizes Wheatley's poetic pleas. Thus, Stewart's intensive WordsWork effects a frontal verbal assault that directly addresses and challenges the complex nature of the occupation and appropriation of African lands and Black bodies with her firm assertion that we will no longer tolerate colonization and slavery—the enslavement of land and peoples: "Away, away" demands the militant activist on behalf of worldwide protests against oppressions (Stewart, *Meditations* preface). Echoing outcries that have continued through the mass lynchings, race riots, and anti-Black violence of the 1830s, 1870s, and mid- and late 1900s to the murder of George Floyd, violence that continues to date, Stewart issues an appeal for Black people to resist: "And shall Afric's sons be silent any longer? Far be it from me to recommend to you either to kill, burn, or destroy. But I would strongly recommend to you to improve your talents; let not one lie buried in the earth" (qtd. in Waters,

Maria W. Stewart 161). Not unlike her predecessor Wheatley, she invokes scriptures through a radical revisioning of the concepts of Black and White. Stewart's WordsWork contradicts the privileging of skin color in the association of goodness with "White" to the empowerment of Blackness based on the intellect. She urges Black people, "Show forth your powers of mind, Prove to the world that . . . [counter to what Jeffersonian and politicized interpretations of scripture claim about Black people's lack of souls and the ability to reason] Though black your skins as shades of night, / Your hearts are pure, your souls are white" (qtd. in Waters, *Maria W. Stewart* 122).[1] Stewart's words provide building blocks of a Black consciousness with pan-African dimensions that resists domination through narratives of the myth of White supremacy, whether such controls are exercised in America or Africa—through enslavement and/or colonization. Of course, "colonization" may have denoted different meanings for Wheatley and Stewart—historically speaking. For the former, it was, on its surface, at least, colonization of America by the British with all its attendant violations of human and civil rights—extended not coincidentally to its enslaved and nominally free Black residents. Repoliticizing the frames of reference and contexts that asserted less than ingenuous motivations of pro-African concerns and anti-slavery agendas, Stewart proactively resists a movement—or more correctly a "scheme"—that involved the displacement of Black people, one that could effectively silence any resistance to the dehumanized conditions of enslaved, indentured, and oppressed Black people in the United States. Though her reworking of words and images were seemingly harmless attempts to "free" her countrywomen and men, Stewart relied on the Word in its historical context to recover a lost history that spoke truth to power. Specifically, because Stewart lived in a "post" colonial America, she turned her attention to the attempts by predominately White privileged American men in power to populate areas on the continent of Africa with free Black Americans—which she and others understood as a means to extend the colonization of sub-Saharan Africa already begun by the mid-1830s. The colonization scheme was meant to ensure that Black Americans existed as a population of wholly enslaved people in the United States, to "separate [free Blacks] from the slave population of [the] country" (Mehlinger 277).[2] In her "Address: Delivered at the African Masonic Hall" in Boston in 1833, Stewart made it quite clear that she was not willing to be stripped of her rightful claim as an African born in the United States: "Before I go, the bayonet shall pierce me through. African rights and liberty is a subject that ought to fire the breast of every free man of color in these United States" (4).

Born free in Hartford, Connecticut in 1803, orphaned at age five, "bound out in a clergyman's family" (*Meditations* 18). Stewart acquired literacy and a basic religious education from Sabbath school classes. Married to James W. Stewart in 1826 and widowed after four years, "America's first black political woman writer" (Richardson, qtd. in Stewart, *Maria W. Stewart*) experienced a religious transformation that made her "a strong advocate for the cause of God and the cause of freedom" (*Maria W. Stewart* 8).[3] Her personal history certainly suggests a woman who had been intimately acquainted with the implications and operations of power underlying any attempts to settle, establish, "repatriate," or otherwise occupy Africa with Black Americans. Among the cadre of anti-colonizationists Stewart was one of only a few Black women who publicly challenged the American Colonization Society, exposing its duplicity and feigned concerns for the education and "uplift" of Black America.[4] "Rather than donate money to fund black colonization in Liberia, these 'real friends' of African Americans, Stewart urged, should use those funds" in support of Black Americans "in this country," a country "that stifled black progress" (Power-Greene 46).[5]

Stewart's words, which inhabited multiple and intersecting worlds, evinced an established body of work deeply rooted in a religio-political discourse.[6] One example, among many, is found in Stewart's preface to the 1879 edition of *Meditations from the Pen of Mrs. Maria W. Stewart*. It is telling that in a work that identifies religion as the premise upon she will offer "meditations" she opens her text by introducing a heavily political and personal experience.[7] "The work was suppressed for forty-six years; and the author was struggling during that time in widowhood and sorrow to maintain her dignity and standing as a woman and a Christian in poverty's dark shade" (*Maria W. Stewart*). It had taken nearly fifty years: from 1829, when her husband died, to 1878, at the advanced age of seventy-five, for Stewart to receive a long overdue widow's pension for her husband's service in the U.S. Navy during the War of 1812. She speaks to her reader as a woman and a Christian; each of these intersectional identities posed its own set of challenges within the context of class. When one considers Stewart within a more contemporary frame of Black feminist ideology, it becomes evident that she is "giving voice to [her] personal experience" through this description of her "own reality" with a "a keen, comprehensive understanding of [Black] women's political reality" (hooks 25). On the one hand, her dignity and standing are at risk because of her current economic hardships; on the other, employing strategic dissemblance is a pecuniary necessity.

Her lack of financial resources had considerably exacerbated a condition of subjugation that stifled and silenced her voice. It had been forty-five years since Stewart gave the memorable farewell speech in Boston, and in this last edition of her work, published in the year she died, the author appears to have revealed only those "details of her own life story . . . that solidify her credentials as a Christian woman of good character" (Valerie Cooper 2). Stewart's framing of her character within a context of engagement with religion on terms defined by, about, and for African-descended Black people was not solely reliant upon an actual Black religious figure. Repoliticization of the spiritual for political aims was also a "reflect[ion] [of] the impact the African-American religious world had" on figures like atheist socialist A. Phillip Randolph (Taylor 7). Although Stewart clearly identifies as a Christian who relies on principles of religion, her methods are not wholly subsumed into an uncritical a-political stance. Rather, her WordsWork evidences a precedent-setting map for those "black men and women [of the Jim Crow post-slavery era] who combined politics with a religious worldview [and who] were able to motivate numerous people at the same time that a black secular left was being silenced by right-wing and moderate forces outside and within the black communities" (Valerie Cooper 6).[8]

At the time of this publication Stewart had, as she announced in her title, been working as a "matron of the Freedman's Hospital." By doing so, she signifies that in addition to "maintaining her dignity" in the face of "poverty's dark shade," her work continued to support and advance the cause of Black people. "Freedmen's [Hospital] established in 1863, is the oldest institution in the world which has had as one of its *primary objectives* the affording of *patient care and professional training to Negroes* . . . its contributions far exceed those of any similar institution" (Cobb 272; my emphasis).[9] Significantly, in her position, Stewart supported this mission, as she "continued to teach school, presided over the housekeeping needs of this community of homeless, needy, ill, and dispossessed within the nation's capital . . . [until] she died in December of 1879" (Richardson, qtd. in Stewart, *Maria W. Stewart* 85). This physical—and perhaps from our contemporary lens "invisible"—labor provided significant value to the postbellum Black folk for whom she so vociferously campaigned in her public speeches. As such, her recounting of the exertion of her body has implications for the connections Stewart signifies regarding the suppression of her intellectual labors: they were equally valuable to the mobilization of the early Black movement for human rights that straddled the ante- and postbellum eras. Specifically, her authorial voice and its messages were for her people who lacked adequate or basic economic resources. The author enables a microcosmic view based on her own circumstances to shine a bright light on underserved and disenfranchised Black women and men—one that captures the very political and spiritual worlds Stewart's work inhabited.

Not surprisingly, "the work" that was "suppressed" and the manner in which the same had "come up" as a result of the payment that had been withheld for nearly half a century resonates with an audience well aware of postbellum denial of civil rights, most prominently (but not only) suffrage. Her social justice work was not only halted when she stepped down from the speaker's platform in 1833, when she was vanquished from the Black woman's public sphere (through coerced self-exile) to other labors. The motivational WordsWork that would have continued to provocatively incite progress—on inter- and intra-racial terms—lay dormant for half a century.[10] Her words were not confined to an "all the Blacks are men" racial uplift. Nor were her words devoted to the empowerment of an "all the Whites are women" proto-feminism. Rather, she was an advocate and activist for Black women, moving from margins to center, who rightly divided the tool of the Word. Stewart thus mapped the inextricably linked race/class/gender boundaries such that she, who was Black, a woman, and economically disenfranchised, was articulated as central to challenging underlying systems of institutionalized oppression. Christina Henderson locates "Stewart's vision of resistance" in this text, observing that in building "on a tradition of African American thought that was influenced by the rhetoric of evangelicalism and the egalitarianism of the American Revolution," Stewart "'crafted a doctrine of religion and rebellion that by 1831 was well established'" (Hinks, qtd. in Henderson 54).[11]

The pivot of her secular voice and words are seen in Stewart's claim that she "believes that God's time has come for *the work* to be recognized among His people" (*Meditations* 18; my emphasis). This is neither avoidance nor escape into religion but rather a repoliticization of the concept of a benign or literal interpretation of divine providence. God's time is Stewart's time. She announces her WordsWork as divinely sanctioned and politically expedient. Brittany Sulzener points out that "in the nineteenth century . . . black women like Maria W. Stewart saw a nation so inherently corrupt that it must be destroyed or transformed in a catastrophic, apocalyptic event that would leave no traces of the former nation behind" (1).[12] This "apocalyptic framework" has critical implications for Stewart's use of biblical sampling throughout her meditations in texts that challenge oppression and signify on the consequences for the privileged classes, reiterated in the overtly political and secular narrative that operates in tandem with the sacred.[13] Importantly, "for Stewart, religion and the loving community it creates are necessary precursors to victory" (Henderson 56). And as such, she invokes as "justification for violence . . . rebellion not just as self-defense but as an act of love." It is significant that "Christian love" motivates, indeed instigates acts of social justice (Henderson 58) for Black people. Stewart's words work to invoke the kind of heavy lifting done by Black women. They not only galvanize a people toward unity, they also collectively struggle for equity and human rights. Like Wheatley, Stewart's words also provide a kind of solace or comfort for the trauma caused by spiritual violence. The carnage wrought by the institution of slavery and its inheritor, institutionalized race-based oppression, was manifested not only in the flesh but the very souls of Black folk.[14] This is perhaps why "prayer [is] central" rather than "peripheral" to understanding Stewart's "analysis of the class, race, and gender dynamic of African American culture and history" (Bassard, *Transforming Scriptures* 53).[15]

Contemporary Black women artivists and lyricists like Lauryn Hill capture the significance of religion beyond mere allusion and thus enact a repoliticization of the Word—like Stewart—in songs such as "Final Hour." In this song, Hill reverses a widely held myth about the evils of money that was often recited prayer-like in economically disenfranchised communities as a way to "comfort" those less fortunate by focusing on the seemingly more valuable currency—their otherworldly salvation. In other words, such myths that relied on scriptures about the "meek" who "shall inherit the earth" (Matthew 5:5, KJV) or the idea that "it is easier for a camel to get through the eye of a needle, than for a rich man to enter the kingdom of God" (Matthew 19:24, KJV) often served to valorize poverty, pacifying those who endured it—and this was especially true for many Black communities. Hill, however, reminds us in her refrain that it is not a question of either/or, but rather one of both/and: "You can get the money / You can get the power / But keep your eyes on the Final Hour." Hill is adamant that one can "Let God redeem you, keep your deen true / You can get the green too / Watch out what you cling to, observe how a queen do." Redemption does not, in the lyricist's prayer about the final hour, depend on a life of poverty and denial; she merely cautions about making a "god" out of one's earthy possessions. She concludes by pointing directly to a biblical verse that she intends to be read in a different way: "And I remain calm reading the 73rd Psalm." This verse is sampled for its multiple connotations and for its complex rendering of concepts such as the intersection and balancing of the spiritual with the material—with its political connotations as well.

As one of the Wisdom Psalms that deals with "faithful living in a corrupt and unfair world," Hill's concluding citation of this scripture punctuates her refrain about "money," "power," and "the Final Hour." Travis Harris observes that "Hill do[es] not have a problem with getting money." Rather, her lyrics are a "cautioning to Hip Hop . . . that pursuit of money and prominence may signify an empty and envious heart." According to Harris, Hill's reference to "the 73rd Psalm which is a Psalm by Asaph pondering the prosperity of the wicked while the righteous suffer . . . [is her] realiz[ation] [that] despite the prosperity of the wicked, they will fall" (21). Celnisha L. Dangerfield points to the importance of songs like "Final Hour," among many in which Hill makes use of biblical "references [and] characters [and stories]" (216) as they point to the significance of "mythical references" and African American "cultural beliefs" represented in the figures and narratives of "Moses and Aaron," for example (217). Following Stewart, contemporary artivists, particularly Black women like Hill, utilize genre expectations to unpack, sample, and articulate their complex responses to the social inequality they observe as prevalent aspects of their experiences as marginalized and disenfranchised Americans. They do so by charting the retrieval of symbolic and literal humanity through religious and political compasses that operate on multivalent axes of race, class, and gender. For example, Hill's shifting of the "focus from the richest to the brokest" and her suggestion to "amend . . . every law that ever prevented" the "survival" of African American people are directly connected to her promise to "document" the history of two very different biblical brothers (Moses and Aaron), who worked together as allies and family for the mutual uplifting of their people in crisis. Like Stewart, who "made use of Genesis and Psalms to assert insurgence in the consciousness of her oppressed brethren" (Harrell 314), Hill issues a final call to oppressor and oppressed.

Hill interweaves and simultaneously veils secular with sacred performances that evince a critical repoliticizing of the spiritual, through which she invokes a god that can provide both physical and moral certainties, even as she cautions that the focus on the "success" that fame and fortune bring to the exclusion of all else is a destructive obsession, a "hypnosis" that her "opus" means to "reverse." Hill's lyrical invocations, like Stewart's meditations and prayers, are not as transparent as they appear, nor are they as seemingly operative as biblical analogy or paraphrase. For example, less "transparent" in this history Hill promises to document, but I would argue is nonetheless present, is a key figure in biblical herstory: Miriam, Moses and Aaron's older sister, to whom Moses owed his "survival since [his] arrival . . . seen through" the legacy of "Lauryn Hill from New-Ark to Israel" (Hill, "Final Hour"). Scholars in hip-hop feminism and related intellectual and cultural artisans and genres, in the works and words of Joan Morgan, Jessica Care Moore, Brittney Cooper, Missy Elliot, McLite, Queen Latifah, Nicki Minaj, and Cardi B, as well as countless others, claim *The Miseducation of Lauryn Hill* as an inaugural work in hip-hop feminism, one that ushered in a contemporary era of Black women's use of art as necessary propaganda in the movements for social justice. Significantly, this foundational artivism pays homage to the WordsWork of foremothers like Maria Stewart.

It is certainly worth considering that in the same years that Stewart that published her earliest specifically spiritual works, *Religion and the Pure Principles of Morality, the Sure Foundation on Which We Must Build* and *Meditations from the Pen of Mrs. Maria W. Stewart* (1831–1832), she also gave voice to secular concerns in which political contexts could and should be realized. She gave the "first public lecture by an American woman before an audience of both men and women" (Roberson 56) on September 21, 1832, at Franklin Hall in Boston. It is often referred to as the "Why Sit Ye Here and Die?" speech because of its call for civil disobedience and resistance to the oppression of Black people, especially Black women. In her "Lecture Delivered at Franklin Hall," Stewart underscores the inter-gender racism that exists between White and Black women, which she argues is evidence of "the powerful force of prejudice" and the "cruel and unfeeling distinction" (*Meditations* 55, 59) based on little else than skin color even as she challenges free Black men to act with earnest resolve on behalf of the rights of all Black people enslaved and free, especially women, who carry the additional burden of their sex.[16]

> I have asked several individuals of *my sex*, who transact business for *themselves*, if, providing *our* girls were to give *them* the most satisfactory references, *they* would not be willing to grant *them* an equal opportunity with others? *Their* reply has been: For *their* own part, *they* had no objection; but as it was not the custom, were *they* to take *them* into *their* employ, *they* would be in danger of losing the public patronage. (Stewart, "Lecture Delivered at Franklin Hall," qtd. in *Maria W. Stewart* 45; my emphasis)

I highlight pronouns in this passage to call attention to the way Stewart's signifying strategy makes use of the first and third person to stress the division between women. On the one hand, she appears to embrace a shared identity as she addresses the businesswomen of whom she inquires about possible employment as not only of the same biological trait, "my sex," but also as related by their gender to "our girls." As such, Stewart seemingly constructs a community of young women who belong to a common community of mature women who operate in a somewhat familial role, who take responsibility for the future and the success of young women whom they mentor and for whom they create opportunities. On the other hand, Stewart's pronouns seem to place distance between White women and Black women. Notably, Stewart's reference to the girls as "ours," which suggests a relationship of belonging, might be read as simultaneously imparting or extending connections beyond and within the nineteenth-century constructed racial boundaries. Even the term *girls* might be interpreted as a reference to the kind of infantilizing and condescending language that marginalizes women, especially Black women.[17] Such intra-gender racial segregation is confirmed through Stewart's repeated references to "they, them, their, themselves," which is meant as a challenge to the White women with "race" privilege who are in a position to hire Black women, women who might potentially support and empower other women. In fact, the potential of this challenge to create an opportunity for her White sisters to join her as allies in the struggle for all women's rights is lost on "them." Stewart demonstrates the bonds of sisterhood that are shattered by racism, and moreover the detached and dismissive tone of privilege it carries.

"Those" women who have economic power offer a tepid reply in response to the chance to uplift other women. After all, not opposing is quite different from being willing to use one's position to improve the lives of others. Of course, it is important to consider the complicated position of relative power held by White women in the late nineteenth century; they were not only bound by tradition but also reliant upon support and backing from a racist and patriarchal society, creating at least one factor that complicates the notion of seemingly autonomous empowered women's refusal to help Black women. That said, Stewart clearly maintains that racism is the cause of this lack of concern from her fellow women, "this cruel and unfeeling distinction" for those of another "complexion." They are not, after all, their sisters or their people, but rather those who have succumbed to the "powerful force of prejudice" (32). Her exclamation of the bigotry and discrimination Black women experience from other women rings loud and clear, despite the shared struggles that should unite them. Such a complex point of view and intersectional weaving of gender and race supports the view that "for Stewart, the future of black Americans was all bound up with the woman question" (Jones 23). I would add that for Stewart, and others like her, there was no "woman question" without Black women.

What is particularly significant about Stewart's repoliticization of the spiritual is the way in which it disrupts the silence of Black women's exegetical power. Like the contemporary artivist who defaces monuments to bigotry and hatred through vandalism, graffiti, web spoofing, and the like, Stewart's words are meant to smash away the conventional language that effectively muzzles Black women. Stewart entreats the "daughters of Africa" to raise their voices against oppression, to be self-reflexive in their judgment, and then to work toward holding themselves and their nation accountable for the redress and development of Black people. She is clear that Black people are accountable to each other, especially their progeny, but is equally adamant that such accountability, couched as it is in the politics of nineteenth-century gendered respectability, should not be interpreted as license to suppress their voices. Black women should not allow others to silence them. Indeed, despite "ignorance . . . prejudices," and at the risk of "calumny and reproach," Stewart responds to a series of hypophoric questions: "But shall I, for fear of feeble man who shall die, hold my peace? Shall I, for fear of scoffs and frowns, refrain from my *tongue*? Ah, no! I *speak* as one that must give an account at the awful bar of God; I *speak* as a dying mortal, to dying mortals" (*Meditations* 12; my emphasis). Emphasizing the morally and spiritually sanctioned woman's voice, Stewart emphatically interjects her own by refusing to be silenced by those whom she characterizes as equals, and whom she renders equally accountable to the moral authority of God.[18] Her WordsWork functions as a tool of activism, going beyond reinforcing the power of a woman's voice through her "I speak."

She supports her right to voice, and by extension the right of all women, through an exegetical intervention of the scriptural edict: "So then every one of us shall give an account of himself [and of course herself] to God" (Romans 14:12). Importantly, this passage of scripture, whose words are echoed by Stewart, warns about the spiritual dangers of judgment, and the very type that Stewart observes come as a result of prejudice and ignorance. Additionally, Stewart is simultaneously referring to the resultant slanderous and defamatory criticism that she experiences because of bigotry and sexism, even within her own community.[19] The Bible states that "every *idle* word that men shall speak, they shall give an account thereof in the day of judgement" (Matthew 12:36, KJV; my emphasis). To those who would discount or attempt to discredit Black women's leadership in religion and politics through baseless and unfounded assumptions or claims based solely on their race and gender, Stewart issues a warning: they too are bound as Christians to justify their "idle" words.[20] Appropriately, through the supremacy of the Word extracted and extended through her exegetical dexterity, Stewart demonstrates the necessity and obligation of Black women to reject suppression of their voices. The Word is not simply a tool in the hands of a skillful orator. Nor is her understanding of biblical language, history, and contexts merely a means to demonstrate intellectual prowess as a challenge to prevailing prejudices against gender and race. Though Stewart most certainly demonstrates her keen use of signifying strategies as an orator and her critical acumen in the writing of words that compel the listener to hear her voice, what is equally important is that she recovers her social self and disrupts the double consciousness that enables self-discernment against natal alienation.[21]

Therefore, Stewart renders herself literally, physically, psychologically, spiritually, politically, and socially viable within the cultural contexts of social death during an era of slavery and nominal freedom for Black women. "As a result, one finds in their hermeneutic response . . . an implicit privileging of sociopolitical experience . . . a subtle strategy to retrieve the biblical text for use in arguments in favor of black uplift and empowerment, African American women like Stewart used their lives and history as the prism through which scripture was refracted and subsequently evaluated" (V. Cooper 19). Such an approach evinces Stewart's engagement with religion as a vehicle through which intersections with the personal and the political function as modes of self-engagement and acceptance—thereby resurrecting the social death to which Black women had been consigned or relegated. Cooper highlights Stewart's use of Ethiopianism as an important symbolic interpretation of an early Afrocentricity that does not denote a return to Africa.[22] Instead, Stewart suggests that "if the colonizationists are real friends to Africa, let them spend the money which they collect, in erecting a college to educate her injured sons in this land of gospel light and liberty" (Stewart, qtd. in V. Cooper 179). She articulates a well-reasoned argument for reparations based on the rights of Black Americans who have been exploited by slavery while simultaneously pointing out the corruption of the notion of freedom and Christianity.

The dual perspective of the rights of fairness within Stewart's understanding of how faith should operate within a democratic society and the rights of all humans is essential to recovering and freeing herself from social death—and manumitting the bonds of Christian slavery.[23] In his 2014 opinion article "Black Men and Women Rising: Resurrection After

Social Death," Maulana Karenga's Afrocentric consideration of Stewart's words is particularly relevant as we consider her confrontation with the cultural, political, and religious challenge to "social death" in nineteenth-century America. He underscores Stewart's challenge to free Black people to resurrect themselves "during the Holocaust of enslavement which was a morally monstrous act of physical and cultural genocide . . . designed to ensure the social death of enslaved Africans—i.e., culturally dead to themselves and dead as humans to their enslavers, reduced to objects of labor, sex and entertainment." Karenga reads Stewart's appeal to the "daughters of Africa, [to] Awake! Awake! Arise! No longer sleep nor slumber, but distinguish [and] Show forth to the world that (you) are endowed with noble and exalted faculties" as a Walkeresque clarion call for Black unity, political self-sufficiency, and moral enlightenment.[24] Fitly, Stewart's words summon her people toward a "striving and struggling together to end ignorance, to bring light to dimmed, self-deceived and narrowed minds, cultivate the love of learning and righteous living; love each other" (Karenga). This framing of light and dark links Stewart to her literary predecessor Wheatley, as both appear to repoliticize the terms under which darkness and light were traditionally used by White slaveholding society to denote the inherent racial inferiority of Black people by exposing and problematizing American cultural conditioning about African and African-descended people.

Stewart's "Why Sit Ye Here and Die?" suggests the significance she attributed to personal agency. Her existential framing of slavery in her juxtaposition of the physical and psychological bondage of African-descended people demands a closer reading to understand her frame of reference for repoliticizing the Word through the symbolic linkage of reason and religion for political ends. First, she draws attention to the power that both secular and sacred knowledge holds to free the enslaved—physically, mentally, and psychologically. Stewart declares, "There are no chains so galling as the chains of ignorance—no fetters so binding as those that bind the soul, and exclude it from the vast field of useful and scientific knowledge" (*Maria W. Stewart* 45). In the same breath, Stewart moves from a general philosophical view of wisdom to a pointed political perspective that both laments her personal lack of formal education and simultaneously disparages the theft of literacy and learning through enforcement of codified legal and social norms to prevent Black people from a proper education: "O, had I received the advantages of early education, my ideas would, ere now, have expanded far and wide" (45). However, Stewart refuses to allow racism to have the last word. Instead, she refers (albeit indirectly) to a scripturally based tenant about the supremacy of knowledge, wisdom, and true education: "But, alas! I possess nothing but moral capability—no teachings but the teachings of the Holy Spirit" (45). She intentionally leaves the hearer of her words to consider the proverbial message, which echoes: "The fear of the Lord is the beginning of wisdom: and the knowledge of the holy is understanding" (Proverbs 9:10, KJV). If the only "teachings" she is allowed in a society that inhibits and prohibits Black women's formal secular education are those "of the Holy Spirit," then Stewart is wise indeed.

Second, Stewart, recaptures the power inherent in the Word, which in itself is laborious work that demands attention to conceiving as yet untried secular and sacred paths and patterns. Then she uses it as a platform from which to advocate for the employment of Black women, to expose the "powerful force of prejudice" (*Maria W. Stewart* 46), to decry the conditions for free Black people who labor under "continual drudgery" (46) with little hope for anything better. Under such conditions, Stewart affirms a give me equity and equality or give me death perspective that challenges social injustice in a militant voice that calls for activism among the free Black population, incites uprising among the enslaved, and reminds the White oppressive slaveholding racist society of the limits of their power. "But ah! Methinks our oppression is soon to come to an end; yes, before the Majesty of heaven, our groans and cries have reached the ears of the Lord of Sabaoth [James 5:4]." Though hers was a short-lived public-speaking career, Stewart's work—from her speeches to pamphlets and essays in the *Liberator* to the 1879 edition of *Meditations from the Pen of Mrs. Maria W. Stewart*—provides evidence that her theorizing the political through spiritual lenses was a significant model of resistance and means for articulating her intersecting identities and establishing her sociopolitical position from unassailable foundations—rooted in and routed through a repoliticization of the Word. As Kristin Waters argues convincingly, Stewart's "struggle for political freedom and equality emerges from a fusion of religion and politics. The powerful principles of morality; not just for venial matters but for more profound ones, have far-reaching implications" (*Maria Stewart* 9).

Stephanie Y. Evans argues that "black women theorizing their social position is not a new phenomenon. As early as Wheatley (1770s), Stewart (1830s), and Frances Harper (1850s), activists have publicly reflected on the meaning and experience of their social standpoints *as black women*" (10). Evans's theoretical model of "standpoint social contract," which draws upon "a framework based on Rousseau's *Social Contract*, Carol Pateman's *Sexual Contract*, and Charles Mill's *Racial Contract*," (5) is instructive as we extend the cultural context of "natal alienation, articulated and reinforced" (Orlando Patterson 8) to a consideration of the climate of intellectual estrangement experienced by early Black women philosophers like Stewart. Specifically, Evans's "standpoint social contract" articulates the position of "black collegiate women [who] were caught in a unique social contract because of the intersection of their race and gender" (5). While Stewart was not, formally speaking, what could be termed a "collegiate woman," she was most certainly considered an intellectual. This distinction is necessary, given Stewart's renown among her scholarly and academic contemporaries.[25] Consequently, Evans's approach to the study of formally educated Black women of the late nineteenth to mid-twentieth centuries is useful in understanding how early Black intellectual women like Stewart experienced social death of yet another type—the death of the mind through social pressure to acquiesce to a mindset of mediocrity. That is, the attempt to suppress their intellectual productions, especially those that challenged dominant discourses related to race, gender, slavery, freedom, and social justice for Black people, was equally culpable in terms of social death experienced, especially by Black women. If, as Evans observes, "the framers of this nation's Constitution . . . penned a foundational agreement that hinged upon black women's subjugated position [and] . . . mandated that black women be ignorant, silent, and subservient," Stewart's repoliticization of religion for social justice provides strong evidence of her breaking not merely with traditional roles that bound White women to relative power but, far more radically, her voice represented a heretical stance that exposed the nefarious nature of intersecting exploitation of religion and politics "that excluded all black women from political participation and social equity" (5).

Not unlike contemporary Black women political leaders like Senator Maxine Waters, Stewart insists on "reclaiming [her] time," and is adamant about being accorded the respect of having her words heard and appropriately interpreted. Stewart signals such with her pronouncement "methinks," which, generally speaking, means "it seems to me."[26] However, the compound word is also a reminder that Stewart the intellectual, the philosopher (if you will) has engaged in thoughtful discernment about issues she raises and their implications for her intersecting constituencies. It would not surprise a nineteenth-century audience any more than it ought a contemporary twenty-first-century reader that *Meditations* should by its very nature be contemplative, profound, and at times, perhaps a bit surprisingly, even metaphysical.[27]

Stewart's sentient and sage reasoning on the injustice and brutality she witnesses in humanity is of consequence as we consider connections between what matters to this early Black Christian woman and what remains critical to her twenty-first-century descendants. First, she not only "hears" in material and otherworldly terms, but her understanding and further probing from the standpoint of judgments, based on her experiential knowledge, connects hearing to feeling.[28]

> But methinks I hear a voice, which says: Blessed are they that mourn, for they shall be comforted. Methinks I hear a voice, which says: Daughter, be of good cheer; thy sins be forgiven thee. Consoling thought! O, thou compassionate Redeemer, was it love that induced thee to leave the realms of bliss, and take upon thee the form of a servant, and descend into this lower world, to die for fallen man? Infinite love! Amazing condescension! A mystery, indeed, that the angels desire to look into. Even eternity will be too short for blood-washed millions to celebrate thy praises. (*Meditations* 23)

In "Meditation VIII" and the prayer that follows, Stewart responds both to a divine voice and to the earthly presence of an oppressed enslaved people. Beginning with the contrasting conjunction "but," which signals a fundamental contradiction between her depressed feelings about human failings and personal loss and Stewart's feelings of exuberant optimism based on the spiritual solace of her faith, she draws on words and their power to incite moves that enable recovery from social death. Somewhere between Jeremiah and Nehemiah, Stewart's biblical hope is framed within a context that insists Black lives matter. As she has done elsewhere in her speeches, essays, and writings, she issues a prophetic call to personal responsibility by engaging in a dialogue about what Black people can do for themselves, about their moral and spiritual fortitude. Her words repoliticize discourses that frame racial uplift within static limitations of self-help advice about how oppressed people can engage in conservative practices of self-improvement. Specifically, her focus is not on a simplistic vision of empowering Black people through challenging White paternal narratives that mythologize and pathologize a monolithic Black identity. Rather, Stewart reclaims, in Sankofic manner, a time such as this for her people, who matter, by imagining self-reliant individuals, constituting a collective community of people who possess power, secular and sacred.[29] As such Stewart returns to fetch some of what was lost through the literal and figurative Middle Passage. Black people have been redeemed spiritually by a savior who looks like them: one who shares physical, psychological, and social circumstances of class and caste, whose power is located precisely in the conscious decision to liberate his people by any means necessary.

The contemplation that leads to an assurance of her personal power within what is not dependent on external circumstances not only reminds her of the self-sacrifice upon which her faith is based, it also grounds her in a knowledge of a family history through which she, as an orphan, may reclaim her place as "daughter" as well as a means for the grieving and impoverished widow to receive the consoling and compassionate love of her heavenly father. Not unlike Wheatley's numerous elegies for women, family, and loss or Lee's sermons about "the widow's God . . . father to the fatherless . . . [who]comforted and solaced" (qtd. in Andrews, *Sisters of the Spirit* 41) her in her "state of widowhood and sorrows," Stewart's meditations provide healing spaces and maps for recovery from social death. It is well documented that the scriptural source in this meditation, taken from the Beatitudes, was of significance to Black people during the slavery and antebellum eras—the identification with and assurance of themselves as blessed people deserving of love and compassion, despite their lowly condition, was critical to survival.[30] Stewart's contemplation of three New Testament verses is worth considering through the lens of scriptural sampling, as they frame a context within which a repoliticization of the spiritual can be explored: Matthew 5:4, Matthew 9:22, and Philippians 3:7.

She begins her meditation with the declaration from a voice in Matthew 5:4 that not only validates grief as a worthy and divinely sanctioned deed, but also, more importantly, is a spiritual endorsement that celebrates the actions of a community of people as they respond to their afflictions, suffering, or sorrows.[31] It is significant that in her contemplation of the New Testament scripture Stewart invokes the instruction of a divine teacher from the well-cited Sermon on the Mount. Scholars have offered much to our understanding of this text in the context of social justice. It is Jesus's consolation and reassurance to poor and underserved people, and it is at the same time Stewart's Afrofuturistic calling into existence. She claims, perhaps insists, through a holy otherworldly voicing an equitable existence for women who, like Stewart, experience added distress as a result of being unfairly treated during their most vulnerable times.[32] Stewart is cheated out of that which is rightfully hers, and there was no legal recourse, given that the executors of her husband's will were the actual defrauders.[33] Moreover, as a Black woman she had little power or authority. Her meditation on the kind of treatment to which she was entitled exposes White men's violation of secular and sacred law and demonstrates her exercise of the agency over which she had *author*ity. She holds under public scrutiny those by whom she should have been treated kindly, who should have taken every opportunity, as the executors of her husband's will, to ensure that this widow would live the kind of life for which her wealthy husband had provided. Her meditation on Matthew 5:4 challenges society's mistreatment of widows, and simultaneously repoliticizes the quintessential social justice scripture. Elsewhere, Stewart directly and harshly chastised White slaveholding society for its oppression, invoking the authority and power of God's wrath upon them for their cruelty against enslaved and free Black Americans as well as for their neglect of the very men and women who had enriched the country. However, in her re-membering of the ancient text and re-inscription of the social justice script, she illustrates another point of entry for her resistance—the sacred Word.

Specifically, her meditation was an intellectual and spiritual reminder that while the world in which she lived may not feel the responsibility to "cause the widow's heart to sing for joy" (*Meditations* 12), Black women like Stewart could take solace in scriptures. Even more than spiritual succor, her reflection on and consideration of scriptures invites the reader to indulge in a transitory but renewing mindfulness that charts a powerful path of self-care for nineteenth-century Black women like Stewart, with perhaps some saliency for her contemporary twenty-first-century descendants. There is no mistaking that the meditations are not so subtly transgressive, necessarily providing an institutional intervention through the Word to speak (godly) truths to (worldly) powers. Between Jesus and Martin Luther King Jr., there is a significance of this mapping for the articulation of a new millennial Black womanist liberation theology and postcolonial framing in a "post-racial" Afrofuturistic cypher. If a postcolonial reading of the Beatitudes, and in particular this verse, confirms a political pathway through which the muzzled voices of the oppressed and silenced are unleashed, then Stewart represents a continuum in the legacy of progressive movements over generations. She hears voices that urge her to engage in acts of self-pleasure and happiness, that remind her she is indeed valued, and that, not unlike the woman with an issue of blood who is healed, there is indeed a balm or salve for her people.[34] Stewart alludes metaphorically through her reflection on Matthew 9:22—the narrative about the woman with an issue of blood who is healed by touching the hem of Jesus's garment—to her own admonitions in several of her speeches about the work to be done by Africa's sons and daughters to rescue or redeem themselves. Seemingly aggressive acts of civil disobedience and violations of traditions are called forth in Stewart's employment of scriptural mediation of secular traditions, cultural norms, scriptural interpretations, and the implications for Black people.[35] Her introspective reflections invite instructive remedies based on paradigmatic ordering and scriptural sampling to pause and reflect on antebellum American society and its human rights violations.[36]

Long before the hashtag that "launched a modern movement . . . [and] shaped a rallying cry" that yielded "a new and concise way of affirming Black humanity in the twenty-first century" (Feminista Jones 26), Stewart's nineteenth-century "Black feminism" campaigned relentlessly and unapologetically—on political and spiritual grounds—that Black women's lives not only mattered, but it was their God-given right to an abundant quality of life. And moreover, Stewart demonstrated that it was through their brave acts that all Black life might be redeemed. Women who step up, speak out, and let their issues be known—that is, those who speak truth to power—are enablers of right action, creators of sociopolitical contexts within which their issues, and by extension the voices of their communities, might be heard and through which they can receive restorative actions. Analogous to the biblical narrative upon which she meditates, Stewart's power came through "Jesus [who] turned . . . and when he saw her" he acknowledged that it was her actions prompted by her "faith" that "made [her] whole."[37]

She follows this seemingly personal and reflective act of divinely sanctioned self-recognition with a summoning voice that calls for public policy that helps to mitigate the conditions that create landscapes fertile for self-destructive personal choices. There are perhaps times when the links or parallels that Stewart draws between externally imposed and legally mandated conditions of Black people—free and enslaved—and the subsequent deficiencies in the educational and vocational opportunities that enable Black social progress are not always as clear as a contemporary reader might hope. There appears to be no shortage of the politics of respectability implicated in her speeches, albeit they are of a disruptive and arguably transgressive form in certain instances.[38] However, such dissemblance does not diminish the weight of this free Black woman's self-authorizing words, undergirded by the Word. She disturbs and disrupts as much as she appears to co-sign a status quo.

One such disturbance can be located in Stewart's attention to the "balm of Gilead," which signifies in its more general meaning a universal cure, or more specifically "resin from the styrax tree, produced in the north Transjordan region of Gilead, widely used for medicinal purposes" (Frame et al. 182). Stewart repoliticizes Jeremiah's rhetorical question to the people of Judah in Jeremiah 8:22 and illuminates the perpetual testimony that the geographical and Hebraic meaning of "Gilead" denotes. The adjacent and intersecting Old Testament themes are most personal and political to Stewart, including but not limited to the capture and selling of Joseph into slavery by his people in Genesis 37 that Jeremiah invokes, with its indirect reference to slavery and Joseph's plea to the people of Judah regarding their culpability in his enslavement, which includes his own family.[39] A similar question is posed by Stewart to slaveholders and slaveholding society about its "sin" and her deliberate contemplation of the underlying disease that has ravaged "blood-washed millions." The blood of Christ that redeems is clearly the first layer of Stewart's meditation, but simultaneously, not unlike Wheatley and Lee, the judgment or "hearing" she proffers is not to be dismissed as mere coincidence.

Nor are the words of the Negro spiritual embedded in this meditation to be overlooked as religious embellishment.[40] As recently as 2018, Crunkadelic ("aka Dr. Susana M. Morris") invokes the concept of "balm" to reinforce the importance of "joy" as a necessary tool in the social justice arsenal. Resisting the trend of think pieces, critical essays, and film reviews "going down" numerous "rabbit hole[s]" about characters, plots, and other "interesting and important questions" about the film *Black Panther*, Crunkadelic chooses to address the feelings it invokes on a very personal yet simultaneously political level. "Seeing my Blackness represented in a myriad of ways on screen has been a powerful *healer* . . . a balm in Wakanda." Crunkadelic highlights the intensity of delight and pleasures that this Afrofuturistic film invokes through shared experiences of collective celebration, inspiration, and imagination of "ways to thrive in the future" in an "uncolonized world," and most of all for Crunkadelic, "the joy that Black art can bring." Notably, the Black Lives Matter Foundation "mission states that we are re-imagining the present and investing in the future of Black lives. To do that, we must focus on the intangibles that create our future. One of those intangibles is *joy*. Black communities the world over have deeply unique understandings and expressions of joy and culture. As an organization that aims to re-imagine the future, we must *intentionally* carve out a lane that centers joy as we move forward." A similar emotional potency can be extracted from a liberally applied balm of Stewart's meditations, in the symbolic recovery achieved through biblically sampled re-presentations of nineteenth-century Black womanity. In the prayer following "Meditation VIII," Stewart offers an image of herself as a formerly diseased woman (36) who is not only desirous and deserving of spiritual redemption but who is healed and therefore has refused to "sink in despair" (37). This restorative healing from abject depression and oppression manifested in the body of Stewart is extended to all Black people through her special plea "for the [liberation of] benighted sons and *daughters* of Africa" (37). In both her meditative and contemplative states of being—as Christian and social justice warrior—she provides counter-narratives (not unlike Wakanda) against prevailing images of Black womanity as irredeemably broken and perpetually victimized, which may serve as navigable symbolic and literal maps of recovery.

Make no mistake, when Stewart took the podium among what was termed a "provocative" or mixed-gender audience, she was well aware of the literal and symbolic meaning of her physical presence in what would have been considered a "man's place." She knew precisely "where and when she entered."[41] She understood that in "1832 women didn't speak in public, especially on serious issues like civil rights, and most especially feminism" (Giddings 50). Importantly, "Stewart articulated the precepts upon which the future activism of Black women would be based. Her ideas reflected both the fundamentals of the Victorian ethic and a criticism of its inherent biases. Out of that mix emerged a *distinct ethos* which underlined Black women's activism for generations to come" (50; my emphasis). I concur with Giddings but want to emphasize that Stewart's "distinct ethos" included a language and philosophy richly embedded with tenets of the Christian faith, thus facilitating her repoliticization of the spiritual.

Like other "antebellum black protest[ers]," Stewart "manifested deep roots in religious beliefs" (Rael 1). Her public voice issued a clarion call that echoed back to her predecessor and departed friend David Walker. Though Stewart's words were chiefly addressed to African-descended men and women about their political position in the United States during the mid-nineteenth century, she spoke and wrote in the language of righteous indignation with the full force of what might be termed a religious warrior, with the authority of God behind and all around her.

In her 1832 speech at Franklin Hall in Boston, "Why Sit Ye Here and Die?" Stewart speaks directly to the issue of the oppression of Black women—arguing that they have been denied equal protection under the law against violations of their person and denied equal access to progress through discriminatory employment practices. She demands the rights of Black women to "rise above the condition of servants and drudges" (*Maria W. Stewart* 47). She was no less critical of Black men who sought to impose such limitations and suppress and oppress Black women.

In her 1833 "Address: Delivered at the African Masonic Hall, Boston," Stewart boldly appealed for African rights, observing that the disdain and disregard of the basic humanity and rights of her people "have fired my soul with a holy indignation, and compelled me thus to come forward; and endeavor to turn their attention to knowledge and improvement; for knowledge is power" (*Maria W. Stewart* 57).

These are her concerns not only in the public oratorical sphere (despite the tendency to want to classify her oratory as sermons, Stewart herself insisted on them as speeches) but also in her written work. In both her 1831 pamphlet *Religion and the Pure Principles of Morality, the Sure Foundation on Which We Must Build* and her 1832 *Meditations from the Pen of Mrs. Maria W. Stewart*, Stewart's sacred mission is inextricable from her civic responsibility to do the work necessary to "go forward, and take off the reproach that is cast upon the people of color" (*Maria W. Stewart* 20). Her right as "a woman" to do this critical work is sanctioned by the will of the "Lord Jesus." So the "spiritual interrogation" demands a political intervention, despite any obstacles she may have met, whether from those outside or within her own race or sex, those who attempted to effectively render her inhuman on the bases of her sex and race.

Stewart's genre enables a more overtly political stance on the quality of Black life, especially Black women's lives, yet her words are grounded in religion. Like Wheatley, she provides a comparative lens through which we can consider the coexisting progress and uplifting of White citizens operating concurrently with the under/devaluing of Black citizens. She points to the contradictions in how "American people . . . [are] thriving in arts . . . sciences . . . and . . . literature . . . aim[ing] . . . to excel in political, moral and religious improvement . . . [even the] poorest ones, who have the least wish to excel. . . . But how very few . . . bestow one thought upon the benighted sons and daughters of Africa, who have enriched the soils of America with their tears and blood" (*Maria W. Stewart* 34–35). Clearly, neither the progress, intellect, nor enhancement of Black people's education matter to a society invested in upholding the myth of White supremacy. Stewart's impassioned words (here and elsewhere) advocate for self-reliance and self-sufficiency among African American people, with clear evidence of their role in the advancement of the nation. At the same time, she vociferously holds White society accountable for its collusion in Black America's underdevelopment: Their "hearts . . . so frozen toward [Black people] they had rather their money should be sunk in the ocean than to administer it to [their] relief" (61).

Following Wheatley, Stewart couches her challenge to White American indifference to Black America by connecting the "heart" to inaction. Wheatley's colonial—"steel'd"—and Stewart's antebellum—"frozen"—American heart are similarly (actually identically) characterized as indifferent and malicious because of the inactions of people who lack feeling or concern for fellow humans whose conditions they are in a position to uplift but instead deny. Arguably, such a linguistic gesture might be said to point to early women's inextricable link between political action and spiritual feeling. However, Stewart moves beyond reactionary responses to institutional racism. Rather, than merely stating the problem, she offers proactive solutions and encouragement to uplift Black people. She says: "Let us promote ourselves and improve our own talents." Stewart rejoices in the knowledge that "there are many able and talented ones among us, whose names might be recorded on the bright annals of fame. But, '*I can't*,' is a great barrier in the way, I hope it will soon be removed, and '*I will*' resume its place" (*Maria W. Stewart* 35). Her unabashed affirmation of collective Black worth and values and her stance on self-determination are emblematic of the early Black nationalist strain (albeit with its attendant and problematic respectability politics), echoing across centuries.[42]

Extending Jane Martin's view that although "scholars have recognized women as teachers and activists . . . not enough . . . have been granted the status of 'philosophers'" (qtd. in Evans 6), Evans underscores the role of race and highlights the failure of historical canons to acknowledge "black women's intellectual production" (6). Perhaps most relevant to Stewart's experience as intellectual and philosopher for whom social death was apparent is Evans's observation that despite the "many obstacles . . . black women wanted the right to whatever education might be available for a citizen of democracy" (7). Even though most nineteenth-century Black women did not have access to college or extensive formal education, "a few activists, such as Maria Stewart . . . had the advantage of grammar school or secondary education" (28). Ironically, her insistence "that the meaning-making process be tied to real-world situations and that democratic ideals be matched with policy implementation . . . explicitly placed subjective knowledge at the center of understanding" (9). Indeed, Stewart's successful challenge to those "who misrepresented black women's interests or perspectives" suggests a significant strain of "moral existentialism" grounded in "social justice and civic responsibility" (9). As such, her resistance privileged the "collective deeds of community service" rather than the "individual existence" of traditional existentialism (9). It follows, then, that at least one thread of Stewart's social death can be directly tied to early seeds of what Patricia Hill Collins articulated as a "black feminist epistemology" (qtd. in Evans 10).[43]

Stewart's connections with contemporary Black women's social justice movements and Black women artivists (from Nina Simone to Queen Latifah and Beyoncé) shed light on the significance of religion. #BlackWomensWordsWorkRemixesSnatchesAndMakesANewTrack #SankoficRepoliticizationMatters

3
Jarena Lee

Calling the Call

> For many Black religious leaders, civil rights and social justice are central to their calling. Their respective faith traditions place religion within the Black American experience while also being informed by African culture and the traumatic experience of the Transatlantic slave trade of African people.
>
> —Lawrence Burnley

Jarena Lee's calling was not merely spiritual and not merely political; nor was it entirely personal. It was a rebirthing and a summoning into existence, a consciousness that could and would operate simultaneously through all three—spiritual, political, and personal. Lee's acceptance of the power of the Word, her willingness to serve as liturgical worker whose ministry was people-centered, and her internalizing of God's sacred voice were such that she shared an intimate relationship with the divine. This relationship—this call—was not meant to transcend the very complicated tribulations and real-world problems faced at a human level. Rather, Lee was called through, to, and from places and spaces that would both test her faith and inspire her toward a life's journey of service to others, despite her subject position in the world. She would live a life that mattered in the nineteenth century and the centuries that followed. The standard she left as a map to her descendants and successors—women of the cloth, spiritual activists, and artivists—drew attention to the significance and power of the call itself, through many connotations.

When something is "called," it is shouted. A call draws attention to itself—in a loud voice to be heard and understood clearly—leaving nothing to be inferred. The word *call* as a noun can refer to the act of naming, claiming, summoning, phoning, appealing an action or judgment, a pull or attraction to something, predicting an outcome, or even a demand for payment. In the context of spirituality, it typically refers to receiving a summons or invitation from God to a holy vocation such as preaching. What I refer to as "calling the call" is meant to define how Lee draws attention to, claims, names, and addresses her summons from God to preach. This call of her calling is not only her own, but an appeal to look beyond race and gender and station in life (this includes statuses such as enslaved, indentured, or class, as well as other divisive categories that attempt to disrupt God's intention as the ultimate authority, the one who will in the end demand payment for the debts owed to "the least of us").

Fittingly, Lee invites a close hearing of her right to respond to God's voice and his call, rather than those subjects that attempt to muzzle or silence and oppress her call and, in so doing, would attempt to directly challenge God's authorizing on Lee's behalf. The calling is also an invitation to retrieve a history, to return to the source of her power and fetch that which may have been forgotten, or that which is at risk of being entirely lost under the conditions of oppression, enslavement, indenture, and marginalization of a people, and to recover that "which [they] have heard and known" to ensure that they "will not hide them from their children, shewing to the generation to come" (Psalm 78:3–4). This call signals her Sankofic re-calling of truths that had been hidden and perverted, to right and rewrite wrongs committed. "From Lee's prophetic ruminations about women's divine right to preach and Richard Allen's pushback to Lee's demands, to the wives of bishops carving out their own spaces to critique Black male ecclesial patriarchy, Black women are central to African Methodism" (Greene-Hayes 8), and African Methodism has been significant in the histories of social justice.[1] As such, to say that she "called" the calling is to signify that her words publicly called upon the church to live up to the meaning of its ministry to attend to spiritual and felt needs—to extend the mission and impact the moral arc toward justice—especially, but not only, for Black women who heard and heeded a higher calling to impact the ethereal and earthly realms into which they were born and bound.

In 1819, Jarena Lee became the first woman authorized to preach in the AME Church. However, it would take 196 years, in 2016, before she was officially sanctioned. On April 6, 2016, Lee was posthumously ordained during the 50th Quadrennial Session of the General Conference.[2] Her 1849 memoir and only extant writing, *Religious Experience and Journal of Mrs. Jarena Lee, Giving an Account of Her Call to Preach the Gospel*, provides valuable insights into the method by which religion was used in the mid-nineteenth century to imbed a social justice agenda within a spiritual calling, through the author's exploitation of Great Awakening literature, specifically the spiritual autobiography/conversion narrative.[3] When Lee recounts the details of her early life, her lack of religion, her struggles with suicidal impulses, her astonishing visions, her marriage, her parenting style, and her eventual itinerant ministry, her reader gets far more than a run-of-the-mill tale of the transformation of a repentant sinner to sainthood in the Christian faith. Instead, her "religious experiences" enable the reader to reflect on overt and covert encounters with the political milieu of early American society (see Chansky).

Consequently, women preachers like Lee might be said to have "politicized the soul by insisting upon the connection between material realities and a spiritual life; the spiritual was not understood as transcending the material or social, nor was it seen as [solely] a rhetorical tool" (Zackodnik 19). Quite the contrary: there are ways in which rhetoric was not necessarily disconnected from the spiritual or the political, but rather an important critical tool in Lee's arsenal that linked her sacred mission to the secular thrust of her social activism. The rhetorical was always already inextricably linked to the Word and the meaning it offered for the least of God's people—all of them—and especially Black women.[4] Lee's act of "written textual subversion and resistance" and her "self revisionings" (Bassard, *Spiritual Interrogations* 93), which involved the "unwriting of a racialized Christian pre-text through the reinscription of her black skin as glorified and transfigured . . . a reassigning of the meaning of blackness" (101), demanded a repoliticization of the Word. Having detailed her quest to find the appropriate church home, one that nurtured her spiritual self within the context of Afrocentric identity (the AME denomination), she reinterprets scripture to "write her own black female subjectivity into the discourse of conversion, even as her subjectivity is produced through these 'contrary instincts'" (101) (see also Carter; Burrow).[5]

Lee uses the language of respect and endearment when referring to Black people. Terms such as *sister*, *lady*, and *gentleman* are knitted throughout descriptions that chronicle her itinerant works in service of her religious calling. While "sister" implies a familial relationship of Christian love and embraces a spiritual language during an era of chattel slavery when biological earthly family ties are neither respected nor encouraged, when children are sold off and snatched from their parents, and enslaved persons are typically prohibited the covenant of marriage and/or the exercise of the fruits of holy matrimony proscribed by the church, "sister," even more than "lady" and "gentleman," signals something of an honorific, a titular respect among Black people.[6] It is not only in Lee's deferent language that we are able to appreciate how she semantically disrupts shattered and fragmented discourses of enslavement. Likewise, in the author's ordering of chapters in the memoir we are provided with a map for supplanting the designated domestic places of women (particularly wives, widows, and mothers). Black women are placed in direct confrontation with the masculine public spaces of men (specifically clergy, slave owners, and husbands). What is noticeable about Lee's sandwiching of the chapter "My Marriage" between "My Call to Preach the Gospel" and "The Subject of My Call to Preach Renewed" is her appositional placement of a narrative of female recovery in the face of patriarchal church authority.

Specifically, she closes the chapter "My Call to Preach" by sharing a vision that allayed her doubts about her call to preach. She rightly challenges Bishop Allen's claim that their "discipline . . . did not call for women preachers" (*Religious Experience and Journal* 11) by sharing Paul's words "that nothing could have separated me from the love of God" (12). This affirmation of faith is critical because four years later in 1811 she marries a pastor—Mr. Joseph Lee—and moves to Snow Hill, a stark contrast to her close community in Philadelphia, and a testament to her adherence to conventional secular and religious norms. During this time, she experiences trials such as depression and physical sickness, as well as the deaths of multiple family members, including that of her husband—"the greatest affliction of all" as she "was now left alone . . . with two infant children" (14). However, Lee is supported by her constant companionship with God and his continual provisions; he "raised up friends, whose liberality comforted and solaced" her as confirmation of her calling (14).

Ultimately, despite being formally prohibited by Bishop Allen from preaching and after years of trials during her marriage and her widowhood, Lee demonstrates that the strength of her call remains. When she resumes her narrative of the "call to preach renewed," she takes time to show that even though being permitted only to exhort and hold prayer meetings, she is able to convert "a very wicked young man" (15) who, during his illness (consumption) was converted by Lee with the support of several other holy women.[7] It is Lee and "two of the sisters in Christ" (16) that provide comfort for the young colored man, not the Reverend. Mr. Cornish, whom they found "laboring with him" to "little satisfaction" (16). Indeed, it is Lee's holy vision of the transfiguration of Christ that leads this sick man to salvation before he figuratively, and she literally, closes his eyes. This experience is described in somewhat of an aside by the narrator—a tangent—after which she "return[s] to the subject of my call to preach" (17).

Likening her own experience of delaying her call to preach (eight years ago) to that of Jonah, Lee provides evidence of her sanctification through the transference of spiritual indwelling from the Reverend Richard Williams to her, as she "sprang" to her feet "in the same instant" that the male preacher "seemed to have lost the spirit" (*Religious Experience and Journal* 17).[8] She also punctuates the experience by reminding the reader that "God made manifest his power in a manner to show the world that I was called to labor *according to [my] ability*, and the grace given to me" (17; my emphasis). I emphasize Lee's signifying that she is graced with the power that befits her aptitude and capacity to serve. It is, after all, precisely what her calling required of her—such tasks for which she was fully qualified based on her aptitude, most evident in her WordsWork—connecting the personal to the spiritual, and repoliticizing so-called biblical interpretations that effectively interfered, attempting to place prohibitions on those whom God had called.[9] Lee called out the deception by exposing the limitations of those who placed themselves in superior positions based on human desire and pride rather than spiritual invitation. Despite the limited roles available for women in the AME Church and the limitations placed on her by formal religious institutional structures and traditions, she fulfills the duty of a preacher. Moreover, she is recognized by Bishop Allen, who confirms God's power in Lee: "He now believed that I was called to that work, as any of the preachers present" (17). Allen simply confirms what Lee already knew, even if it is his confirmation that grants secular authority for the spiritually sanctioned work she was already accomplishing. Ultimately, male authority must align with divine authority and support the holy works that, when fulfilled by a woman, simultaneously represent political progress.

This view of woman's place challenges existing proscriptions based on the patriarchal narrative by demonstrating God's wisdom as ultimate authority over both external and internalized oppression.[10] Such can be seen in Lee's recounting of her earliest interactions with Bishop Allen, during a time when she was not quite sure of her call. When she shares that it had been "revealed" to her that she "must preach the gospel," she observes that Allen encouraged her, by example of "Mrs. Cook, a Methodist lady, [who] had also some time before requested the same privilege" that she do likewise, and confine her religions work to "exhortation, and holding prayer meetings." Despite this condescending response and indirect refusal of her request to be authorized to preach, Lee responds that she "was glad to hear, because it removed the fear of the cross." Such denial initially confirmed her own doubt, "but no sooner did this feeling cross my mind" than she was engulfed with a "holy energy which burned within me, as a fire, began to be smothered" (*Religious Experience and Journal* 12). This holy fire represents not only the biblical mandate not to "quench the Holy Spirit," but also demonstrates how marginalized people are self-silenced through internalized oppression.[11] It was not Lee's own ambition and will but God's insistence that propelled her movement toward her call. Simultaneously sincere and straightforward, her expression of Christian humility operates in tandem with a less obvious manifestation of internalized oppression experienced by others like Lee, both free and enslaved, who are poor, Black, and women. Not entirely akin, but related to contemporary Black code-switching, nineteenth-century Black women's signifying of this type was a kind of survival tactic, one that preserved Lee's spiritual calling and enabled her to operate as a free Black itinerant preaching woman within the boundaries of societal norms. Lee's words suggest the literary tightrope of which she was well aware: she needed to walk among mortals even armed with God's divine providence.

For Lee and women like her, the question of one's place had to be carefully considered in both preordained otherworldly or "divine" spaces and established sociopolitical public and domestic spheres. Regarding the "two stages of the Christian's psychospiritual development" present in early Black women's spiritual autobiography, William Andrews puts it this way: "First these women had to become assured that they were the beneficiaries of Christ's atonement and were therefore heirs to his heavenly kingdom. Then they had to confront the problem of what their role should be as Christian women in the earthly realm" (11). Andrews contends that it is the women's role as Christians that takes precedence in terms of their literary aims; they provide few if any intimate details about their lives that might offer insight into family history or background. He explains that "life before conversion was of no real significance except as far as it could be used as a kind of negative moral object lesson for her reader" (11). Andrews's contention about the significance of Lee's "before conversion" life experiences notwithstanding, the 1849 version of Lee's *Journal* reveals particulars about her life before and after conversion (especially the latter), that enable some perceptions about and insights into certain consequential personal and political issues at stake for the nineteenth-century Black woman preacher. As such, they reveal complicated and intersecting sacred and secular testimonies of why #EarlyBlackChristianWomensLivesMatter, and how these early Black women's lives are relevant to contemporary Black women's lives.

Expressly, with regard to the more intimate details of Lee's life, it seems plausible that her relief at the safety of her sick child, whom she left in the care of friends, the reconnection and warm reception from her mother, who was "happy to see" her and with whom she "left her poor sickly boy" upon leaving to do her "Master's will" (*Religious Experience and Journal* 22–23) contribute to our understanding of this holy preaching woman's maternal bond despite separation. It also speaks to her connection to a community of kinship with strong ties—as extended family—as well as a sign of God's providence (22), with its attendant message of prioritizing God's will over man's and at the same time her connection with humankind. Indeed, Lee's chronicling of her reuniting with her sister after having been "separated from [her] some thirty three years" (23) is interwoven with her descriptions of ministry work, including "a prayer meeting at my brother's" house (her brother "did not enjoy religions") (33–34) and her considerations of the "various . . . operations of the Spirit [and . . .] the goodness of God" with regard to "the human family" (49–52).[12] There are, to be sure, limitations to how far we can draw any definitive conclusions about the "real significance" of family, to use Andrews's words (11). However, such limitations should not prevent us from probing alternate ways of acknowledging the personal, private, and intimate within the religious and political, and perhaps considering the extent to which they overlap and intersect. Despite such obstacles, however, Lee marks her experiences through lenses that provide insight into how she navigated this incongruence. And, perhaps of equal importance, her text provides evidence of early Black women's repoliticization of religion. Undoubtedly, the details about her marriage to a pastor not only provide the necessary evidence of Lee's sincere attempt to maintain early American cultural conventions regarding family structures, and thereby bolster her right to accept the call to preach when she is subsequently (and providentially) widowed. Such details also remind the reader of the arduous journey of the female preacher. The self-denial required is an explicitly stated part of Christian doctrine, but the doubly treacherous road that a woman must travel to fulfill her calling requires perhaps a stronger will to navigate the spiritual with the political—to honor both the sacred call and the secular demands within the construct of a patriarchal society.

Lee's concern for children extends beyond her own immediate family to a concern for the education of all Black children: "My mind was *much exercised*, seeing the *need of schools*. I counted *25 children and some young people whom I loved*. I lamented their obscurity, and advised them to get a white man to teach them, and endeavored to shew them, that, without the advantages of education they never would be a moral people, and, in the course of time, their own children could, by proper advancement, become teachers for themselves" (*Religious Experience and Journal* 69; my emphasis). In this passage describing her experiences in Ammonsburg, Lee's expressed anxiety about the dearth of educators and suitable opportunities for educating Black children extends earlier voices of subtle and not so subtle protests from Black writers like Wheatley, Jupiter Hammon, and Lucy Terry, among others, and predates later postbellum movements for educational reform such as those during the era of the Freedman's Bureau.[13] Lee treads cautiously, moving from direct to indirect modes of signifying in order to both emphasize racial disparities and offer practical advice and reasonable alternatives, given antebellum-era laws, codes, and societal norms regarding the education of Black people. While she "lamented" the "obscurity" of Black schools and teachers and "advised them to get a white man to teach them" until such time as they attain appropriate education and credentials to "become teachers for themselves" (69), she also celebrates that within "two or three weeks" they had "established as school of between 30 or 40 scholars" taught by a "colored teacher" (69).[14] Moreover, she observed that it was both secular and religious education that strengthened the "manners of the people" (70). It is suggestive that Lee reinforces the educational empowerment and uplift made possible through the efforts of Black people and communities. She praises this community because they "worshipped in *their own* Chapels [with] *their own* preachers, exhorters, and class-leaders (*colored*)" (70; my emphasis). I emphasize Lee's repetition of key words that stress the value of self-empowerment and ownership. Education is reinforced as a right and responsibility that belong to "colored" people, and it is they who possess the power to maintain and preserve knowledge for themselves. She observes that "we are all children of one parent, no one is justified in holdings slaves" (113), and as such all children should have the same rights. If there is any question about whether her recollection of such experiences is merely fodder for Christian morality, Lee's tone here and throughout her narrative evinces a preaching woman who speaks truth to power in opposing both physical and mental enslavement.

Lee's words are more than extended sermonizing or proselytization; they are evidence of her nuanced and intellectual engagement at the intersection of religion and politics. The extent to which Lee engages in an intensive thought process is punctuated as she draws our attention to her own intellectual activity and the considerable use of cognitive power through a "much exercised" "mind," one that is preoccupied with matters of this world—the felt needs of children for whom she expresses the deep emotion of "love." While their morality is clearly a concern, it is likely not the only "advantage" for which education may prove beneficial. That these "young people" matter to her is clear, as she "counts" them and in so doing signifies that they "count." Her revelation that they "need" education is tempered by her knowledge that there are insufficient Black teachers to instruct them. However, Lee does not merely recount the short-term "problem" of the lack of education, she also provides evidence of the long-term implications of this failure and suggests, practically speaking, that educating children will in turn produce more teachers.

Not unlike in our current era of Black women's social justice movements, she reveals a great concern for education and literacy as well as an understanding of the critical need for Black educators. Certainly, her words enable us to perceive Lee as a woman who is as troubled about issues related to children in school, progressive notions of school integration and perhaps segregation and separation, as both her contemporaries in Methodist and other Protestant denominations and her twentieth- and twenty-first-century counterparts. We can see the linkages from Catherine Ferguson's first American Sunday school in 1793 (see Hartvik) to, nearly a century later, Lucy C. Laney's first school for Black children in Augusta, Georgia in 1883 to the National Black Lives Matter Week of Action in Our School. The latter brought the current social justice movement and "several key goals" to education into hundreds of schools in Washington, DC: "End zero tolerance in school, and implement restorative justice. . . .[15] Hire more Black teachers. . . . Mandate Black history and ethnic studies in K-12 curriculum. . . . Fund counselors, not cops" (Jones and Hagopian 17). These contemporary issues echo Lee's signifying moves to simultaneously justify the rights of women and children to equal access to education (from student to teacher) and to provide evidence of the value of her call to preach. While it is important in terms of the demands of the genre, as a Black woman, Lee's story extends beyond the genre, proving herself worthy to preach on both God's and man's terms. Her memoir extends the great commission to include and embrace the need for "abundant" life for all genders, races, and classes. She reveals how physical liberty enables spiritual freedom.

Lee's politicization of religion also calls into question our conventional narratives and contemporary readings of the history of the Black church and its role in historical social justice movements, and whether the gulf between less religious-based movements like #BLM is as great as we might imagine. The Reverend D. Anthony Everett observes that "a spiritually driven social justice mandate reaches beyond what is right or wrong for individual and business interests in a consumerist society. A spiritually driven social justice movement is concerned with the good of all of society, those who have financial means and those who do not, and it is not exclusive of race, ethnicity, gender, orientation, ability, or other discriminatory factors. The #BlackLivesMatter movement exemplifies spiritually driven social justice that applies a hermeneutic from the eyes of oppressed black bodies but remains inclusive of other forms of discrimination." Kaavya Asoka puts it this way: "A growing number of Black Lives Matter activists—including the women behind the original hashtag—have been refocusing attention on how police brutality impacts black women and others on the margins of today's national conversation about race, such as poor, elderly, gay, and trans people" (qtd. in Chatelain).

They are not only highlighting the impact of police violence on these communities but articulating why a movement for racial justice must necessarily be inclusive. The point I'm making here is the significance of ways that women, from Lee to Chatelain, challenged and transgressed even seemingly progressive agendas, with an understanding of the long-term impact of their movement-making moments. Consider, for example, Bishop Allen's reversal of his initial response to Lee's call to preach. His shifting view of women's preaching from one informed by gender bias and conventional "knowledge" to what might be considered a progressive view of the woman's role in the church and society was a critical move, set in motion by Lee's nonconforming words and actions. However, Allen's decision to permit Lee to preach did not in itself change the fact that women in the AME Church did not "pierce" the "stained glass ceiling" until July 11, 2000, when Vashti Murphy McKenzie became the first woman bishop of the church. Religion is one, but certainly not the only, institutional barrier that demands unwavering and consistent challenges, but it is undoubtedly one of the earliest spaces of resistance for Black women. And in taking back "God," Black women began the struggle to liberate themselves and moreover to tell their own stories. As Joanne Braxton observes, Black women autobiographers "construct . . . a uniquely black and female autobiographical self, leaving a literary legacy and providing guidance, encouragement, and direction both for readers and for future literary trends" ("Autobiography" 128). Perhaps one of the maps that women like Lee provide is a clear understanding that resistance is a verb; it is a progressive empowering force that increases as it identifies, deconstructs, and attempts to abolish oppression—and, most important, it continues to challenge oppressive forces that attempt to relocate and reproduce their abuses.

Lee challenges sexism within the clergy using her biblical interpretation of the word *preach* and its gendered associations. Such exegetical performance, not coincidentally, exposes literal and uncritical readings intending to oppress women like herself. Thus she provides a map of recovery with guiding steps for the rescue of Black women (by Black women) from tripartite systemic oppression. She confronts the heavy-handed adaptations of the Word intended to silence—and by extension kill—the preaching and prophetic voices of women, especially Black women, by drawing upon strong parallels between her contemporaries—Christian male clergy—and ancient Jewish priests—the Pharisees. Consequently, this early Black preaching woman exposed one of the central means—or technologies—through which religion has been weaponized against society's most vulnerable classes. She reminds a Christian reader, and one who might be tempted to escape into religion, that Christianity in and of itself is neither apolitical nor a salve intended to mitigate or cover injustice. Adherence to the arbitrary and self-serving nature of the "law" is met by confirmation of the admonishment of certain laws that had been used against the most susceptible of God's people—a clear violation of Christian grace.

Such pharisaical readings produce knowledge about practices that govern and impact the day-to-day lives of common people, and place those in power in positions of privilege. Lee unravels this pattern, and precedent, of unchecked power as dangerous to and for the very people it might have been intended to protect and serve. Consideration of whether or perhaps how the nature of allyship is complicated—inter- and intra-racial and gender—is a matter for the late nineteenth, twentieth, and twenty-first centuries. The refusal to accept unchecked power by remaining silent and the conviction to interrogate the terms and thereby expose the covert means through which this ecclesiastical authority operates, in order to construct a viable paradigm for liberation, invites us to use Lee's life in her words and on her terms as a viable and progressive model for movement forward. Bishop Allen could be both brother/friend/ally and at the same time be the hand that held her down, that kept her from advancing God's work. Correspondingly, higher education, the military, government, and religion are institutions that gift and grieve to enrich or exacerbate already infirm conditions of those most vulnerable among us.

Her scrutiny and deconstruction of word power in the preaching text also point to issues of class and limited access to literacy and education; the few who enjoy that access manipulate language to reinforce and maintain their power. She reveals how such power dynamics, manifested intra-racially between Black men and women of the cloth, also provide an opportunity to unveil underlying systemic oppression that links humanity regardless of class, caste, race, or gender: "If the man may preach, because the Saviour died for him, why not the woman? seeing he died for her also. Is he not a whole Saviour, instead of a half one? as those who hold it wrong for a woman to preach, would seem to make it appear" (*Religious Experience and Journal* 13).[16] She challenges those who question the issue of the right of any person to receive a calling to preach by dissecting the language of "those who are determined not to believe" (12) in the right of a woman to preach. If a woman's right to preach can be undermined in such a manner, then so too can the descendants of those "unlearned fishermen" who were equally as "ignorant of letters" as women like herself, and yet they "too, were inspired" (12). Markedly, Lee's text exposes the psychical confusion and internal dysfunction triggered by the conflict between political interpretations of scripture. In many ways, one can hear the echo of James Cone's claim that "Christianity is not alien to Black Power; it is Black Power" (84). Lee's words may have fallen on the less than attentive ears of Black male clergy who failed to consider their own race-based oppression in the images of the "unlearned fishermen," but it was not lost on Black congregants who were reminded of the adverse effects of distortions of God's Word. She uses the Word to connect class and gender within her own race and can be seen to predate Black feminist/womanist traditions.

Likewise, in her analysis of resurrection, Lee enables a transitional bridge back to the future (so to speak) by renarrating her value in society with her reference to "labor." She not only undermines the attempt to "make" meaning serve a secular and ungodly purpose, she also exposes the deliberate mischaracterization of God's authority in the attempt to "straiten" or restrict God's gift to all his people—including Black women. The level and extensive WordsWork that called forth truths in her retrieval of the most valuable aspects of the Word, in Sankofic fashion, remains as significant to the nineteenth-century Black woman preacher as it does for twenty-first-century preachers, artists, and freethinkers. Issues of class and modes of being (caste based upon gender, sexuality, race, and the like) draw upon the legacy of this early preacher, as she introduces critical thinking as a necessary tool against which "faith without works" lacks meaning—in this case the work is that of the mind, the intellect, and the willingness to see other humans in the fullness of how their creator intended. Like those of the unlearned fishermen, the lives of the uneducated—and especially their callings—mattered.

Placed squarely within the tradition of Black writers' use of biblical archetypes to mitigate their marginalized positions in White society, Lee articulates her call to preach within the context of several divine communications, which she appears to ignore because of societal concerns with the obligatory deferent stance of one who is too low to do God's work on account of sex, class, and race. However, she quickly recovers, and her experiences reveal a fearlessness that is described as guided by the force of the Holy Spirit. Forces of slavery, preaching, and converting a master at one point, traveling alone through slave territory as a free Black woman in the South, the pull of motherhood when one of her children falls ill, as well as the constant opposition she meets from those who deny her access to churches and pulpits because she is a woman, are all part of a testimony that is at once deeply personal and spiritual and at the same time necessarily and purposefully political.[17] Extending the Word and repoliticizing the coveted scripture and pulpit for women, Lee invokes the power to preach justice for all, especially enslaved Africans.

Equally important here and throughout Lee's work is her attention to what Moody terms an "inclusive theology" (54), one that "celebrated multiethnic and inter-faith Christian worship" (55). Moody reminds us of the time Lee spent with "Native American Christians" and her "offer[ing] the Gospel to every group that [would] embrace her" (54) as evidence. Moreover, Lee not only saved herself and liberated slaveholding Christian masters from the sin of slavery, she also fought for the rights of women to preach—not just to exhort or to teach Bible lessons to children, but actually preach. She did all of this while putting her physical body on the line traveling through slave territory as an itinerant preacher and subjecting herself to intra-gender and intra-racial ostracizing and condemnation for not adhering to the standards set for her sex and despite the unreasonableness of Black women's ability to actually attain American cultural standards of the pure, pious, domestic, and submissive woman. Lee's relatively small but mighty work demonstrated her willingness to fight not only external obstacles but also the tremendous internal pressures she had to overcome to reconcile brokenness within her psyche and spirit, and ultimately to confirm her sense of self-worth to her God and the diverse communities she addressed. Importantly, her narrative might be read as a journey of one who went "to hell and back" to redeem and resurrect herself.

Lee's narration of her itinerant preaching experiences provides a structure for analyzing her own path to self-recovery as well as some insights into contemporary connections and pathways to wellness by Black women. Moody explains how Lee's narration of her own health and illness enables a revision of dominant narratives about Black women in general. Specifically, "Lee seems purposefully to draw on nineteenth-century notions of womanhood as a social and biological construction in order to garner sympathy from those who might otherwise have disdained her as unfeminine and thus unnatural" (67). This biblical sampling undermines the myth of American "exceptionalism," which relies on stereotyping "others" (in terms of race, gender, and the like), and reframes some of the contemporary contexts within which Black women are expected to perform superhuman expectations while their labor and its fruits are often rendered invisible. She offers a new track, a retooled and amended vision of Black women's health, appropriating the so-called dignity in working until you drop or die trying—no human should privilege this type of suffering in silence as the will of God—that is often replayed as somehow heroic and virtuous. Lee recovers her humanity and renders her work—sacred and secular—as hyper-visible. She "supplants the image of the black woman as field hand with the image of her as the 'angel in the household' . . . transforms her genuinely suffering self into the trope of the sick woman and exploits this trope in the representation of herself as an exemplary Christian" (Moody 67).[18]

The following example points to Lee's possible inversion of the patriarchal church order of service: she gives a sermon, which is followed by a male minister's exhortation. Recall, as evidenced by Bishop Allen's suggestions about the type of tasks women perform, that it is typically men who give sermons and women who exhort. Further, Lee's recounting of her performance of "2 sermons a day for several Sabbaths" (69) and the heavy workload that she performs demonstrates her successful accomplishment of God's calling to meet felt and spiritual needs, by encouraging a consideration of work that privileges sisterhood and expresses concern for those in bondage.

Lee is more than ready, willing, and able to do as much and whatever kind of holy work men are sanctioned to do in the AME Church.

In fact, she provides a context that establishes the additional pressure of the work she is already doing, and it is particularly significant given that such "woman's" holy work is being performed during "the time of [a denominational] split" in Methodism. She "preached five or six different times . . . for several Sabbaths two sermons a day . . . continued . . . meeting . . . rode five miles . . . preached again . . . continued to visit the sick the remainder of the week, and on Sabbath . . . rode five miles again . . . filled an appointment . . . and was retained another week" (*Religious Experience and Journal* 88). After these rather long days Lee continues by preaching a farewell sermon, praying for the sick, traveling "six miles distant, and one also for 6 o'clock in the evening," enduring a "very hard ride through the swamp" with a sister that accompanied her, as she continued in her schedule: "held prayer meetings, visited the sick, and passed many joyful moments of sweet communion especially in one sister's company, who was a member of the National Church in Ammonsburg" (88).

Reading and reflecting on the experiences journaled here, it is likely that nineteenth-century readers as well as contemporary readers, especially overburdened, underappreciated, and undercompensated Black women, will understand why she is sick and tired, and perhaps sympathize with the toll her work has taken on her physical body—sustained by God's strength. Crystal J. Lucky observes, "Throughout her life, Lee worked tirelessly to gain formal recognition from male church leadership, created alternative spaces in people's homes and communities to share the gospel she fervently believed she was called to preach, and helped to change the perceptions male preachers had about their future female colleagues" (20). Lee's command of this genre, a religious memoir in the tradition of the conversion narratives of the Second Great Awakening, demonstrates her subtle but nonetheless potent repoliticization and recovering of the early Black woman's evangelical voice.[19] Lee's experiences reveal contradictions between the pious and proselytizing aims of the genre and those conspicuously profane hypocrisies with which this woman of God had to contend. That is, "American spiritual autobiography chronicles the soul's journey not only from damnation to salvation but also to a realization of one's *true place* and destiny in the divine scheme of things" (Andrews 10–11; my emphasis). As the first African American woman to publish her autobiography, Lee's work "constitute[s] a tradition within a tradition, operating within the dominant, familiar, and essentially masculinist modes of autobiography." Such writing "simultaneously, . . . reshape[s] and redefine[s] [its] inherited formulae" (Braxton, "Autobiography" 128). In so doing, she inaugurates a genre within a genre (Braxton, *Black Women Writing Autobiography*)—conversion, memoir, womanist/feminist, spiritual, autobiography—that demands and draws upon the inextricable nature of the spiritual and the political as a historical and contemporary marker of Black women's continual struggles to recover the terms under which their lives matter.[20]

Specifically, women like Lee revealed a "remarkable sense of self-worth, self-confidence, and power, despite the traditional autobiography's treatment of the self as a deceiving antagonist" (Andrews 15). This self-empowerment—notwithstanding the presumption of their incompetence—became a part of their sacred "duty" and enabled women to challenge both religious and societal authorities. As Andrews observes, "Their consciences did not require biblical sanction to denounce contemporary injustices, such as slavery, racism, and sex discrimination, wherever these evils seemed to be hindering God's work. Theirs was a *gospel of human liberation* addressed particularly to the spiritual enslaved. Still, they knew from personal experience how social bonds contributed to spiritual enslavement . . . they 'realized more and more what a terrible thing it was for one human being to have absolute control over another'" (Andrews 16; my emphasis).[21]

Centuries later, women of the cloth continue to frame their challenges to social injustice and calls for action within religion. Bishop Vashti Murphy McKenzie has addressed issues such as immigration, racism, and institutionalized and state-sanctioned violence against women, children, and people of color. At a 2015 prayer vigil she insisted that Sandra Bland's death must not become "another hashtag and another statistic"; her death must "motivate us to action" (qtd. in Caruba). Lee's and McKenzie's words and actions were critical to regaining control of their lives, and by extension their communities. "Holding a large banner bearing the popular hashtag '#JusticeForSandra,' McKenzie led the group from the chapel up University Drive to Hope AME Church, a small white chapel off the road leading into campus" (Caruba).[22] This action, which literally and figuratively joins sacred and secular institutions, is an extension of God's work, not unlike that performed by Lee.

If, as Bassard suggests, Lee's life story permits "us to recover the theorizing ground of a narrative whose text-ness . . . ultimately give[s] way to a traditional narrative of suffering and redemption" (*Spiritual Interrogations* 89), then it also provides a map of symbolic recovery as a substantiation of her repoliticization of the Word through our textual analysis of her prophetic reading and work.[23] The specifics that her 1849 *Journal* provide about the day-to-day tedious facts of Lee's performance of her call—doing the work to which she was called—reinforce political arguments revealed in her spiritual narrative.[24] In chronicling her preaching experiences, she interprets the work of anti-slavery as holy work. Citing the "golden rule" and invoking an image of the Christian family, Lee observes: "I felt that the spirit of God was in the work . . . and I pray God to forward on the work of abolition until it fills the world, and then the gospel will have free course to every motion and in every clime" (*Religious Experience and Journal* 113). Here she links a spiritual aspiration with a biblical mandate to propagate her religion globally. She gently persuades by offering her inward sentiments and her divine supplications as a consciousness of the work it will take for enslaved men and women to be free to learn and freely exercise their faith, without the physical shackles of slavery. Not surprisingly, repeated emphasis on "work(s)" throughout her narrative, with the significance of physical labors, invokes a spiritual force or power behind her social justice range, not only in somewhat dulcet tones but also in those more strident ones. "But the *wickedness* of the people certainly calls for the lowering Judgements of God to be *let loose* upon the Nation and Slavery, that *wretched* system that emanated from the *bottomless pit*, is one of the *greatest curses* to any Nation" (80; my emphasis). Her language is meant to invoke and agitate for a struggle both moralistic and militant against a vile and corrupt people who uphold the values of a shameful institution that is a blight to the citizens who support it. Lee's words echo her works and stand as signposts of the potency of repoliticized religion.[25]

Further, Lee's sermonic interventions punctuate this politicization of the spiritual, laced with sarcasm and signifying, that is easily recognizable to a historical and contemporary audience: "O how careful ought we to be, lest through our by-laws of church government and discipline, we bring into disrepute even the word of life. For as unseemly as it may appear now-a-days for a woman to preach, it should be remembered that nothing is impossible with God. And why should it be thought impossible, heterodox, or improper for a woman to preach? seeing the Saviour died for the woman as well as for the man" (*Religious Experience and Journal* 11). Her oft-repeated description of the impoverished peoples she meets and the conditions under which she fulfills her ministry suggests intense concern for those most oppressed, among whom she includes herself as a "poor female instrument," referencing her "poor labors" (12), "poor soul and body" (14), the value of the "instrumentality of a poor coloured woman" (17), "poor unworthy being" (32), and "poor pilgrim" (59). Of equal importance, and what links Lee's story to her predecessor Wheatley and her contemporary Stewart, is Lee's refashioning of conventional tropes, especially those that situate the Black female body within simultaneous narratives of suffering and pleasure.

Surely Lee could not have predicted the secular and spiritually based words, works, and political movements of Black women that proceeded from her own repoliticization of the Word—to do God's work in man's world. What she might have imagined, though, given her biblical wisdom, was that the "seeds" she planted would surely have been given "watering" and then eventually "increase" by divine providence and the earthly labors of holy women like herself.[26] Similarly to those of her contemporaries and predecessors, Lee's accounting of her passage through spiritual and secular waters—not unlike the Middle Passage of millions of captured and enslaved Africans—would prove a sustaining element in the passage and return from enslavement to full liberation well beyond physical freedom. Such intergenerational challenges to obstacles remain, and the blueprints laid out in the words and work(s) of Lee and her sisters Stewart and Wheatley inaugurate a legacy that enriches and replenishes lands contaminated by race, class, and gender inequities by turning the soil and planting seeds for equality, social justice and, most important, freedom for their sisters and brothers in bondage.

4
Binding Up Together

Addressing Our Past to Face This Present

> We are all bound up together in one great bundle of humanity, and society cannot trample on the weakest and feeblest of its members without receiving the curse in its own soul. . . . Society cannot afford to neglect the enlightenment of any class of its members.
>
> —Frances Harper, "We Are All Bound Up Together"

Harper's cautionary exhortation about the interdependency of people who, despite their connected cultural, historical, and national conditions, are unable to see each other's shared humanity is important to consider as we explore the intersections of early Black Christian women's WordsWork. Harper's words remind her nineteenth-century audiences that those structures that undermine, unravel, and marginalize the "weakest and feeblest" are at great risk for contributing to the demise of society as a whole. She is thus exposing the way that societal compliance with bias and prejudice feeds a national and anti-Christian affliction. While this study does not encompass Harper's writings beyond this introductory inclusion, one can see the work of Stewart in particular as mapping such inclusive religio-political ideas as those espoused by Harper.[1] As contemporary readers, we can see the intersecting and interconnected words, ideas, and emotions that are braided together, those which I argue highlight the continuation of Black Christian women's narratives of redemption and contrition since at least the eighteenth century: Wheatley through poetry, elegy, and epistle, Lee through sermon and memoir, and Stewart through political speech and contemplative spiritual prose. When I write "braid," I mean to evoke an image of Black women's braided hair that connotes artistry—woven strand by strand—which gives the greatest pleasure and meaning, announcing its value in the interlocking symbols of resistance, diverse and divergent maps, and a spiritual connectedness marked by the joining of individual strands, parts, and links to create the unified braid.[2] As such, the power of their words—through filters of sacred and secular dimensions—sounds an alarm and issues a call for a binding together of humanity. Their words work to confront and counter the kind of brutal oppression perpetrated on African-descended people—the most tragic and literal manifestation being chattel slavery and those conditions arising as a result of this horrific institution—on God's and humankind's terms.

However, as Harper's words signify, it is not only the capture and control of personal and political bodies but an equally fearsome toll of spiritual bondage that steals all humanity. This message of the spiritual weight of physical oppression as counter to the true mission of her faith, captured in Harper's critique of Christianity as "a system claiming God for its author and the welfare of [humankind] for its object" (96), is an extension of the work that the words of Wheatley, Stewart, and Lee perform. These early Black Christian women writers offer searing criticisms of the institution of slavery and the consequences of the dehumanization of African peoples in America.[3] They do so by addressing the implications of the lack of secular and sacred education as factors that impede the liberation of souls, minds, and hearts. Critically, Wheatley, Stewart, and Lee use their words to call for true empathy rather than superficial sympathy for others. Throughout the poetics, politics, and propagation of their words, which oscillate between hermeneutical, exegetical, and eisegetical, each woman inflects the power of God to intervene as well as the need for people to act in ethical, moral, and responsible ways to fight the oppressions of others, thus, inserting and asserting the inheritance of themselves as Black women who are equally worthy humans. To be sure, as illustrated earlier, each author's text provides examples of how the words of eighteenth- and nineteenth-century Black Christian women have worked as foundational grounds upon which later Black women artivists, preachers, teachers, and politicians would compel attention and progressive action. However, when placed alongside each other for comparison, a pattern of artivistic intergenerational WordsWork appears that shows the force of combined forms of language, speech, and art as multilayered links binding our past to this present with prescience for the future.

This chapter links their revelations about the hypocrisy and conspiratorial nature of religion and politics, their anti-slavery/pro-liberation and human rights arguments, as well as their attempts to extol the value and potential of freedom from oppressing others and enduring the weights of oppression as interconnected goals of a more nuanced and authentic form of human liberation—one that is as grounded in faith as it is in the contemporary political plight of their respective societies. There are significant intertextual links in their works that invite consideration of connections between the historical worlds of Wheatley, Stewart, and Lee. Building upon my reading of their WordsWork in chapters 1–3, I further develop and demonstrate the ongoing symbolic and literal cartography of self-recovery that can "help somebody cross" (Nordyke and Crist).[4] That is, not unlike literal bridges that require different structures depending on distance and span and geography (for example, beam, truss, arch, and suspension) Wheatley, Stewart, and Lee evince interconnections between early Black women's repoliticization of words that figuratively invoke each woman's unique contribution to a continuum of empowerment through their respective challenges to social injustices, and at the same time, they demonstrate their shared politically informed Black spiritual aestheticism. Similarly, Tara Bynum recovers for Phillis Wheatley a "'potentiality' wherein writing moves language and ideas across time and geography toward those who can read its form" (62). Citing Bassard, Bynum highlights critical touch points between early Black spiritual women and their contemporary twenty-first-century activist inheritors. The "potentiality" of a continuum across time and space that can be read backward and forward maps useful strategies for activism, social justice, and the resistance of intersectional boundaries. As such, early Black women's words recover structures that omit the power and promise of faith-based resistance within the context of political resistance. Significantly, this type of resistance neither excludes nor denies the full exercise of power through the interconnected and repoliticized power of words and the work that the Word does. This WordsWork captures the strength of the wordsmith to create new fabrics and designs out of old cloth and the supernatural extratextual authorizing and exegetical work of the Word.[5] I take serious account of how religion and politics intersect as artivistic lenses from the past to present and future social justice movements, and most importantly, how they link and twist along parallel and intersecting strands to repoliticize and recover a nuanced indictment of the very faith they uphold.

Poet, preacher, and politician stand side by side, connected through shared actions and feelings in mourning, shared confrontation of power—God's and mankind's—shared longing and confusion, and shared feelings that most sharply construct a powerful and necessary humanity. Their literary labors are visible if one looks closely at the combined WordsWork. Beginning with Wheatley's eighteenth-century epyllion and rewriting of an Ovidian myth, the poet reflects on the grim aftermath of disunity and discord in "Niobe in Distress for Her Children Slain by Apollo" when she reveals the fate of young siblings who meet their untimely deaths as a consequence of war and broken strands of what might have bound together two women (both representing forms of deities) in sisterhood and motherhood.

> Transfixed them both and stretched them on the sand:
> Together they their cruel fate bemoaned,
> Together languished and together groaned:
> Together, too, the unbodied spirits fled,
> And sought the gloomy mansions of the dead. (lines 132–135)

Brothers wrestling playfully, enjoying frolicking together, are shot down by Apollo's arrow, and they experience shared suffering as they lie dead on the ground. The duality of this verse is a clear signal from the pious poet whose imagery works to evoke a scriptural reminder that "to be absent from the body, [is] to be present with the Lord" (2 Corinthians 5:8). At the same time, the sight and site of "unbodied spirits [who] fled," like the many elegies Wheatley offers to those who have lost children, actualizes their parents' mourning of what remains (quite literally and figuratively). The disembodiment of consanguineous members immobilizes the living as well as the dead. Mutual suffering is at least one way to be bound together, albeit less than desired.

Along comparable axes, Stewart's attention to the power of being bound or "knit together in the holy bounds of love and union" draws attention to a "revolt" against "tyrann[y]" rather than compliance with it, as in the case with Niobe and Latona, who murder each other's children out of hatred and pride. The politician emphasizes the power of unity as an example she hopes to inspire and agitate Black people toward collective action. "Look at the French . . . the Haytians . . . [and] Poles . . . insult one of them and you insult a thousand" ("An Address Delivered Before the Afric-American Female Intelligence Society of Boston"). It is not only that collective efforts will lift the conditions of Black people, but unity will also have an impact on their self-esteem, how others see them, and how they see themselves. Stewart punctuates the interconnectedness of collateral damages caused by individualism and class distinctions, not unlike those brewing between Wheatley's mythical mothers, whose arrogance and conceits grounded in society's perceived value of a woman's fecundity undermine and destroy the very things they value most: their progeny and their legacy. In the same address Stewart laments what she calls an "envious and malicious disposition [of Black Americans who] had rather die than see each other rise an inch above a beggar." The infighting and intra-racial discord are exacerbated because "no gentle methods are used to promote love and friendship among us, but much is done to destroy it." Stewart's words here work to link the spiritual with the political as she points to the love that Christians should extend toward one another in the same passage that she draws upon historical narratives that incite activism among Black Americans. The comparison to others in places like Haiti and Ethiopia identifies the power of collective action among African and African-descended people at the same time that she evokes a Christian commandment of love that should fuel and empower her people. In short, what should unite divides: nationality, race, and religion. Stewart does not hesitate to punctuate the importance of unity among the "free people of color in [the] United States," whom she admonishes for failing to exercise their collective power and "boldly contend for their rights" ("An Address: Delivered at the African Masonic Hall, Boston" 70). This is not only a cooperative political unity grounded in a necessary "encourage[ment] and patron[age] [of] each other" (70) to do the right thing and abstain from doing harm to one another. For Stewart, activating such a call is more deeply grounded in a Pauline theological entreaty to be "deliver[ed] . . . from this body of sin and death . . . for the good that I would do, that I do not; and the evil that I would not do, that I do" ("Meditation I," in *Productions* 25).[6] Her WordsWork here grapples with the tension between the internal motivation to do good and the external challenge one must overcome in order to act upon those good intentions. Stewart understands the spiritual power at play if one is to liberate to transform intentions into actions for the good of all. Moreover, there is no separating sins of omission from those of commission, especially with regard to the uplifting and liberation of her people—Christians and African-descended people.

A similar dynamic is at work—and perhaps most palpable— in the experiences of the preacher Lee. We are presented with the comparative effects of unity and disunity and how the former enables and promotes her mission to convert, permitting her also to analyze the underlying systems of oppression, bias, and prejudice at work even in those who are themselves oppressed. Lee celebrates "people of color of different denominations" (*Religious Experience and Journal* 48) who unite as well as those who "could not"—and would not—"unite in fellowship" (28). She narrates her journey to places and spaces where Black men preachers refuse to allow her access to the pulpit, with some expressing so much animosity against her because she is a woman that they are ineffective at spreading God's word. She also recounts diverse experiences with White Christians—some embrace and nurture her and others discount and refuse her calling on the basis of her race (45).

Lee's calling out of the intra-racial community of Christians who are less than faithful in their service toward one another is more than the preacher's condemnation of those who are refusing the sacred call to love one another. She also, by juxtaposition with the interracial fellowship of those who uphold God's tenets, complicates the need to enable embracing of the Word through a Black woman preacher, and by extension complicates and indicts the type of cultural conditioning and internalized prejudice and bias that undermines the spiritual, political, and personal well-being of Black people, especially Black women. She demonstrates that the power of faith to overcome external and internal oppression is a matter of repoliticizing Christian values at the service of marginalized people, rather than weaponizing faith in order to further devalue and dehumanize others. It is only a question of who—what race or gender—holds one down; it is also, perhaps more importantly, as Lee's words seem to suggest, a question of the will to create bridges and opportunities through which one might, regardless of race, gender, or condition, perform works that can liberate others. As such, she reveals a common humanity that is available to all, if they would or could receive others as God has received them.

The pious poet Wheatley offers an example of the value of this liberating move—as she observes that the Earl of Dartmouth will be rewarded for his work "to sooth the griefs" ("To the Right Honourable William, Earl of Dartmouth" 35) of enslaved Africans with "heav'nly grace" (36) that will give "sacred sanction" (36) to his work, and eventually "find [his] God" (43) in the "ethereal plain" (41). As James A. Levernier so aptly observes: "It is difficult indeed to imagine that the irony implicit in the metaphor of slavery so often repeated from the pulpits of New England would have been lost on Wheatley" (28). Her connections with the New England clergy did indeed help to inform the production of "religion" in her works. "Baptized by [Samuel] Cooper near the altar where [the Reverend Samuel] Sewell had presided [at Old South Church] for more than sixty-five years" and exposed to the thinking of ministers such as "Cooper, Chauncy, and Eliot [who] were all at times known to have used their ministerial authority to support the revolutionary cause," as well as those "intensely interested in human rights" (24), several of whom ultimately certified the veracity and authenticity of Wheatley's first volume of poems, support a view of Wheatley's WordsWork as extending through a Black woman's voice a repoliticized religion of the people, most notably articulating a path through which the purported religion of slave-holding Christians, whom she calls "Modern Egyptians" ("Letter to Reverend Samson Occom"), could ultimately be reoriented.[7] Similarly, in drawing attention to shared humanity and the distinctions and divisiveness that inhumanity breeds, Wheatley is careful in her letter to her Native American brother the Reverend Sam Occom to move respectfully into the community of humans with him: thanking him first for his "vindication of their [Negroes'] natural rights." She notes that he is doing this on behalf of others, that is, the rights "respecting the Negroes," by her use of "their." Further, Wheatley's adoption of this third-person pronoun suggests a clever way of demonstrating the way that differences need not separate us from our humanity. Occom is part of the "their" that connects him with others—especially, but not only, African people. In this case, the Mohegan minister is both part of and apart from those whose humanity he defends: "the negroes." Occom is an ally (or more correctly a comrade); she quickly disassociates him from "those" who would "invade" the rights of others, those tyrants who are wreaking chaos and spreading darkness over a continent. This attention to invasion not only identifies Christians by reminding Occom of a fact he well understands, but also affirms that "civil and religious liberty" are interconnected—indeed, "inseparable." The poet goes beyond the anti-slavery argument, which is prominently figured in this letter and elsewhere, as I analyzed in earlier chapters. In yet another reworking or repoliticizing of terms typically cast in a different light, Wheatley draws parallels between African and European oppression—which signifies that "those" who usurp and dehumanize others are not only "White" or "Black" (European or African): in her turn of phrase, it is evil and greed that connect and bind people together in the oppression and violation of others. Importantly, "as her letters make clear, Wheatley understood the stakes inherent in her efforts to remain humble and embody virtue. She accepts that she functions as a member of her 'Nation' and frequently speaks on behalf of Black Africans [even] as her poetry gains her an audience with prominent political and religious figures" (Cassander Smith 107).[8]

The "Modern Egyptians" or ancient Africans are no different in the poet's view than those contemporary eighteenth-century slaveholders who traffic in the theft of human beings. And by the same measure, her contemporary enslaved African brethren are no less desirous of their freedom, "impatient [with] oppression" and yearning for "deliverance" ("Letter to Reverend Samson Occom") from their oppressors than were the ancient Israelites—or the colonial American patriots, for that matter. That Wheatley yokes both under the same bands of oppression and the same ability to be granted "deliverance" by their shared God is no accident or coincidence. She means in this letter, as she does in her poem "On Being Brought from Africa to America" and throughout her works, for her words to reinforce the importance of understanding the shared oppression and deliverance that binds together free to enslaved, African to European, and Native American, White, and Black with Christianity. She indirectly reminds readers of the scripture that warns the faithful to Christ that they can hardly love Christ and hate their brothers and sisters: "How well the cry for liberty, and the reverse disposition for the exercise of oppressive power over others agree" ("Letter to Reverend Samson Occom"; 1 John 4:20). Rather than the "penetration of a philosopher," Wheatley offers exegesis and eisegesis to provide clarity on the political within the spiritual dimensions. The Christian mind must be the muse as Wheatley engages it with power and thrust backed by the authority of the Word of God and the wisdom of experience. Not unlike Whitfield, she too "prayed that grace in ev'ry heart might dwell"; and most certainly, as her words proclaimed, Wheatley "longed to see America excel" ("Death of Rev. Whitfield" lines 20–21). With a "mournful strain," she did indeed cast before her audiences the great "undressed complain[t]" ("To the Right Honourable William, Earl of Dartmouth" lines 14–15) that exposes America as a nation that disregards "heaven's beauteous dyes" ("Hymn to the Evening" line 8), euphemistically castigating the "west [that] glories in the deepest red" (line 8). It is, therefore, not the "colour" of enslaved Africans but rather those sins of the nation against humanity and God that mark America with "diabolic dye" ("On Being Brought from Africa to America" line 6).

Likewise, Stewart's America bears a "stain" that is "dark and indelible," existing under a "dark and dismal . . . cloud" for its "cruel wrongs and injuries to . . . Africa . . . almost drunken with the blood of her slain" (*Maria W. Stewart* 39). And Lee condemns "the wickedness of the people [which] certainly calls for the lowering Judgments of God to be let loose upon the Nation and Slavery, that wretched system that emanated from the bottomless pit, . . . one of the greatest curses to any Nation" (*Religious Experience and Journal* 63). Of course, it is not only the system of chattel slavery that is challenged by Lee. Her attempt to save cruel slave masters from God's reckoning acknowledges and addresses the actions of those individuals and societies that enable the atrocious machine that dehumanizes her people—free and enslaved, men and women. Like Wheatley, she is careful to acknowledge progress, however minimal and illusory at times: the "great slave holder, [who] had been very cruel; thinking nothing of knocking down a slave with a fence stake, or whatever might come to hand . . . became greatly altered in his ways for the better" after hearing Lee's sermon (18). This "Deist" who did not believe that Black people had souls had a change of heart and "notwithstanding his age, walked about three miles to hear [Lee]" (18). While we don't know if this reformed slaveholder made the ultimate act of contrition by freeing his enslaved people, Lee recounts progress in his treatment of those he enslaved, adopting a somewhat hopeful tone, as does Wheatley in speaking of her political ally the Earl of Dartmouth. Importantly, the "sacred sanction" given to Dartmouth's work on behalf of enslaved African people is extended through Lee's insertion of an "Omnipresent One" who protects her from capture or worse, "though in a slave country" (35). The greater gift, not unlike those announced in Wheatley's verses and Maria Stewart's meditations, is spiritual. Lee observes the endowment of "great liberty in word and doctrine" to "the slaves and the holders, [who] felt the power of God [which] seemed without intermission" (36).

Lee's audiences, like Stewart's and Wheatley's, were mixed; and while Wheatley does not directly address the issue of audience, Lee is clear in her journal references to the various communities, races, and genders of people she encounters as she moves from place to place. She also provides information about the age and religious experiences of those to whom she preaches or whom she reaches. In keeping with some nineteenth-century women's concerns, Lee addresses the importance of educating children and reveals those strategies used to block education as well as those people who support it. In this, Lee is part of a legacy of Black women who advocate for education, especially for Black children. Betsey Stockton, for example, "was hired by a team of women to organize and become the head teacher of the Infant School for the Coloured in Philadelphia" (Escher 10). Although Stewart more directly explains in her political speeches the way that systemic oppression works and with whom it is located, Lee's religious text is interlaced with ethical dilemmas and other concerns—legal and extra-legal—as a path to full liberation through her critiques of racism, sexism, and the institution of slavery and those laws that limit the liberty of free Black women and men.

At the same time, aspects of Lee's recounting of other subjects in her *Journal* demonstrate divergent paths to related socio-religio-political goals. The paths that distinguish the itinerant preacher from her spiritual sisters who strike poetic and political chords are worth contemplating. For example, Lee appears to celebrate the Christianization of "Methodist Indians," highlighting the work of the Reverend John Steward [*sic*] a "coloured man" whose "ministry" she describes as a "miraculous call," referring to his conversion of Native Americans in the Sandusky region (*Religious Experience and Journal* 47). It is notable that this reference provides an opportunity to cite another Black spiritual author—"a book called the *Essence of John Steward*" (48; see Mitchell). Lee's references to this text comments on several issues, including the diversity of Bibles, the contexts within which Native Americans were proselytized, and the fear that they might help hide enslaved Africans (Mitchell 27).

Interestingly, Stewart's allusions to Indigenous peoples demonstrate varying levels of oppression but might initially be read as her complicity with European conquest of Native American people. However, a second reading offers a subtle compelling critique of the oppression of others—a lesson to be learned from, not an action to repeat:

> Alas, what keeps us so? Prejudice, ignorance, and poverty. But ah! methinks our oppression is soon to come to an end; yea, before the Majesty of heaven, our groans and cries have reached the ears of the Lorde of the Sabaoth. As the prayers and tears of Christians will avail the finally impenitent nothing; neither will the prayers and tears of humanity avail us anything unless, we possess a spirit emulation within our breasts. Did the pilgrims, when they first landed on these shores, quietly compose themselves and say "the Britons have all the money and the power, and we must continue their servants forever"? Did they sluggishly sigh and say "our lot is hard, the Indians own the soil, and we cannot cultivate it"? No; they first made powerful efforts to raise themselves, and then God raised up those illustrious patriots, WASHINGTON and LAFAYETTE, to assist and defend them. And, my brethren have you made a powerful effort? Have you prayed the Legislature for mercy's sake to grant you all the rights and privileges of free citizens, that your daughters may also rise to that level of respectability which true merit deserves, and your sons above the servile situations which most of them fill? . . .
>
> And even the wild Indians of the forest are more united than ourselves. Insult one of them and you insult a thousand. They also have contended for their rights and privileges and are held in higher report than we are. (*Productions* 56, 61)

Here Stewart first expresses her dismay—"Alas"—by questioning the conditions in which Black people appear to be hopelessly and perpetually interred—"kept." She thus poses a rhetorical question to which there is no simple answer: why Black people have been and continue to be kept so low—at the bottom rungs of society—for so long. This question allows her to open a dialogue and, moving from despair to hope, she highlights the value of unity. It is regrettable that she emphasizes such through the example of "Indian" people, whom she problematically refers to as "wild"—perhaps as a euphemism for "savage" or perhaps to signify the way they are described by their European oppressors. However troubling her essentialization is here, it is worth considering how the political writer turns to a history of betrayal and resentment among African peoples that might be said to have a parallel narrative of Native oppression and genocide. She laments the lack of "love and friendship among" her own people, who "now possess" a spirit of disunity. To be sure, there is here a mixture of advocating for unity that will enable the oppressed to revolt against their oppressors as well as a call for racial uplift among her privileged brethren. Not unlike David Walker, Stewart holds freed and upper-class Africans responsible for resisting the oppression and advocating for the freedoms of her enslaved brethren. She provides them with a short history of what oppression looks like and an example of unity through her references to Indian peoples. She points to the history of European conquest, which is a narrative of moving from oppressed colonized peoples to oppressors who colonize and enslave, all in the name of Christianity. She also points to the history of Africans on the continent who sold other Africans into slavery and those, enslaved and free, who have learned well to use the master's tools. Of course, there is much to unpack in Stewart's words, and much that is problematic, to say the least. Indeed, her comparisons rely on some miseducation about the unique situatedness of Africans in America, whose conditions and recourse are not entirely analogous to either British colonists or Indigenous peoples (Indians). That notwithstanding, Stewart's attempt to repoliticize the spiritual is ever present. She invokes the same sense of African history as Wheatley does in her reference to "Modern Egyptians" in order to demonstrate the learned patterns of oppression that are fluid throughout diverse cultural points as well as the religious history of a God who delivers his people and a disobedient people who repeat the tragic consequences of their own oppression by enacting it upon others.

Lee also addresses a freeing of the spirit through her simultaneously political and secular tone. Her ministry speaks truth to power, not unlike Stewart's political speeches and religious meditations as well as Wheatley's spiritual poetry. Lee observes that she "saw many displays of [God's Word's] power . . . [among] the people in Niagara. . . . The slaves that came there felt their freedom, began to see the necessity of education, and hired a white man to teach them to read and write among themselves, and have Sabbath schools." Lee also reveals her "astonish[ment] to see so many there that came from a free state, [who did] not take more interest in instilling the science of education among their fellow beings" (*Religious Experience and Journal* 49). This surprise at free people's apparent lack of concern for those who are enslaved echoes similar themes from Stewart about the responsibility people owe to others and Wheatley's more abstract addressing of privilege in general, through which parallels might be drawn between the poet's critique of the institution of slavery and disregard for the enslaved person's physical, spiritual, and intellectual development.

Invoking heavenly retribution as earthly resistance, Stewart's repoliticization of religion in her reorientation of Christian humility threatens violent retribution from an omnipresent, omniscient, and omnipotent God. Cleverly, Stewart calls for her African "brethren [to] sheath [their] swords, and calm [their] angry [albeit justified] passions. Stand still and know that the Lord is God. Vengeance is his and he will repay" (*Maria W. Stewart* 40). Wheatley's claim in "On Being Brought from Africa to America" that "some view our sable race with scornful eye / their color is a diabolic die'" (5–6) is echoed in Stewart's 1831 introduction to *Religion and the Pure Principles of Morality*. Stewart maintains, "Many think, because your skins are tinged with a sable hue, that you are an inferior race of beings; but God does not consider you as such" (qtd. in *Maria W. Stewart* 29). Wheatley's "some view" versus Stewart's "many think" may appear so subtle a distinction that it is hardly worth mentioning. However, while "some" and "many" are both imprecise terms mathematically, the indefinite "many" could easily connote so numerous as to signify the thinking of countless people on this issue of skin color. Likewise, whereas "view" (in this context) typically denotes a perspective or interpretation, "think" suggests a more deliberative consideration, signifying regressive rather than progressive movement on the issue of race. This is somewhat indicative of what Kristin Waters terms a type of "knowledge-producing posture that stems from an analysis by the formidable Stewart of organically generated Black feminist theory" that subverts racialized oppressions (*Maria Stewart* 9).[9]

In another comparison, Wheatley's "Remember, Christians, Negroes, black as Cain; / May be refin'd and join th'angelic train" ("On Being Brought from Africa to America" lines 7–8) is a stark contrast to Stewart's harsh language and castigating tone. Certainly, if God and the Constitution "hath made all men free and equal . . . then why should *one worm say to another*, 'Keep you down there, while I sit up yonder; for I am better than thou? It is not the color of the skin that makes the man, but it is the principles formed within the soul" (*Maria W. Stewart* 29). Whereas Wheatley signifies equality among mankind regardless of race or religion, placing Black and White Christians at the same level due to their equal capacity to be freed from spiritual impurity, Stewart's claim about the "principles formed within" more overtly challenges racism within the context of an indivisible politics of religion. Wheatley's unifying language dismantles eighteenth-century racial hierarchies that invoke the curse of Cain to mark black skin as inferior and evil, and Stewart's worms connote shared conditions of parasitical, contemptuous, groveling, and devious corruption from within.

Further, juxtaposing Wheatley's "'Twas mercy brought me from my *Pagan* land, / Taught my benighted soul to understand" ("On Being Brought from Africa to America" lines 1–2) with Stewart's request for God to "have mercy on the benighted sons and daughters of Africa" (*Maria W. Stewart* 34) suggests trans-historical moves in which "mercy" and "benighted" are repoliticized.[10] Stewart makes patently clear that such conditions of "benightedness" are caused by the circumstances resulting from slavery and racism: she laments "how very few" American people "bestow one thought upon the benighted sons and daughters of Africa, who enrich the soils of America with their tears and blood" (*Maria W. Stewart* 34–35). Wheatley's "mercy" and "benighted" express something like a prayer of thanks to a merciful God for her survival in the hold of the slave ship throughout the long journey of Middle Passage. She praises a God with the power to lift her out of spiritual and physical darkness. Stewart's prayer is to an omnipotent God for deliverance of a "thorough reformation" by which Africans can reclaim their right to "respect," "unity," and "honor" (36–37). Stewart's prayer is followed by a call for economic self-determination "to raise a fund ourselves . . . to lay the cornerstone for the building of a High School" (37) as well as a "spirit of independence" and unity among Black people to build their own institutions, sue for their rights, and use their minds, endeavors that she claims are sanctioned by God. Contrastingly, Wheatley's mind vis-à-vis her prodigious lays are depicted in many ways like Aphra Behn's Oroonoko, a noble savage. Notably, Behn's prizing of the supposedly Western values in the non-European indigenous man whose best characteristics can be attributed to his proximity to what we might term in contemporary contexts as "White" values or the myths of White supremacy—grace, nobility, and physiognomic features similar to White men. Like Behn, Wheatley's master John Wheatley describes the young poet in words that reflect a comparable sentiment about the girl who was brought from Africa as an "uncultivated barbarian" ("To the Public"). Her poetic genius is thus determined to be based on the influence of her European masters, who have "cultivated" this former "barbarian."

At their heart, Wheatley's verses are about humanity and equity in the earthly realm. She is deliberate in her avoidance of any oversimplified repoliticizing of pro-slavery and anti-abolitionist strains. What this young versifier and lyricist wanted most was to create a language that would touch not only "the hem" of her savior's garment but also the hearts and minds of her fellows—those with whom she shared this planet. By now it is clear that Wheatley used signifying to speak to several audiences simultaneously through the subtle eighteenth-century language of indirection in order to make a case, to speak for those oppressed and unheard voices of enslaved and nominally free Africans and women (Black and White). Bassard especially has discussed the significance of her elegiac work and how it speaks most identifiably to and for women of the eighteenth century who could claim, at best, nominal and relative freedom. However, not unlike our contemporary social justice advocates, Wheatley conveys concerns well beyond her own "village" of Africans (enslaved and nominally free in the colonies and on the continent). The work her words intended to accomplish extended even to those for whom nominal privileges were secured in their support of the myth of a White supremacist ideology that undergirded the institution of slavery through their actions and desires to acquire power via "Whiteness," "maleness," and class. Her lyrics lay this message bare, if one is attuned to the historical and cultural contexts within which this "genius in 'bondage" (Sancho) penned her powerful words. She understood the toll that war had taken on the lives of White people—men, women, and children—circumstances that also kept them from seeing or responding to the humanity of their fellow Black citizens, family, and friends.

In the dysfunctional community that Wheatley shared with them—one in which she, as an enslaved teenager (as she was at the time she wrote most of her works), would have been considered "privileged," working for/owned by prominent wealthy Bostonians John and Susanna Wheatley—she could straddle both worlds because of her "race" and caste. She saw both wealth and want with a dual vision—perhaps a kind of double consciousness (such as Du Bois would later articulate) that informed a very nuanced and sophisticated understanding of power and its consequences—intended and unintended. In "On the Death of a Young Gentleman," Wheatley asks a fundamental question that addresses the loss of a young man in war to "ease the anguish of a parent's heart" (line 15). Her questions are also meant to contemplate the meaning of her WordsWork —the intention and purpose for her artivism: "What shall my sympathizing verse impart? / Where is the balm to heal so deep a wound? / Where shall a sov'reign remedy be found?" (lines 16–18). She poses formidable questions about the nature of combat, ones that indirectly decry the waste and "wisdom" of war. She calls for answers from her nation's leaders to this excessive loss and preventable violence, which she traces to greed and desire for power. The emotions she describes range from agony for the loss of a child to a "raging tempest of . . . grief" that needs "control" (line 21). The costs are great because human lives are at stake in such modes of conquest, and throughout her corpus Wheatley both sees the underlying structures of power that enable such devastation and destruction and calls for their cessation. One might wonder if there is indeed a "balm" to heal the depth of the national "wounds" Wheatley signifies here.

Lee seeks a similar solace. She wants freedom for the enslaved Africans, a converted spirit and heart for Christians, a world that sees the equality of all humans, especially Black women like herself who are called to do God's work. However, as an early example of the significance of intersectionality, this nineteenth-century itinerant preacher does not view these issues as separate or mutually exclusive. In fact, her ministry demonstrates a theological perspective that sees the need for simultaneously healing—or at the very least treating both sacred and secular injuries that are obstacles to true liberty—in the here and the hereafter alike. Her map for achieving such a palliative can be seen as Lee invokes the power of God to liberate "the slaves and the holders"; she writes she "felt great liberty in word and doctrine; the power of God seemed without intermission" (*Religious Experience and Journal* 36). Her messages of hope and salvation—her preaching and attempts to provide that "balm"—are not limited by congregation or denomination. Lee witnesses to the curiosity seekers as well as the "Deist, who said he did not believe the coloured people had any souls" (18). And, in the end, she observes progress toward engaging the human spirit through her ministry: When she "had done speaking" the Deist "went out, and called the people around him, said that [although Lee's] preaching might seem a small thing, yet he believed I had the worth of souls at heart. This language was different from what it was a little time before, as he now seemed to admit that coloured people had souls, as it was to these I was chiefly speaking" (18).

Not only do the Deist's ideas about the nature of Black people change, so also does the way he speaks this truth to others, becoming effectively (and perhaps unwittingly) an agent of anti-slavery. The change in this Deist's language counters some "truths" upon which slavery had been justified, a major one being that Black people had no souls. His view, based on what he articulates and "now admits" publicly to a mixed audience, has shifted based solely on the power of Lee's words. She has "worth," and this has been pronounced by a person who is situated in a privileged place—a free White man who, not coincidentally, shares the same religion as that of former statesman Thomas Jefferson. The Deist has been converted, despite the fact that he was not Lee's primary audience. It was to Black people that Lee was "chiefly speaking," and yet her message of faith was not lost on an opponent. This is significant because she, not unlike Wheatley, demonstrates a pattern of influence that does not depend on a unidirectional "speaking to the empire," with an understanding that certain universal truths can be supported without relying on the "choir" to co-sign, merely based on shared experiences and interests.[11] Part of the balm will entail educating both oppressed and oppressor—sometimes simultaneously. There are more than forty instances of Lee's use of the term *liberty* throughout this text: Lee describes having been "permitted" (15), "found" (15), "given" (18), "had" (18), or "felt" (36) liberty to various degrees, sometimes "little" (18) or "peculiar" (21), "greater" (36), "considerable" (89), and to a "great degree" (92). Moreover, she felt such liberty in diverse contexts, "among strangers" (26), on a particular "subject" (36) or "portion of Scripture" (36), "in the word" (41), "in speaking" (43), "around the circuit" (45), "to hold [a] quarterly meeting" (55), "in word and doctrine," and even the "liberty to leave" (48) when time, place, or climate dictated—or of course when God's urging led her to do so. Ultimately, it appears that Lee seeks to conclude that it is in "the Lord" (79) and "with both life" (65) that liberty is key—repoliticization of the Christian God's intention that humans have abundant life "on earth as it is in heaven"—one that is possible only through complete liberation of the body, mind, and soul.[12]

This type of freedom is also experienced, though in different contexts, by her predecessor Wheatley and by her contemporary Stewart. And this extension of liberty allows them to repoliticize their renderings of God's Word through the holy scripture in ways that obtain justice for all people. The words upon which they meditate, either in poetic form, rendering via eulogy, as did Wheatley, or as Lee does in changing the language and nature of relationships between raced and non-raced persons, bind them together in their shared goal of extending an inclusive humanity. While Lee does not convey that the slaveholding Deist freed his human property, she does provide evidence that may permit her reader to consider how the change in perspective—the conversion—that led to new views about colored people could have impacted his relationship with those he enslaved. Perhaps his acknowledgment that they did indeed have souls could at the very least have resulted in more humane treatment, if not gradual or complete manumission. The context and registers of the liberty Lee describes, suggest an understanding by the itinerant preacher that change is gradual rather than immediate.

It is evident that Lee understands both the biblical mandate of seed planting and witnessing as well as the worldly schedule of how things happen. She invites her reader to meet some interracial acquaintances on several occasions, with "white ladies" as an example of the type of women traveling—once when she is a passenger to Hagerstown with "three white ladies, members of the Episcopal Church" (59). In this context, it appears that the gender and race of the women seem less consequential than those of the elderly Deist, "73 years of age, who would reproach Religion, until I . . . exhorted him to get religion; for God's name is worthy to be praised by all intelligent beings" (59). Given the audiences to whom she preaches, it is clear that Lee examines not only the spiritual but also the intellectual capacity of people of all races—White and Black women (whom she often refers to as sisters during her journeys, as she does those who accompany her and those who support the work she does in her ministry), as well as White and Black men—slaveholders, enslaved, and free. Another incidental experience was with "a white lady" who shared passage on a "boat with me, bound to Philadelphia" (87). Both the White lady and Lee were seen safely to their destination by a "gentleman who was coming to the city, seeing her lonely situation and also mine, he never left the cars until he saw each of our baggages in the omnibus and starting for our doors" (87–88). She describes this man as "a gentleman indeed," and although we are not told his race, it is safe to assume that he was a White man, given the time of travel (September 1839) and the fact that he was at liberty to ride in the car with a White woman.

One experience in particular sheds light on the progress that her preaching may have yielded among her gender. Lee recounts a meeting with a "white lady, of great distinction, a member of the Methodist Society," who was converted by Lee a decade earlier (19). This woman was so pleased to see Lee that she "invited her home with her" (19) to stay overnight. Lee described this fortunate encounter as "bread cast upon the waters, seen after many days" (19). As Lee demonstrates throughout her text, securing appropriate lodging and reception in the various places she travels is critical to her ministry, and indeed without them she (and the sisters who sometimes travel with her) are not safe. So being invited to the home of a prominent White woman was essential at this time as she had arrived to speak to "large congregations of various and conflicting sentiments" (19). The map for future generations of the necessity of planting seeds that generate fruit years later—in this case a decade—is one of perseverance and endurance, reflecting the importance of creating pathways for change. Lee, of course, gives God the credit for this "wonderfully shocking" experience that, she claims, "felt as if aided from above" (19). Her experiences also reveal a pattern of pivoting when necessary. As a preacher and activist, Lee understood the power of flexibility.

On the heels of this experience at the Dennis Creek Meeting House, Lee brings us back to the harsh reality that doing God's work is not without sacrifice, despite the progress of seed planting and harvesting. She is left traveling with her son and without money—without the "means to procure my passage home" (20).

Consequently, Lee "opened a School, and taught eleven scholars, for the purpose of raising a small sum" (20). She shifted from preacher to teacher without losing the point of her mission, her call. As she shares that "meditating upon [God's] goodness," seeking clarity about where she should go next, Lee receives a message from God, who "made known to me" the next part of her journey—to Philadelphia (19). Lee preached at schoolhouses throughout the country, not only because they were the popular places that doubled as churches and other multiuse locations, but also because of the significance of preaching as teaching and the value of learning on spiritual and secular levels—especially, but not only, for free and enslaved Black people. Lee shares her feelings about the acquisition of knowledge throughout her text. However, one instance in particular, following her comments about the necessity of "intelligence" to receive God's words (noted above), stands out. While in "West haven, [Lee] visited a School of boys and girls, and was much pleased to see them engaged and improving in their studies." She remarks, "How great the difference now, thought I, for the mental and moral culture of the young than when I was a child!" (29). Addressing both the "mental and moral culture" of children is significant not only because Lee punctuates this passage with an exclamation point that reveals a kind of emotion she usually reserves for religious acclamations, but also because it is a focus on faith that links God's power to brain power—both of which had and continued to be throughout Lee's time restricted and prohibited from Black people. Indeed, she speaks rather fondly of Bishop Allen's "interest in [her] son's welfare, by sending to school, and otherwise improving him in education; by which he has made considerable improvements therefrom; which give me great reconciliation of mind" (59). Lee speaks of the importance of building schools throughout her work.

What becomes exceedingly clear when we connect the poet, the preacher, and the politician is that being bound up together, as Harper phrases it, is multilayered and riddled with complexity. Unity is indeed power, and the legacy of early Black Christian women writers draws us a map for seeing both the intentional and unintended consequences of exploiting power for good and for evil. These Christian women were not solely intent on a soul-saving mission meant to guide people to heavenly salvation. Their interconnected artivistic voices issued a call for a deeper understanding of the connected humanity that must be understood at a deeper level, not only as a necessary strategy for the endurance of Black people in worlds they were not meant to survive, but also a call to begin re-creating a world in which all people, regardless of race, gender, or position in society, would thrive. For these women, the Word was not only a tool for doing God's work on earth but also a way of making meaning of their lives and of demonstrating beyond a shadow of a doubt that #EarlyBlackChristianWomensLivesMattered. As such, probing the layers of meaning laced throughout their works, echoing along parallel and intersecting lines, we can imagine conversations that address complementary concerns and strategies among Wheatley, Stewart, and Lee that point us toward a greater understanding of the legacy they birthed of artivistic moves deploying WordsWork that calls for a deeper understanding of how and why #ContemporaryBlackWomensLivesMatter.

5
Black Women's Lives and What Really Matters

> If scripture got you spiritually and rhetorically beating the sh*t out of gay people, women, and Black folks rather than Bible-thumping the sh*t out of capitalism, white supremacy and heteropatriarchy, you're using it wrong. God ain't on your side and you might have the Devil on your team.
>
> —Brittney Cooper, *Crunk Feminist Collection*

What really matters is people—all kinds of people, and especially women, Black women people, from whom it seems the world has tacitly turned away. As if to do so would somehow erase all those moments in his- and herstory we would rather transcend. Religion can't erase the sins of chattel slavery, as there is no scripture one might cite, no sermon one might preach, no poetic verse, no apologetic speech that will allay the abuses, exploitations, devastations, and aftershocks of chattel slavery—and the child shall follow the condition of the mother, in perpetuity. However, the children of early Black Christian women like those I've briefly engaged in earlier chapters are survivors, and they matter precisely because the condition these women—these descendants—will follow has been inherited through a spirit of liberation, an understanding of the power of words, the intelligence, and most of all the imagination to fetch what was lost, remix, repoliticize, and re-create a new track. This track is one that holds the past accountable, engages with the challenges and opportunities of the present, and embraces the joy that is our future. Cooper powerfully identifies a singular thread—a through line, if you will—from Wheatley, Stewart, and Lee to contemporary Black Christian women who demand a faith that is based on empowering and lifting rather than oppressing and dehumanizing people. Her attention in particular is directed to the way that the Word, "scripture," is weaponized on multiple levels. First, there are those "spiritual" soul-reaching beliefs from within that are manifested in visible ways and are a product of a particular indoctrination that is anything but godly, even if it can claim to be legitimately religious, or more precisely a tenet of organized religion. Next, and closely associated with this accepted myth of the inferiority of others whose beliefs stand apart from one's own supposedly more Christian and therefore superior faith, is the propaganda or propagation of lies about them—the words that human beings can use to crush rather than heal others.

Contemporary scholars like Cooper repoliticize the meaning of spiritual or religious texts and contexts as they relate to actual Black women, among other minoritized and marginalized people. Put bluntly, Cooper calls a "saint" a sinner. That is, she exposes the power of the Word both to construct and, more importantly, to deconstruct false doctrine that serves the interests of those in the most privileged positions in society—contemporarily those are typically (but not always) wealthy cis-gendered White men. Historically, Black women have been at the bottom rungs of society based on multiple levels of oppressions based on their positionality (race, gender, class, sexuality, ability, and so on). For it is those in positions of power who have attempted to hold faith hostage by misappropriation of spirituality. In this manner, Cooper's words demonstrate the empowering carrying forward of the WordsWork of early Black Christian women like Wheatley, Stewart, and Lee. Stewart, for example, laments the lack of "men spiritually minded . . . not given to filthy lucre holding religion in one hand and the world in the other" (*Religion and the Pure Principles of Morality* 10). In this Stewart, not unlike Cooper and Wheatley, would chastise and challenge young educated White men to forgo the "transient sweetness that turns to endless pain and . . . sinks the soul" into "immense perdition" ("To the University of Cambridge in New-England" lines 29–30). Surely, a great deal of those "sinful actions" were at best (if one can call it that) supporting their hedonistic lifestyles, embracing their own humanity from their privileged positions, and at worst directly included the enslavement and violation of others, displaying their inhumanity by their dehumanizing actions. Lee reiterates the critical import of actual spirituality and faith by juxtaposing it with the perversion of Christianity for the oppression of others. She cautions the church fathers to be "careful [about perverting the Word of God] . . . lest through our by laws of church government and discipline, we bring into disrepute even the word of life" (*Religious Experience and Journal* 13). Lee's caution is her way of carrying forward this idea of the disjuncture between what faith was, is, or should be, and peering into the complicated historical, cultural, spiritual, and political meanings such notions of "faith" hold for Black believers and freethinkers in the twenty-first century. Too often attention is given to the "laws of church" rather than the deeper spiritual meaning of the Word of God and the divine authority on which the power of the Word stands. To be sure, contemporary linkages between previous generations of righteousness, equity, and justice with its civil rights roots/routes in the Christian faith suggest a religion-based faith that seems further from any Black experience in the United States than in all previous generations. Indeed, some would argue that "the Black church" is little more than an idiom that holds little in the way of reality to effect change or address the unique obstacles faced by this current generation of Black people. However, despite such challenges, the voices of those who provide an intergenerational bridge across race, gender, and class obstacles resonate from Wheatley to Cooper, and beyond affirm the dynamic power of faith as a central space of spiritual and political renewal and strategy.

Cooper's words serve as reminders of the institutionalized suppression and oppression of Black voices and lives, even as we attempt to recover religion as a tool to contradict such regressive politics. Therefore, not unlike Stewart and Lee, who more than a century and a half earlier had criticized the misogyny and hypocrisy of Black men who were deemed leaders (for example, Black Masons) and Black fathers of the church (Richard Allen and others), Cooper encourages us to question a monolithic Christian-based, culturally informed, inflected, and practiced faith: "the Black church." It would be irresponsible to overlook the internalized racism, sexism, homophobia, xenophobia, classism, colorism, ableism, and other learned and socially transmitted forms of adapted, adopted, and accepted oppressions that religion has enabled under the guise of community building and divine sanctioning. Ironically, religion has indeed functioned to culturally condition society both in support of and against such prejudices, biases, and social inequalities. It is widely known that there is a disproportionate number of Black women in the church performing labor duties compared to their appointment to leadership roles—the labor to power ratio is palpable. Notably, "African American churches' problematic relationship with women continues in part because few of the denominations have undertaken the task of thoroughly examining the doctrines of their institutions . . . [which] are often based on the cultural norms of the first century" (Green 118). Clearly, those "first-century" norms speak to the ongoing significance of Black women's repoliticization of the spiritual, signaling the value and import of their intertextual connections to earlier Black Christian women like Wheatley, Stewart, and Lee, who provide support beams for the construction of bridges between early Black Christian women and contemporary twentieth- and twenty-first-century women.

It is critical to consider the evolution of "faith"—or, more precisely, Christian religious practices and beliefs as they articulate and construct new meaning of the spiritually political in the words (spoken, written, and signified) of Black women. Relatedly, it will be necessary to reflect on and examine how contemporary theories, concepts, and linguistic turns as they are manifested in this historical moment and cultural milieu provide expressive connectives, literal and figurative, between women across centuries. Bettye Collier-Thomas punctuates and incorporates decades of the conceptualization of the relationship between Black women, politics, and religion and their role in social justice. She observes, "One cannot fully understand sexism and gender discrimination in the black community without a careful evaluation and understanding of religious institutional praxis and the internal discourse over the meaning of black manhood and womanhood" (94). This articulation of the inextricability of religion—not only in theoretical approaches but in the lives and literary works of Black women—is critical for the placement of holistic herstories that recover a full humanity for Black women, one that respects the role faith and spirituality play in their movement for full liberation of all people.

For social justice workers like Tarana Burke, her faith represents the cornerstone of her activism. Religion is the ground on which she "stands in the gap" (Matthew 6:10, KJV) on behalf of those silenced and violated Black girls and women, and the unnaturally suppressed voices of their mothers, sisters, aunties, and grandmothers. These terrorized victims are so traumatized by visible acts of violence that they hush themselves and thereby silently and unwittingly acquiesce to the will of their victimizers—an acquiescence that renders them invisible. It is out of such a moment of self-silencing that a powerful movement to reclaim self evolves, compelled to join forces and be counted among that broader community of authentic members with personhood that must be revived and recognized for the progress of all people.

An artivistic interpretative recovery of self can be seen in Libianca Fonji's "People," which poses some critical questions about the ways in which pain goes unacknowledged or unrecognized. The artist asks heart-rending questions that are seldom if ever considered in any great depth as they relate to Black women: "Did you check on me? / Now did you look for me?" (lines 6–7). How disparate are the calls for response to the tears, tragic events, and consequences for missing and abused White women from the relative nonresponse to similar cries for the global rescue of their Black sisters? Libianca's voice and tone as well as resonating rhythm permit us to hear she has been "drinking more alcohol," and her eyes are red, not from "banga" (marijuana) but rather from her tears that are neither seen nor recognized. It was during the COVID pandemic, when people were experiencing deep bouts of depression and internalizing some of their lowest points, that the Afrobeat artist reminded of the significance of people seeing each other. She explains that "people" don't really know, nor does it seem they care, to understand the pain and tears of others. Her words are especially poignant as we consider the personal emotions and trials the artist endured as an immigrant to the United States, and perhaps what pain drove her to drink and tears. Her lyrics speak to a pain that has silenced her in ways unimaginable. She announces: "You won't see how buried I am inside my grave." So, in her pain and anguish, she turns to a "Holy Father" who, she prays, can understand her from the inside—how she tried to be strong, to hold her head up—and whom she pleads with not to leave her, but instead see and redeem her. The backstory is autobiographical in many ways. This young Cameroonian American woman speaks truths that connect to others, endangered and perhaps on the brink of suicide, those who have removed themselves physically or emotionally from humanity. Certainly, Black women experience bipolarity, not unlike most other non-Black humans. Research shows that as a doubly, perhaps triply, minoritized people, Black women are misdiagnosed and in some cases experience symptoms differently. Libianca draws our attention to a most horrific vision of what it looks like to be cancelled, discarded, and at risk of self-annihilation. She highlights her invisibility by engaging the interrogative, not unlike her ancestor Stewart, choosing to elicit responses rather than wholly condemn or accuse, but the call for accountability, for empathy and concern, for the recognition of her humanity is clear: "Did you check on me? . . . Did you look for me? / . . . / did you notice me?" The people to whom she refers, to whom she poses these questions don't even know, nor do they seem to care, about this young woman's tears and the pain that is hidden behind a smile—a smile that, when we look closely at her words, we realize perhaps disguises a deeper desire to end her own life. The tune is haunting, her voice riddled with raw honesty such that our experience goes beyond merely listening to a song—we sample the death and anguish with which many women like her live, or rather exist, daily. Her ancestors signal a similar refrain.

We might be tempted to consider only the literary devices used—the hyperbolic visions, the assignment of her feelings of deep despair to the Christian God's providence and call on her life—when considering Jarena Lee's attempts at suicide as she constructs them within the context of the narrative of conversion. This would not be an unreasonable conclusion, and it fits the general narrative of conversion. But I argue there is more here than simply the circumstance of conversion, as she shares aspects of her life that are distinct and particular to her experience as a Black woman in the antebellum era—albeit a free person. I remind again that there is method in her approach to devoting an entire chapter to the prejudices she encounters. Looking through lens of a contemporary understanding of how mental health is impacted by race and other social constructions, it is equally reasonable that—although couched in the language and conventions of early American literary and religion—she is attempting to be seen on a far more personal yet equally political level—one that shares her spirituality as one mode of relief—the kind that would not come from fellow humans. The visions that foretell her calling are juxtaposed with her recollection of "a young man professed to be righteous, [who in 1831] says he saw in the sky men, marching like armies" (*Religious Experience and Journal* 63). Lee is likely referring to Nat

Turner's rebellion as a way to address the "wickedness of the people . . . the Nation and Slavery, that wretched system that emanated from the bottomless pit, one of the greatest curses to any Nation" (63). Lee's call to preach came from voices she heard that she assumed other people would doubt, as well as from visions that are confirmation of God's validation (not unlike the confirmation of her sanctification) as an irrefutable source (10).[1] Despite her understanding of the subject position she held as a Black woman, Lee's visions enabled her to see herself differently regardless of the failure of others to do so. Not unlike Lee, who interwove visions and voiced directives from God that were uncomfortable, bringing forward the knowledge of good and evil in the same space of her narrative, Libianca demands to be seen, heard, and understood, and for her pain to stand in the gap for others. The call of Black women, historically and contemporarily, whether for spiritual intervention or human compassion—for understanding—is a reversal and a challenge to essentializing notions and myths of Black peoples as always already knowable to others but not to themselves. The message that Black women have cross-generationally extended through their systems of faith-based articulations is the idea of knowledge of self as an empowering political and rehumanizing tool. It neither negates nor reproduces the kind of double consciousness that W.E.B. Du Bois articulated as being born of internal striving against the myths of White supremacy.[2] Rather, as can be seen in the lyrics of Libianca and articulated in Black women's words throughout time, knowledge of God, in whose image they understand themselves to made, is indeed the truest knowledge of oneself. This way of knowing repoliticizes misinterpretations of power that are invoked through Christianity—which has historically been used as a tool to misname and dehumanize women and people of color, especially African-descended people. In Erykah Badu's words: "If we were made in his image then call us by our names / Most intellects do not believe in god, but they fear us just the same" (lines 10–11). Black women thus repoliticize in the tradition of their eighteenth- and nineteenth-century models.

One clear example is Burke's revelations about the unspoken sexual abuses that silence women and girls, contributing to chasms across which bonds between Black women and children need to be built and revealing the politics of spiritual disruptions of sacred and secular proportion. What is significant is that this disruption occurs in the development stages, at transitional moments from Black girlhood to womanhood—an interruption in physical and psychological development of Black girls that has remained misidentified, and quite frankly overlooked or ignored, since the era of chattel slavery in the United States. What the poetic utterances of a Wheatley could only hint at contemporary Black women scholars have challenged directly.[3] Nazera Sadiq Wright analyzes how "nineteenth-century African American women writers" like Maria Stewart "define black girlhood. . . . Identifying black girls as youthful and therefore childlike removes sexual suggestion from their bodies. . . . [Emphasizing] a black girl's age as a textual marker recognizes that, similar to all women, black women in the antebellum period experience a youthful period and undergo distinct stages of growth and maturity into womanhood" (150–151). Young Letitia's experiences in Stewart's serialized 1861 story echo aspects of the childhood remembrances of both Wheatley, who captures the memory of being in her father's arms, and the young Lee, who is naïve with regard to the absence of any religious education or upbringing in her family. In "The First Stage of Life" Stewart introduces her reader to an innocent girl, not yet six years old, moved from place to place without even the basic knowledge of colors or nature, who loses her father and then her mother and who is at the mercy of adults she barely knows. Letitia "knows not where, she knows not when this gentleman became her step-father, she only knew that he was her step-father, and when she comes again to her recollection, she finds herself in a strange place, surrounded by the beautiful light of day, the blue sky above her head, cloued [*sic*] with white" (2). So, what does it mean to embrace childhood, and how does one connect to that about which one may have been seriously miseducated, or even completely disconnected from this first stage of one's humanity—plunged directly into adulthood? For early Black Christian women, as it is for women and girls of our era, the challenge to recover the earliest parts of one's humanity is critical. They invoked scripture and made it pertain to themselves as Black girls, finding ways directly and indirectly to challenge what a child's role should be, or addressing through their WordsWork how important it is to "train up a child in the way [s]he should go: and when [s]he is old, [s]he will not depart from it" (Proverbs 22:6, KJV).

Aria S. Halliday's *The Black Girlhood Studies Collection* (2019) evokes poignant links between contemporary and historical worlds and words.

"Some of the earliest autobiographical work by Black women in North America begins with Black girlhood. Black women, including Harriet Jacobs, Phyllis [*sic*] Wheatley . . . and many others have reflected on . . . the ways that the world fights against Black girls for existing. Through their imaginings, we see the world as Black girls do—a world that is violent, dehumanizing, disrespectful, and hateful toward girls whose hair puffs, whose full lips part to make way for a big smile and a belly laugh, whose voices rise and fall with the heartiness of ancestors, and whose skin glistens like gold when caught in sunlight. Across space and time" (1).[4] Halliday's collection, which attends to theorizing and centering experiences of Black girls in contemporary cultural studies, laments the lack of archival sources that refer to "girls" rather than "women." For one thing, "through the histories and narrative of enslaved women" we have learned "that enslaved Black girls were treated—in many ways as women. As early as age eight, some enslaved girls were responsible for maintaining entire households as well as performing playmate tasks for their enslavers' young children . . . forced to reproduce, cook, clean, care for children, and/or tend the land" (7).

Although Wheatley was a child prodigy, arguably a product of the Enlightenment, there has been little attention given to the significance of her situatedness, her subject position as a Black girl. To be sure the reference to "PHILLIS, a young Negro girl" was meant to draw attention to her juvenile status and thereby reflect societal views in the eighteenth century about childhood and children in general. Thus, this attention to the young poet and spiritual autobiographer's youth is mostly within the context of White childhood.[5] Here I want emphasize the way Wheatley's life and words provide maps of symbolic and literary recovery for Black women, and especially girls, by connecting her to a contemporary understanding of "'Blackgirl' (one word, no space)." Halliday cites Robin M. Boylorn's coinage of this term "to mean the 'indivisibility of race and gender' in the lives of Black women" (3). As Halliday explains, "The conjoining of Blackgirl and its application to those we may contemporarily consider adults or children calls together the memory, the feeling and the future of Black girlhood" (7).

Given that children are our most oppressed people, with Black women positioned at the lowest rungs of humanity and disproportionately underserved economically, it is not surprising that early Black

Christian women and today's contemporary Black women artivists, activists, and religious and spiritual thinkers, leaders, and preachers continue to strive for the liberation and knowledge of the value of Black girlhood as critical to the thriving of Black people. The protection of Black girlhood and its future is not thus isolated by the limitations of age. Rather, Blackgirl is a continuum that serves as a catalyst not only to embrace the "least among us" (Matthew 25:40, KJV). but also to challenge and protect our raised voices from being coopted. Tarana Burke identifies the racism and sexism at the heart of criticisms of this global movement against injustice that targets Black people.

Tarana Burke, like her ancestors Wheatley, Stewart, and Lee, addresses all genders even as she makes a case for the critical significance of Black women in particular, making clear the interconnected collective contemporary struggles and movements for Black people regardless of gender. In a 2020 BBC interview, Burke reminds listeners that "what we're seeing in Black Lives Matter . . . is *our* response to the response that *we* get. Black people aren't the only ones being killed by the police." But it is "the response when a *Black* person is killed by a police officer" that is most troubling. She first addresses state-sanctioned race-based responses to the violence and oppression against all Black people, regardless of gender. Burke then focuses on the response to Black women's calls for justice: "White supremacy says, 'Black women you might have vision, you may have voice, you may have leadership, but I can't see that vision, voice, or leadership until you have a conduit that shows it to me through a white gaze.'" Burke requires no such conduit or instrument to fulfill her vision, raise her voice, and lead this movement, as she is centered religiously, morally, and politically. Burke's faith, however, should not be read as an opiate that will magically relieve the pain that Black women experience. Far from it. The resistance against the myth of White supremacy echoes Wheatley's call to tear down curtains and barriers constructed by Christian intermediaries, those "Modern Egyptians" who fail to honor a God-given equality of all his creations: "Christians, Negroes, Black as Cain," who are worthy before the throne of the divine in that they may all equally "join th' angelic train" ("On Being Brought from Africa to America" lines 7–8). Moreover, it is critical to understand this within a context that is free from myths of Black Christian women's insufficiency, myths that had previously interpreted earlier pious and holy women like

Wheatley as imbibing an opiate or religiously ignorant, merely following the faith of their Christian White fathers and mothers. Rather, Burke reminds us of the spiritual force that empowers and enables her to go beyond a moment, or movement, toward what really matters: "You can't do this kind of work without being grounded in a faith that showed possibilities. Christianity is, really, when you take away all the pomp and circumstance, it's about hope and possibility."[6]

There is, to be sure, a depth and breadth of possibilities that the interwoven spiritual and political hold for Black women, who affirm through their faith the deep, profound spiritual understanding that the personal, political, and spiritual cannot be disconnected from the heavily political burdens under which they labor and worship and to which they feel connected through centuries of women who attempted to repoliticize the links between spiritual and felt needs of Black women, in perpetuity leaving no stone unturned in their quest for social justice and human rights. Contemporary artists, thinkers, political activists, and holy women continue to turn over again existing and new stones that both inspire and conspire to lift Black women up and over beyond survival to thriving as living human beings with "inalienable" God-given rights. Cross-culturally, Black women, whether claiming Christianity, Islam, Judaism, Buddhism, Rastafarianism, African or other indigenous spirituality, agnosticism, atheism, freethinking, or any diverse variety of practices and belief systems, find ways to integrate spirituality as they resist, challenge, and overthrow structures of oppression and actions designed to dehumanize Black people both spiritually and physically.[7]

Thus, Black women, historically and contemporarily, have not only named themselves, they have also called out those tyrants and persecutors who would use coercive tactics to enslave, disenfranchise, and victimize them on all levels. Most important, they have christened and identified the spiritual as a source of liberation and power that placed them on the moral, figurative, and literal high ground to defy and attack race, class, and gender subjugation and oppression. By naming and articulating their God (or gods) and the meaning that such figures of otherworldly divinity connote and denote for their earthly existence, and/or their refusal to succumb or submit to an otherworldly presence through resistance to such constructs, they command a sovereign power through which they channel their autonomy and self-determination. Ironically, such a God was often characterized by others as "White" and "male" and by some as inaccessible and incomprehensible to the supposedly inferior souls of Black women. Indeed, Black women—especially Christian Protestant women during the antebellum era—articulated the meaning of a seemingly foreign faith on their own terms. Nonetheless, Black women would not be denied ownership of their souls, of their inner selves, even under conditions of chattel slavery. If man could claim ownership of the most precious aspects of her humanity and claim for her a place of subhumanity, his earthly authority did not translate into a perpetual divine sanctioning and commission to terrorize and supplant the power of an omniscient and omnipotent God who had implanted the breath of life into her—that supernatural being who had created in her a perfect image of humanity. Of course, the idea of full humanity based on full corporeal embodiment is equally critical to understand as we consider contemporary Black feminist atheism, which Marquis Bey counters in his argument opposing Christian "no-body" religiosity.[8] "Atheistic Black radical feminism operates via entrenchment rather than theological abstraction; it emphasizes and validates the embodied life" (3).

Significantly, Black women engaged in the prescient act of naming that both included and extended beyond mortal words, ways, or wonders. Theirs was an act of invoking a life force that was bound to earthly reason and natural as well as supernatural sources. They operated through the force of their own internal power manifested outwardly through subversive actions. They called and continue to draw upon, manipulate, and exercise political actions through powerful forces, both conventionally religious realms (such as Christianity) or diverse spiritualities and ways of knowing. These include but are not limited to ways in which they named and reclaimed their whole human selves—based on their earthly calls to a spiritual or other powerful presence (for example, imagination)—one that Wheatley for sure was fond of conjuring in her works (albeit through lenses of neoclassical forms). Whether it was the Divine Mother, Orisha, Allah, Christ, Buddha, Krishna, Yahweh, Supreme Being, Oshun, Ala, Jesus, God, Father, Father/Mother, or any other appellation, Black women throughout time have insisted on signifying a supremely spiritual authorizing and qualifying divine being that nourishes, heals, and embraces the fullness and duality of their sacred and secular experiences.[9] Their works extend beyond simple, albeit well-articulated, understandings of religion as a tool of oppression to instructive remedies with precedent-setting paradigms for empowerment and social justice.[10] The historical, social, and political contexts imbedded in their lyrics and words testify to the significance of Black women's spirituality that prays, works, and imagines the power of a people thriving through the remembrance and respect of their past and acknowledgment of the present and future.

Their voices are the "evidence of things not seen" (Hebrews 11:1, KJV) but imagined in their artivistic works that fully embrace the power of faith to inspire change and chart the future conditions under which Black women, from Wheatley, Lee, Stewart, and Frances Harper to Audre Lorde and Maya Angelou, Lauryn Hill, Beyoncé, and beyond, exist as fully liberated humans. They speak, write, sing, dance, pray, and advocate for social justice in ways that "#SayTheirNames" and speak those truths, reclaiming their time for our time, as absolutely necessary for "a time such as this."[11] Significantly, they push back against a government and a religion that conspired to monetize the Black woman in perpetuity, using their words as liberatory weapons—expressed on behalf of those who remained in bondage.[12] Black women like Stewart, in their diverse manipulations of the "liberatory discourse of inclusion and the racist discourse of exclusion employ several argumentative strategies—scientific, historical, moral/religious, economic, and political—with the first four serving as pillars to support the final, political argument for or against an individual or group gaining the rights and privileges of citizenship" (Waters, "Crying out for Liberty" 39). Central to the revolutionary aspect of Black liberalism is religion, or more precisely spirituality, and the work that has been done to repoliticize institutionalized religion and belief systems that are more in line with early Black women's religious thought and its application to real-life experience.

In what is perhaps one of the most challenging times for Black women in our recent history, they are certainly no strangers to both the extreme pleasures and tremendous sorrows that accompany their ways of being in this world. Contemporary Black women are also no strangers to the many coping mechanisms that have attended their attempts to balance and navigate the dehumanizing instability of being Black, woman, and disproportionately economically and socially underserved and marginalized. Yes, race, class, and gender biases and systemic institutional “isms” are the frames that attempt to hold Black women hostage in order to keep them in or return them to systems of bondage. What has enabled them to recover their physical and metaphysical selves across generations can be evidenced in the words of an African American Christian hymn, “I Know It Was the Blood,” which invokes the torture, blood, and hanging of a redeemer who suffered for his people, who loved them enough to leave a legacy of personal, political, and spiritual struggle that not only survived but thrived. It is through “the blood,” understood as a physical and ethereal manifestation of a life-giving and sustaining force, that Black women accept, protect, and bring forth life in the flesh and in the spirit. It’s how they protect those most vulnerable and motivate those with privilege and power to join them to honor life and the blood without which there can be no redemption, no progress, and, as we have witnessed—presently and historically—no justice for Black people, especially Black women.

The enslaved poetic genius of the devout Christian Phillis Wheatley asserts that a God-given “Love of Freedom . . . impatient of Oppression [yearning] for Deliverance” is a “principle [that] lives in [all of] us” (“Letter to Reverend Samson Occom”). It is not solely ideological or political freedom that is cause for which Wheatley must “pray” that “others may never feel” the tyranny of oppression (“To the Right Honourable William, Earl of Dartmouth” lines 30–31). It is the enslaved adolescent’s remembrance of the family she lost (because of slavery) that invokes such “wishes for the common good” (line 22): the father from whom she was “seiz’d” when still a “babe” (line 29), the image of her mother pouring out water in morning rituals, and those “excruciating” “sorrows [that] labour in [her] parent’s breast” (lines 26–27).[13] As “a victim of the largest involuntary human migration in history . . . kidnapped from her family in Africa and forced to spend up to two months crossing the Atlantic” (Carretta 1), Wheatley extends her sufferings beyond a singular view from the perspective of a victim; rather, her perspective is that of one who has persevered through a human tragedy in the traumatic conditions of a system of human holocaust, one who has held on to her very life as a young girl enduring the Middle Passage. Beyoncé’s water imagery as well as Badu’s lyrics about being underwater speak to an imaginary middle passage that has been maintained throughout centuries.[14]

Wheatley renames herself a survivor, with a testimony of empowerment for other Black people, enslaved and freed. As Katherine Clay Bassard argues, "Connotations of survivorship—black bodies, African cultures, and black texts—converge in the figure and poetics of Phillis Wheatley" (*Spiritual Interrogations* 36). What is also quite clear is she imagines and repoliticizes—by recentering Black/African kinship that has been stolen—even as she is literally for all intents and purposes an orphan. That is, while the enslaved poet was able to establish a much-needed familial relationship with her master and especially her mistress (Susanna Wheatley), it would hardly replace the great loss she refers to in her "Dartmouth" poem, one to which she referred frequently in her elegies, which not coincidentally permitted yet another way of connecting to families and centering their importance in her life from spiritual and political perspectives. Curtis Anthony Woods observes that "she aligns her soul with oppressed blacks, regardless of the sanitized and sentimentalized 'family' offered by many New England slave-owners" (78).

Her letters to her friends the Reverend Sam Occom and fellow Black woman Obour Tanner reveal a tone of familiarity that can be recognized by those who appreciate how extended family operates for Black people. In both blood and communal sharing of the best and worst of times, through thick and thin, they support, encourage, validate, chastise, and memorialize—and those are the folks who become one's family. Of course, Wheatley's faith served as at least one significant means of establishing an extended kinship lost in chattel slavery through her embracing and acceptance of the understanding of the Christian doctrine of family. "Wheatley adopted and later adapted evangelical theology as an instrument of remonstration that exposed the political and sociological tyranny wrought against African peoples in early America" (Woods 2). Rosetta Haynes points out that "in drawing upon religion to achieve greater personal freedom and to advocate for societal transformation, [writers like Wheatley] engaged in a praxis that today might be labeled a theology of liberation" (7).[15]

Not unlike Wheatley's, Frances Harper's poetry too allowed for the Sankofic recovery of the meaning of her identity as well as other African-descended people through religious and political contexts. Harper's work ushers in an early call that is responded to by her twenty-first-century Black women descendants. In the preface to her 1854 *Poems on Miscellaneous*

Subjects, abolitionist William Lloyd Garrison describes and decries the position of Black people under U.S. chattel slavery: "In one word, they are property to be owned, not persons to be protected" (3). Such is echoed and responded to in the refrain "Black Lives Matter." That is, Black people are not property; we are human beings deserving of the same rights and protections as every other citizen of this nation and the world—persons to be protected and valued. Garrison's claim that Harper is "identified in complexion and destiny with a depressed and outcast race" (4) asserts the primacy of race, a most debilitating and denigrating obstacle, not only for "the entire colored race" in general but also for the art and beauty that Black people contribute to the world (4). Indeed, there are significant linkages and haunting echoes between the assertions made by Garrison during slavery and by Black Lives Matter today.

Carla Peterson further highlights Harper's call for the value of Black life. She observes that Harper's attention to "the Syrophoenician woman as the weak and oppressed subject" and the "theme of the fallen woman" that is "common in . . . Harper's poetry . . . universalizes the themes of hunger and poverty" and at the same time particularizes and politicizes the plight of Black women and their families in such a way that "allows those readers who so choose to apply these circumstances to the specific historical experience of African Americans" (Kindle location 2024). Melba Joyce Boyd characterizes Harper's words as evincing "the heart of an artist who could contextualize a world that had too often been ignored and personaliz[ing] voices that had too long been silenced" (26). Moreover, Peterson reads Harper's poetry "in both its recited and printed forms" as "serving as a structural frame through which she could fashion herself in the public role of poet-preacher in order to articulate her vision of nineteenth-century America" (Kindle locations 1994–1995). "Harper conceived of poetry as moral and didactic preaching in which originality was less important than the ability to create character in the reader . . . in order to encourage her audience's social activism" (1996–1999). Similarly, Amanda Gorman's "Hymn for the Hurting" strikes and echoes the proverbial chorus across centuries by capturing the political in a humanistic and spiritual frame: "Everything hurts. / It's a hard time to be alive, / And even harder to stay that way" (lines 12–14).

Likewise, Angelou's "Still I Rise" is created within a context that celebrates the strength of Black people who endure through and build upon adversity to create foundations for success in the worst of times. What is most important is the connectedness to the Black family through centuries and the realization that overcoming oppression is rooted in the legacy of intergenerational communal and familial "hopes and dreams" that enable us to stand on the shoulders of those who came before. This is the center that reaches through and across continents, centuries, and other worlds. Angelou reminds us of where we've been, where we are and, most important, who we are: "past that's rooted in pain / . . . / Into a daybreak that's wondrously clear / . . . / Bringing the gifts that my ancestors gave" ("Still I Rise" lines 31–39). Connecting her faith as an extension of family and the sociopolitical reach of churches such as that she experienced in Glide Memorial, Angelou observed the eclectic congregants of "elected officials, lawyers, judges, criminals, housewives and house-husbands and many elements of the underworld," pointing out that "there is no place greater than the home of God, except in our individual selves, than the places where women and men set aside to go and worship, to just come together, and praise of the spirit of God." Not unlike many Black women, she explored a variety of faiths, including "Zen Buddhism . . . Judaism and . . . Islam." Following her "spirit," Angelou ultimately concluded that she "really want[ed] to be a Christian" and that she found its "teachings accessible."[16]

Such is seen in Lorde's apotheotic rendering of Yoruba deities Yemoja, Oshun, and Shango in her familial circle of life: embracing and celebrating the protection of children from womb to birth, strength, beauty, sexuality, marriage in the familial life-giving and sustaining forces. She speaks of a West African–inspired spiritual reawakening in which she announces, "I will become myself / . . . / and Mother Yemonja raises her breasts to begin my labour / near water/ the beautiful Oshun and I lie down together / . . . / Shango will be my brother roaring out of the sea" (lines 21–29). The imagery of water as recounted in Margaretta Odell's biography of Wheatley can be found lingering here throughout time and space. Water is a life-giving force and a reminder throughout Lee's narrative of her inherited power. The "deep hole, where the water whirled . . . coming to the water [where] I sat" (*Religious Experience and Journal* 4) contemplating suicide suggests chilling consequences for this holy woman. However, she escapes the second deadly encounter with the "tempter [that] pursued [her to] a vessel of water" (4), moving across the water as did Tarsus (8), eventually arriving to spaces from which she experiences spiritual growth and nurturing as well as physical sustenance (57). The site of water therefore is likened unto an otherworldly transitional space through which she is empowered to receive her call to preach and to embrace a life of serving God and others. The natural path through which power is infused, whether real or imagined, is but one space through which consciousness among Black women is raised, and through which they are empowered to levels beyond the material world and the limitations and boundaries set for their existence—moving them like flying Africans to a higher abode beyond tyranny and oppression, while at the same time keeping them grounded to a more powerful form of their earthly existence—one that will shatter myths and challenge injustices.

Recall that Lauryn Hill's admonition in "Final Hour" attempts a similar dual purpose of reaching higher spiritual and secular groundings. Her words recognize and privilege love, people, and family over the kind of "power" that secular and fleeting celebrity can bring by capturing the significance of religion beyond mere allusion to the Word. Hill considers what "wealth" and "power" might bring, especially if you can "let God redeem you" and "watch out what you cling to." As a young Black woman, what Hill "clings to" in her personal life as well as in her lyrics is grounded in spirituality and connected to family. In this way, Hill's WordsWork explores what is possible when one has a balanced focus on the overall goal—of abundant and fulfilling life here and in the hereafter.

In "Everything Is Everything" she posits herself, a Black woman who, despite coming from poverty—"I begat this flippin in the ghetto on a dirty mattress" (lines 39–40)—offers a vision of life that is rich on all terms. Hill's talents are unrivaled, as she reminds her haters, those who would attempt to undervalue her accomplishments, that "you can't match this rapper-slash-actress" who is "more powerful than two Cleopatras" (lines 41–42). But not unlike her ancestors (Wheatley, Stewart, and Lee), Hill sees the interconnectedness, like interwoven fabric, and the balancing of the spiritual with the material. In this song, Hill is clear that she is not boasting about her accomplishments but rather calling our attention to the "words" she "wrote" "for everyone who struggles in their youth" (lines 14–15). She speaks to a generation of truth-seekers for whom lies and "deception" have clouded their views of their value, concluding with an invitation to self-love in order to "make a better situation" (lines 65–66).

Joining her foremothers Wheatley, Harper, Lorde, Angelou, and others, Hill attempts to offer balms of hope to offset some of the tragic situations faced by Black people, Black women in particular. In an era of widening health disparities for Black women across class and rapidly growing concerns about fertility and infant mortality, as well as anti-Black violence perpetrated against Black children, it is particularly relevant that Hill's "Zion" celebrates maternity and her Black baby boy in particular. In fact, she frames her soon-to-be born son within a spiritual symbolism that evokes imagery of the birth of Jesus and of the Rastafari African homeland.

She refers to the birth of Zion, her firstborn, as that for which she "had been chosen," despite being "overwhelmed." Hill then narrates the visit from "an angel" who spoke words of prophecy from Isaiah 9:6–7 about the coming of the Messiah: "For unto me a man child would be born." Her "crazy circumstance" is not unlike that of the biblical Mary, an unmarried woman of faith whose future is uncertain. As in "Final Hour," Hill reminds us of what matters most, as she refuses the advice of those focused solely on career and worldly possessions, instead choosing her "heart." This is a choice to embrace a heavenly calling to Zion with all its "perils" and its "joy." Hill's religion is political and potent, bearing witness to the significance of Black women's power and her ability to bridge a multiplicity of levels of oppression and internalized consciousness. She thus lyrically testifies about attempts to contain and lay claim to her physical and spiritual self, and thus spiritually venerates life and "Black" lives that matter through generations—all the while embracing her Black woman's kinship that evolves through her faith and is manifested in her activism—one that connects to and complements early Black women's WordsWork.

The same is true for the similarly grounded but iconic Beyoncé's *Black Is King*, which arguably deifies Black people, declaring: "Not just some words in a Bible verse / You are the living word / . . . part of something way bigger" ("Bigger"), Black womanity is rehearsed, rewritten, and restated in religio-political and family-centric terms. Across the nation traditional Christian women preachers and theologians have been embracing the music of Beyoncé through what has become known as

Beyoncé Mass. The Reverend Yolanda Norton is credited with having organized the first service of this type in San Francisco. Norton reveals that she wanted to create a faith experience far from the debilitating and oppressive one in which she was conditioned. She recalls that at one point she considered leaving her ministry, and when she turned to theology, analyzing scriptures, she began to make use of this pop culture icon's lyrics. "The Mass, which was based on Norton's class 'Beyoncé and the Hebrew Bible' drew roughly 1,000 people. Norton says 'Flaws and All' is 'the essence of my interaction with God. I'm not quite sure why God loves me, and I love God.'"[17]

These Masses include songs like "Survivor and Freedom" as worship music complementing Norton's sermons and "include readings from scripture." Importantly, like those who came before her, Norton intends that such services are "about making the church a space for empowerment, inclusion, and healing," with a caveat that the Masses are "not [about] worshipping 'Queen Bey', as Beyoncé's fans call her." Norton's ultimate goal is to create an inviting space for those "people [who may] have been hurt by the church." As such, not only does this young Black Christian woman preacher fulfill this need for those who require a healing of sorts, the church has become a space of resistance, of the type that Brittney Cooper advocates: a religion that's "Bible-thumping the sh*t out of capitalism, white supremacy and heteropatriarchy," using God's words in the right way, one that resists the Devil—in its many manifestations. Norton affirms that she "wanted to be a part of something that made a statement and said, 'God is love.' And that's the final word." Thus, like her ancestors, she indeed "kicks the sh*t out of" tyranny and oppression and thus repoliticizes the Word through a Black artist's lyrics.

From Wheatley, who wrote herself into humanity and birthed a subtle but powerful response to slavery, poverty, and sexism in her literary works during her very short life, to contemporary Black women's social justice movements, we see the evidence of a historical legacy of foremothers for whom the religious was political, and for whom their socio-religious politics are reflected in nearly every walk of life. Notably, Cori Bush, former U.S. representative for Missouri's first congressional district from 2021 to 2025, the first Black woman to represent the state, is an ordained minister; Alicia Garza, Patrisse Cullors, and Opal

Tometi, co-founders of BLM, are credited with having reinaugurated a global Black movement for social justice and reform; and GirlTrek is a health movement that has inspired Black women to take back their health and their neighborhoods by walking, connecting more than 1 million members. Black women continue to demonstrate the power of the blood that flows in and through them. It sustains them, I argue, through their interconnectedness with a spirituality, religion, and faith in a higher power. Beyond physical conditions, limitations, and multiple and multilayered oppressions, Black women remain spiritually centered and guided—naming God as the source of their strength and as the authorizing figure who enables and grants them moral authority. Therefore, evidenced here is "the presence and power of God" as the ultimate sustaining power personified for Black women and Black girls. Moving forward this connection to "Queen Bey" and other contemporaries, young girls can once again claim the necessary human and humanely embraced spaces of their development as girls to women—one of the most critical bridges and links that remain from their ancestors. Indeed, the religio-political work and words of Black women are, as ever, critical to the survival and thriving of our people, especially in the current era of post–civil rights reconstruction, when our nation has returned to regressive politics. It is a work of remembrance—perhaps now even more relevant with the recent passing of such beloved artivists as Toni Morrison, Nikki Giovanni, bell hooks, Maryse Condé, and Shay Youngblood, among others—to cherish our Black women words and the power they ignite in as many ways as possible, as a subtle reminder that they remain, as they have been throughout history, "fearfully and wonderfully" insurgent.[18]

Conclusion

Collectively and individually, the power of Wheatley's, Stewart's, and Lee's words and the model of Black women's repoliticization of the spiritual they left for their #BLM descendants are given special meaning when we consider the historical contexts in which they engaged in social justice work. Black women in the colonial and antebellum eras were considered less than human, whether enslaved or free. Authors like Jennifer L. Morgan have written about some of the animalistic views of Black women that were presented as "facts" in eighteenth-century travel narratives. For example, while some White male narrators claimed that due to their grotesque anatomical structure African women "could suckle over their shoulder," others paralleled African men's appreciation of the Black female body with a preference for primates, maintaining that they "copulated with Orangutans." Morgan points out that "Europe had a long tradition of identifying Others through the monstrous physiognomy or sexual behavior of women" (170). Citing Winthrop Jordan, Morgan underscores the cultural climate and context within which Black women were imagined by the eighteenth-century White mind. "African women's African-ness seemed contingent on the linkages between sexuality and a savagery that fitted them for both productive and reproductive labor. Women enslaved in the seventeenth and early eighteenth centuries did not give birth to many children, but descriptions of African women in the Americas almost always highlighted their fecundity along with their capacity for manual labor" (184–185).[1] In comparison to her African sister, the European American woman was believed to have evolved from her licentious origins and to have shed her immodest and shameful history.

Notwithstanding obvious class differences among all women of the period, in deliberate and striking contrast to Black women, White women, while typically relegated to domestic roles with limited opportunities for formal education in the first half of the eighteenth century, were fashioned as fair, delicate, and possessed of the highest moral character. Whereas "in previous centuries, women were perceived as sexually aggressive and lustful . . . the daughters of Eve, constantly tempting men to sin . . . [b]y the mid-eighteenth century, the older image of woman as sexual temptress was in the process of transformation" (Merril D. Smith xv).[2] Such a "generous" reconceptualization of the foundation of Black womanhood, however condescending and problematic it may have been for White women, was beyond any stretch of conventional "White" imagination.[3]

Despite White women having only limited power relative to their male counterparts, the conditions under which they lived in colonial America were incomparable to those enslaved Black women endured, and only marginally comparable to the situation of free Black women of equal class status. The power and property White women did sometimes possess meant they could exercise control over Black women and their children in perpetuity.[4] "Although the number of laws governing slavery—and enslaved women—accumulated over the course of the colonial period, the legal doctrine of *partus sequitur ventrem*—progeny follows the womb—was one of the first, and it inextricably bound racial slavery to maternal identity. The doctrine first established the inheritability, and hence the permanence, of slavery as a legal status" (Snyder 5).

To be sure, free Black women fared much better than their enslaved sisters, because they shared rights similar to those of White women: they could own property, marry, own their children, and in some states they could sue in courts. However, Black women (free and enslaved) were required to pay income taxes—an expense for which White women were not typically liable—with few exceptions.[5] Free Black women were openly accosted on public streets or conveyances and denied proper lodging befitting their gender during a historical period in which women were treated as delicate, frail, and requiring the utmost courtesies. They were even relegated to segregated and inferior spaces in the church. With only limited political, economic, social, and even religious privilege, free Black women in colonial America occupied a position of presumed inferiority, marginalization, and disenfranchisement. In the eighteenth-century theocentric world in which multiracial alliances among poor White people (indentured and free), Native Americans, enslaved, free, and half-free Africans existed, religion was a significant factor in the potential for upward mobility in society. For example, early on those Black people who were baptized could gain their freedom. Patrilineal lineage based on English laws permitted children of mixed racial parentage to be born free if their fathers were free even if their mothers were enslaved. Interracial marriages were legal—with regard for class more than race in such unions. Importantly, Black, Native, and White people of similar socioeconomic circumstances protested social injustice wrought by wealthy propertied men whose laws, tariffs, and political power ensured an equal level of poverty and lack of resources for these similarly disenfranchised colonial Americans, without significant regard for "race" (see Schlesinger; Jordan).

Black women, especially those enslaved and considered property, were regarded no more or less than their male counterparts—a type of gender equality existed among the enslaved man and woman that did not exist among the free Black population, and certainly not between Black and White, rich and poor. Power wielded by the wealthiest (White, propertied, and male) citizens was undergirded by both secular and religious authority, with economic wealth considered a sign of the Christian God's favor. Wealthy White men were free to violate Christian doctrine and commandments of the most heinous type—rape, violence, psychological and physical abuse of Black women. Black women (free and enslaved) were presumed unevolved, licentious, and without status beyond that of what some historians have termed "producers and reproducers." Consequently, there was no presumed innocence for the youngest females of the African race (who, historian Winthrop Jordan has argued, were seen as "another" form of humanity). Indeed, one Black writer (Olaudah Equiano) documented his knowledge of such heinous violations as the rape of girls not yet ten years old. Often such young girls were purchased as "bed warmers" or concubines or for the purpose of breeding and thereby increasing slave owners' profit margin.

Early Black women spiritual activists bear witness to a regrettable and shameful but complex truth in their written prayers, sermons, songs, and homilies. Wheatley, Stewart, and Lee confronted the hypocrisy of White slaveholding Christian masters who violated with impunity their religious covenants and commandments through ungodly and heinous acts of sexual coercion and aggression against adolescents and the rape of mothers, daughters, sisters, and wives. Their words and their rewriting of conventional normative values through exegesis of biblical doctrine exposed slavery as well as the laws that codified, embraced, and encouraged the decimation and victimization of the Black female body, which had been so unabashedly sacrificed on an avaricious altar of national consumption and wealth building, and the inherited system of internalized (intra-racial) gender oppression. It was not enough for Black girls and women to address the sins of their White forefathers and mothers; they also needed to visit and expose the places and spaces to which they had been relegated by their Black brothers, fathers, and sons. Black men had to be held equally accountable if Black women and girls were to be truly safe and free from violence, victimization, and the vigilance of tyranny that erupted within the contexts of chattel slavery in America. The political shrewdness of these early Black women spiritual activists was consecrated through a common union of women writing, speaking, and praying their bodies down from the sacrificial cross of patriarchy, racism, and slavery (de facto and de jure) through their resurrecting voices. In perhaps no other realm of the political spectrum is a "raised fist" more appropriate as a sign of solidarity, support, and unity than in resistance to sexism, bigotry, class, and caste prejudice. For the works of Wheatley, Stewart, and Lee provided a "ram in the bush" (Genesis 22:13, KJV) as both symbolic salvific remembrance and political strategy to be deployed, and relatedly that which their faith demanded.[6] Indeed, they invite us to focus on our failure to adequately #SayHerName, even as we mourn, or march and protest, the unconscionable killing of unarmed Black boys and men.

Perhaps more critically, their repoliticization of religion provokes prescription rather than proscription. What I mean by this is Wheatley, Stewart, and Lee expose a tendency in even the more progressive responses to racialized violence—whether expressed through public think pieces, social media, or peer-reviewed scholarly journal—to #NameTheProblem, #LimitTheSolution, #FocusOnTheLackOf, #PersonalResponsibility, or #PublicPolicy in ways that reinforce rather than productively resist the oppression and suppression of Black people in America. What I hope to have shown is how in many ways these early Black American women offered useful templates for social justice, as their works highlight the positive aspects of spirituality, holistically speaking, as a psychological force that combats destructive stress-inducing hormones (self-help, self-mediation, Zen space). These works function also as a community-building force that unifies through shared struggle and common goals and celebrates the diversity within, offering a validating structure that nurtures the power of resistance by the refusal of the victimized to be silenced. Certainly, the work of contemporary social justice activists asks us to reconsider our view of Black women's herstory. We see a legacy of Black women who have held onto the promises and built upon the labors and courage of earlier generations and moved forward the legacy of their eighteenth- and nineteenth-century foremothers: the poet Amanda Gorman; the organizers of the decentralized Black Lives Matter movement (Alicia Garza, Patrisse Cullors, and Ayọ Tometi); religious leaders like AME bishop Teresa Jefferson-Snorton, the Reverend Gina M. Stewart, and AME bishop Vashti Murphy McKenzie; and Black women mayors, congresspersons, and political representatives from former representative Cori Bush to Senator Laphonza Butler to former vice president Kamala Harris. These contemporary women who are successfully navigating complex and multilayered obstacles and opportunities offer us a new lens through which we might view the lives of early Black poets, preachers, and politicians like Wheatley, Stewart, and Lee. We are thus empowered and challenged to see our Black women's herstories outside static lenses that frame and name who we are—and, of equal importance, who we were.

Imagine trying to conceptualize what it means for us to think about the joy, empowerment, and internalized value that formerly enslaved or nominally free women enjoyed in and through their repoliticization of the spiritual. How much brighter their shine—moving out from the shadows of spaces reserved for the privileged others—and how clearly we can see a path through and with them, even throughout their travails. It is instructive and appropriate here to turn to Bynum's reading of the pleasure, joy, and love in Wheatley's lyrics and their connection to contemporary twenty-first-century activists who insist on a "both/and" existence, not wholly subsumed by one's constructed subjectivity or bound to static existence within racialized and gendered identities. Our twenty-first century extends and descends from a matrilineal line that connects the desire to explore one's full humanity and the pleasure in doing so, not as a proof text or some sort of rite of passage from chattel into humanity, but rather as a refusal to deny one's internal intimacy—negating social, psychosocial, political, and physical death. This can also be reimagined as the embracing of one's full spiritual self, which includes both the body and the soul as interconnected and inextricably linked.[7]

I want to close by highlighting one last moment of the repoliticization of religion for social justice aims by sharing a postmortem fact-checking "mic drop": Wheatley's response to Thomas Jefferson's claim that "religion indeed has produced a Phyllis Whately [*sic*]; but it could not produce a poet. The compositions published under her name are below the dignity of criticism." His condescending description of the slave poet appears in a section of his *Notes on the State of Virginia* that outlines "the administration of justice and description of the laws," including no fewer than twenty-three references to laws as they pertain to slaves—one in which Jefferson claims that "Epictetus, Terence, and Phaedrus, were slaves. But they were of the race of whites. It is not their condition then, but nature, which has produced the distinction." In Wheatley's poem "To Maecenas," she describes Terence as "of Afric's sable race" (line 40). It is hardly coincidence that in the same section Jefferson is dismissive of Wheatley's works, he directly addresses her claim that Terence is a Black African, thereby attempting to assert the superior nature of Roman slaves versus Black or African slaves—and thus perpetuate the myth of White supremacy. Jefferson's claim that "the compositions published under her name are below the dignity of criticism" is belied by his challenge to Wheatley's claims about the race of Terence. This intertextual moment between Jefferson and Wheatley is a reminder that consigning Wheatley to the realm of religion wrongly erases the political significance of this devoutly Christian poet. Both religion and poetry have indeed "made" a Wheatley! More importantly, Wheatley, Stewart, and Lee made religion an instrument to challenge social injustice, to highlight their unique experiences as Black Women in America. And they did so in their own voices—speaking truth to power across their century to ours. #EarlyBlackChristianWomensLivesMatter

Matter (A Poem)

By Dr. April Langley (a Black writer who matters)

She who occupies space,
Irrespective of race
a consideration,
Without reparation
situation, affair,
Of which she's well aware
Of her significance,
Despite indifference
secreted from a wound
From which she's not immune
Whose soul is not fractured
Though body's been captured
Imagined a problem
A Being unsolemn
ironically engaged
perpetually upstaged
attempting to escape
An all-conflicting fate
circumstances of her
existence as transfer
That they cannot scatter
She's matter, that matters[1]

1 This poem (taken from my unpublished book of poetry) represents my concluding meditation and call, my remixing and recalling, a Sankofic re-memory of the moment when I heard about Breonna Taylor and felt a void when I realized how quickly the "dust" settled as if she—and, by extension, those like me—just simply didn't matter, and with a view that perhaps we were simply matter.

Notes

Preface

1 "The first wound for all of us who are classified as 'black' is empire. This is a truth many of us—whether we are included in that category or not—prefer to avoid" (Dangarembga 19).

Prologue

1 Here and throughout this book when I refer to "women" it is with the understanding that Phillis Wheatley was indeed a girl when she produced her literary works. The term *woman* in this context is meant to include but not "adultify" Black girls, as I will discuss in chapter 5.

2 The late scholar-activist Audre Lorde argues that the "master tools will never undo the master's house." Elsewhere I have argued that such tools as are available to the master can be successfully deployed when accompanied by new blueprints. Sondra O'Neale addresses the skillful deployment of "biblical myth, language and symbol" by eighteenth-enslaved poets like Wheatley to protest slavery albeit subtly (145).

3 I draw upon the title and signify the lyrics of this hymn by Albert A. Goodson, who "wrote both text and tune in 1956 for the Radio Choir of the Fellowship Baptist Church in Chicago, Illinois, where he served as minister of music. The hymn was published as a gospel anthem by Manna Music III, 1963" (https://hymnary.org/text/weve_come_this_far_by_faith). Since then, this hymn has served both secular and sacred purposes aimed at both looking back on the history of the Christian God's deliverance and interventions and looking forward to

the promise of a future that relies on the omnipresence and omnipotence of the divine to lend strength to those struggling for political as well as spiritual power—most often in the face of overwhelming oppression and obstacles.

4 Here I refer to Paul Laurence Dunbar's vernacular poem that celebrates a black woman's voice in "When Malindy Sings." I borrow from the following stanza: "You ain't got de nachel o'gans / Fu' to make de soun' come right, / You ain't got de *tu'ns an' twistin's* / Fu' to make it sweet an' light" (lines 9–11; my emphasis). It is my intention here to signal those "tu'ns an' twistin's" that acknowledge the rich vocal riffs of the Black woman's songs, her ability to speak in tongues (Mae G. Henderson), scripturalize (Vincent L. Wimbush), and sample (Katherine Clay Bassard), and how these linguistic pivots and moves (redirection, rearticulation, and restatement, of formerly politicized "facts" and biblical "truths") are bent and repoliticized in the service of Black women's power—articulated through "dat music, / . . . / Ez it makes its way in glory / To de very gates of God!" (lines 55–56).

5 The term *sampling* has a long and storied history that is rife with controversies and engagements with cultural appropriation, racialized music forms, and other elements of what in the late 1990s was termed culture wars—the remnants of which remain with us today. Camea Davis's concise description of the "hip hop aesthetic of sampling, characterized by taking previously recorded music and piecing it together with a variety of techniques to create a new instrumental track" (114) is a plausible entry point for defining this term. Tom Perchard offers an in-depth analysis and rigorously researched study of the framing of sampling in the context of the African American musical genres hip-hop and jazz that is quite useful for my purposes. Another lens through which sampling is considered is from "Tricia Rose . . . [who] positioned rap's sampling practice as *cross-generational* 'homage,' 'a means of *archival research*, a process of musical and cultural archaeology.' Whether cultural-nationalist, constructivist, or genealogical, much early scholarly writing on hip hop sampling sought to position the practice as one in which the musicians' *relation to a black musical past was of primary importance*" (Perchard 278; my emphasis). "Sampling is commonly and casually said to either function as a medium of significant, binding collective memory or else

enact some kind of musico-cultural traditionary incorporation" (279). While Perchard presents varying perspectives on the value or connection of sampling to cultural history and memory, he ultimately concludes: "The depth of its [sampling's] historical grounding, the brilliance of its experimental methods, and the liveliness of its insider debate meant that hip hop was a musical culture far more alive to the benefits, demands, and impositions of memory and history than simply atavistic or simply pragmatic theorizations could describe; the words of the artists . . . suggest that we should instead consider these ideas as part of a critical, musical-historical discourse . . . in which contemporary creative agency was ever intertwined with representations of and relationships to the past, both productive and problematic" (300). In this context sampling—especially literary/biblical sampling—could hardly be considered anachronistic, but rather a layering of that which was fetched, called into the future through the toils and struggles of early Black Christian writers: their dialogue, monologue, preaching, teaching, and repoliticizing of the Word.

6 In *Transforming Scriptures* Bassard argues that "Stewart's meditations push the boundaries of written language to create multilayered, multivocal text that 'sample[s]' the scriptures, pushing the genre of prayer to the level of cultural performance" (4). In Bassard's "scriptural sampling" she "characterize[s] Stewart's prayers" as imbued with "orality and musicality," demonstrating an "overall vision of the use of scripture to encode and explicate the historical and social situation of African Americans" (57).

7 Carla Peterson observes that women like Lee and Stewart "recognized the extent to which their efforts to 'elevate the race' and achieve 'racial uplift' lay" in both the "political and social" realms, as well as in "their faith in the performative power of the word—both spoken and written" (3). I extend this aestheticization of the work that their words consciously invoke through the authority and power of the Word (holy writ) to Wheatley as well. Relatedly, Robert Patterson observes that "the *Word and word* helped them to unsettle the foundations upon which racism, sexism, and racist-sexism depended and thrived. . . . Black women's engagement with the *Word* was therefore appropriative . . . insofar as they self-consciously invoked biblical narratives in which (black) women rebelled against oppressive

institutions, led communities, and triumphed in the face of adversity, in order to destabilize biblical authority as the chief arbiter of their civil disenfranchisement" (57–58; my emphasis). Rosetta Haynes locates a "distinctive working-class consciousness" (21) that can be seen throughout in the writings, sermons, and speeches of Jarena Lee and Maria Stewart, especially as they integrate the latter roles into the weaving and braiding of elements into their WordsWork that repoliticizes the spiritual for political aims. Tsitsi Dangarembga poignantly observes: "Healing is weaving, a knitting together and reintegration of the parts that were mangled and crippled. Weaving of words—and through this process, reweaving time, action and reaction into a new whole—makes writing back against empire a site of potential for healing. Some writing raises a scar, puffy, often suppurating, over the damage. The best writing opens the lesion again and again and cleanses. Here the trauma subsides with each set of words, sentences, paragraphs and pages. The rawness is transformed into something that in a certain light looks like skin that was never lacerated. What is done is done. Such transformation is our best option in this era" (22–23).

8 While Teresa Zackodnik's work is meant to address Black preaching women of the nineteenth century, I have extended elements of her argument to the eighteenth-century poet Wheatley. These women "politicized the soul by insisting upon the connection between material realities and a spiritual life; the spiritual was not understood as transcending the material or social, nor was it seen as [solely] a rhetorical tool" (19).

Introduction

1 According to the George Washington Presidential Library,

> "Under their vine and fig tree" is a phrase quoted in the Hebrew Scriptures in three different places: Micah 4:4, 1 Kings 4:25, and Zechariah 3:10. George Washington used this phrase multiple times in correspondence throughout his life, and one can find Washington reference it almost fifty times. Of the three passages, it is most likely that he

> was citing Micah 4:4 in his writings. The section states: "but they shall all sit under their own vines and under their own fig trees, and no one shall make them afraid. . . ."
>
> The phrase refers to the independence of the peasant farmer who is freed from military oppression. . . . In the biblical passage there is a juxtaposition of the simple life with that of royalty or the state. . . . Thus, it would seem that Washington's use of "vine and fig tree" in its full context would be an appropriate message in the setting of the American Revolution and the founding of the United States (https://www.mountvernon.org/library/digitalhistory/digital-encyclopedia/article/vine-and-fig-tree/).

2 Addressing the "political" within the spiritual, Elizabeth Grammer challenges views of Christianity as "the opiate by which women were comforted and encouraged to accept their subordinate position in society . . . an outlet, a retreat from the inequalities of this world . . . an escape valve for their discontent, a tool in the service of the dominant culture . . . [that] may have altered the women's interior lives . . . [but] did not affect their exterior lives." Rather, she maintains that the spiritual autobiographies of women like Jarena Lee "make clear that Christianity significantly marked their lives in ways that led them to *reject* their subordinate lot in the world" (5). She notes that "historians like Catherine Brekus, Nancy Cott, [and others] have been arguing for several decades that evangelical religion, like bourgeois individualism generally, opened a whole new world for northern women discontented with their roles as wives, mothers, sisters, and daughters. Evangelical sects—with their ties to 'religious dissent,' and their desires to 'preserve the element of "protest" in Protestantism,' and 'to separate themselves from American culture by challenging its understandings of gender and race'—offered women an allegiance beyond the home, a new field in which they could become active, assertive, and relatively free agents responsible for nothing short of redemption of the word" (6). Bettye Collier-Thomas's work is equally instructive as she characterizes a kind of syncretic relationship between the spiritual and political dimensions of the "first generation of black women preachers," who were unlicensed "exhorters" and "evangelists" whose

"claims to religious authority were disputed and denied on biblical grounds." Nevertheless, they "clung tenaciously to their doctrinal claim of spiritual sanctification and . . . ordination by God" (*Jesus, Jobs, and Justice* 28). She writes, "The mere presences of female preachers challenge the notion of women's inherent inferiority [and] their sermons and writings attest to women's intellectual capacity. As [antebellum black women preachers] who traveled and preached to black and whites their lives and images empowered other women to think, to speak, and act. The very persona of a female preacher—especially a black woman—who professed to holiness and to speak the word of God, was disconcerting for some and empowering for others. It resonated [in] all levels of society and posited ways of being and acting for young girls and women to whom her mantle might be passed" (28–29). Gandhi puts it this way: "Those who say religion has nothing to do with politics do not know what religion is" (371).

Cedrick May's *Evangelism and Resistance in the Black Atlantic, 1760–1835* is an important contribution to more nuanced ways of understanding early Black writers' repoliticization of the Word. In addition to Wheatley's "skill and her dedication to spreading her message of universal freedom and human dignity," her "work also shows, as do the works of . . . Maria Stewart, that black religious writers and evangelicals were actively *rethinking, adjusting, and developing their own ideas* about religion and society as well as affecting the world around them with those ideas" (63; my emphasis).

3 Teresa Zackodnik observes that "African American preaching women [who] foregrounded the politics of 'soul winning,' contesting the inequities of a democratic public sphere . . . effectively drew attention to the *politicization of the soul*" (6; my emphasis). In so doing, I argue that they *repoliticize* the spiritual to effect social change. Moreover, I assert the use of the same can be said to be deployed by their descendants—those Black women of the twentieth and twenty-first centuries engaged in social justice and equity resistance sometimes, but not always, under the banners of spirituality.

4 As the first Black woman permitted the ministerial authority to preach in the AME Church, Lee was the first to be licensed but not ordained. Importantly, as Bettye Collier-Thomas observes, "Antebellum preaching women such as Jarena Lee" "opened the door for

Harriet Baker, Margaret Wilson, and Sarah Ann Hughes to pursue careers as preachers" (*Daughters of Thunder* 89). In 1881 Hughes was the "first AME women to be ordained as a deacon" (89). Later, in 1889, Baker was appointed by the Philadelphia AME Conference to take charge of St. Paul's Church—"perhaps the first black woman to be appointed to pastor a church" (69).

5 Maria Stewart is already considered the first Black American woman political writer. Marilyn Richardson identifies Stewart as the "inheritor of a black female tradition of activism founded on a commitment to religious faith, human rights, and women's struggles" (introduction viii). The late June Jordan ruminates on the "[un]natural" position of Wheatley as the "first Black human being to be published in America" (254), arguing that the "specific daily substance of her poetry establishes" her as "the first decidedly American poet on this continent, Black or white, male or female" (258).

6 Here I extend Joanna Brooks's argument about the role of eighteenth-century African American and Native American literature to include later figures like Jarena Lee, and to adapt Brooks's analysis of literary aims to suggest that their works (Wheatley, Stewart, and Lee) also inaugurate a more contemporary sub-genre of social justice writing. Brooks argues that writers like Wheatley, Stewart, and Lee "redirected the democratizing, charismatic, and separatist energies of American evangelicalism and its powerful doctrine of rebirth into the formation of new religious communities, new theologies, and new literatures for people of color. By adapting, politicizing, indigenizing main line religious discourses, African-Americans and Native Americans also established a platform for their critical interventions into early national formulations of race" (3).

7 Importantly, Roberts's claim that "Wheatley did more than ventriloquize or utilize homiletic rhetorical styles; she specifically engaged the tradition of the poet-minister, which treated verse as a premier tool for activating revival and affecting the course of history" (140) speaks to at least one important aspect of how the poet repoliticized the Word.

8 This phrase "opiate of the masses," first coined by Karl Marx in *Critique of Hegel's Philosophy of Right* (1843), was a point of view carried through Black nationalists from David Walker to Malcolm X and current movements.

9 Katherine Clay Bassard, Cedrick May, Joycelyn Moody, and Jennifer Rycenga (among others) have analyzed the intertextual fluidity of spirituality within the politicized voices of Black women like Stewart, Lee, and Wheatley. Indeed, these scholars have gone beyond merely suggesting the simultaneously spiritual, political, and personal dimensions of these author's productions. They have shifted our lenses toward a more critical understanding of early Black women's deployment of faith-based knowledge as vital elements in their spiritual mission truths. In short, these scholars have provided us with the necessary tools and lenses through their theories and methodologies to give proper justice to more rigorous and in-depth probing of these women's words for meaning that matters to and for (from my perspective) Black women. They permit us to derive meaning such that early Black Christian women's writing may direct us to where and when they enter discourses of gender, class, race, sexuality, and social justice. Rosetta Haynes points out that "the sophistication with which Lee expounds the scriptures on the issue of preaching reveals her intellectual engagement with theology. Yet she is very much an activist intellectual, thoroughly engaged with the social and political concerns of the communities she serves" (61).

In particular, attending to their manipulation of the genre of African American written prayers, Bassard articulates the significance of understanding the diversity within Black spiritual writing. Black people were "never a monolithic group of Bible readers, but have, from their first encounters with the text, evidenced a range of Bible-reading practices" (*Transforming Scriptures* 2). Indeed, this is precisely why I employ Bassard's technique of "spiritual sampling" to a reading of Maria Stewart's "Meditation VIII." Notably, "women . . . like Maria Stewart . . . often blend cogent social critique with more traditional Protestant hermeneutics" (2). It is important to read Black women's religious works, particularly the earliest texts, as both spiritual and political because of what they reveal about the "biblical intertextuality" imbedded in these authors' use of signifying scriptures (for example, "the trope of the talking mule") to advance anti-slavery, women's rights, and social equality among free Black and White America.

10 "And a woman having an issue of blood twelve years, which had spent all her living upon physicians, neither could be healed of any, came behind him, and touched the border of his garment: and immediately her issue of blood stanched. And Jesus said, Who touched me? When all denied, Peter and they that were with him said, Master, the multitude throng thee and press thee, and sayest thou, Who touched me? And Jesus said, Somebody hath touched me: for I perceive that virtue is gone out of me. And when the woman saw that she was not hid, she came trembling, and falling down before him, she declared unto him before all the people for what cause she had touched him, and how she was healed immediately. And he said unto her, Daughter, be of good comfort: thy faith hath made thee whole; go in peace" (Luke 8:43–48, KJV).

11 Zackodnik argues that "it is important in understanding the reach and influence of African American preaching women to consider physical spaces, as well as ideological location or positioning as liminal. Liminality can enable one to access sites and listeners that would ordinarily be off limits if not physically imperiling" (8–9).

12 Here and throughout this study I will refer to these early Black women writers and their descendants as artists and *artivists* interchangeably. I see their works as engaged in similar aesthetics located at the intersections of art and politics toward social justice. "Artivism is a portmanteau word combining art and activism. . . . In many cases artivists attempt to push political agendas by the means of art, but a focus on raising social, environmental, and technical awareness is also common" (Wikipedia). See Marta García-Cano and Victoria Martínez Vérez, "Artivism: A Crossroads of Creativity Between Art, Education, and Social Work," *Australian Art Education*, vol. 45, no. 1, 2025, 43–56. This is a contemporary contextualization of W.E.B. Du Bois's claim that "all art is propaganda" ("Criteria of Negro Art," *The Crisis*, 32, 1926, 295).

13 Among other resources, AAPF highlights a number of contemporary tools of analysis and dissemination of information through social media (https://www.aapf.org/sayhername).

14 It is ironic that Patterson's example of the "natural injustice" caused by social death through chattel slavery in America should place before us the choked, tied, and whipped body of a young Black girl—all this

savagery observed by a family who is powerless to defend her. This question of "the slave's social death, the outward conception of [her] natal alienation, articulated and reinforced" (8) exposes literally, and perhaps literarily by the authors studied here, the violent intersections and multilayered dimensions of sex and gender faced by Black women.

15 See Vincent Brown's challenge to Orlando Patterson's theory of "social death" and slavery.

16 Of the three women, only Lee had children. Rosetta R. Haynes observes that "Lee reflects the challenges of being a biological mother and trying to be true to her calling as a spiritual leader. When Lee's husband dies, she is left to care for two young children on her own." One son she says is sickly. Lee "does not mention what has happened to other child" (83). What is significant here is that conditions that follow from these eighteenth- and nineteenth-century "radical spiritual" mothers to their twenty-first-century "woke" daughters are maps of resistance in perpetuity.

17 While Wheatley was not technically manumitted until 1774, she lived what might be termed a "freer" existence than other enslaved Africans in Boston. Her position as prodigy and what some consider Enlightenment proof text provided her a measure of freedom that was equal to and in some instances less restrictive that those of emancipated or nominally free Black people living in the colonies. Ironically, Wheatley's own emancipation resulted, not unlike that of many other Blacks, to a state of unfreedom. See Hardesty for a more detailed analysis of "unfreedom" and its implications for Black people like Wheatley. Both Stewart and Lee were born free but indentured: Stewart, an orphan, lived as an indentured servant until she was fifteen, and Lee was similarly "bound out" from the age of seven because her parents were too poor to care for her. "To further diminish the family's financial burden, it was also common for children to be bound out as indentured servants. Jarena Lee, for example, was only seven years old when she moved sixty miles from her parents in order to become a servant maid" (Rosetta Haynes 60). Nonetheless, Wheatley, like Stewart and Lee, had fewer limitations with regard to issues like literacy, travel, and intense scrutiny and oversight that most enslaved Blacks experienced.

18 Their voices resonate like Hagar crying out in the vast wilderness; their works and lives are transformative for a seemingly lost people. Riffat Hassan (Pakistani American theologian and a leading Islamic feminist scholar of the Qur'an) maintains that in the Islamic version of the "dramatic story of Hagar's life . . . Hagar does not see herself as a victim of Abraham and Sarah, or of a patriarchal, class and race-conscious culture. She is a victor who, with the help of God and her own initiative, is able to transform a wilderness into the cradle of a new world dedicated to the fulfillment of God's purpose on earth . . . an indestructible emblem . . . of a mother's love for her offspring . . . a true believer's faith in the saving power of God" (155). Significantly, Bassard extends Chanta M. Haywood's "focus . . . on African American religious women of the nineteenth century . . . [a]s 'voice[s] crying in the wilderness." She notes that "black women's consistent turn to scripture for literary material is an attempt to position themselves as inheritors of the prophetic mantle" (*Transforming Scriptures* 12). "Ironically, while the figure of the slave woman Hagar would seem a more natural representation of black womanhood in the nineteenth century, African Americans, male and female, are more often described as 'children of Ham' or 'sons [and daughters] of Ham" (16). In postcolonial terms, women like Wheatley, Stewart, and Lee spoke and wrote *as*, not *for*, "subalterns."

19 I am grateful to Brigitte Fielder, whose presentation at the Society of Early Americanists has helped me consider early Black women's writing within this context. She argues convincingly for early African American literature as "protofuturistic" and for an understanding of the "theological writing" of this period as a Black print technology, alongside "faith" as "extending Black futurity."

20 Marilyn Richardson "affirm[s] the influence of such well-known figures," including Wheatley, as "neither isolated nor atypical, but inheritors of a black female tradition of activism founded on a commitment to religious faith, human rights, and women's struggles" (foreword viii). Along similar lines, Jazz A. Milligan observes: "When scholars discuss the contributions of black women in American society, they usually write about well-known figures such as Sojourner Truth, Harriet Tubman, Rosa Parks, Angela Davis, and other women. They rarely focus on the women [like Phillis Wheatley] who did not

make grand speeches or do dangerous activities in the name of liberating their people. Instead, there were women who used their voices through different mediums such as writing, legal cases, or using their bodies physically to liberate themselves from the oppressive patriarchy and uplift the legacy of black women. . . . [They] went against the societal norms of their times and put themselves into situations where there were none like them before" (1). She further reminds us that "in the public realm, there has been a push for more recognition of Wheatley's influence on future poets such as current National Youth Poet Laureate Amanda Gorman" (19).

21 "Demita Frazier, Beverly Smith, and Barbara Smith were the primary authors of the Combahee River Collective Statement in 1977. They articulated the concept of multiple oppressions, critiquing both sexual oppression in the black community and racism within the wider feminist movement" (Blackpast, https://blackpast.org/aah/combahee-river-collective-1974-1980) as well as the internal strains of heterosexism and homophobia in the National Black Feminist Organization. "The Combahee River Collective statement was created and written by Afrocentric black feminists who parted ways from the NBFO (National Black Feminist Organization) in order to create, define, and clarify their own politics. These women are actively committed to struggling against racial, sexual, heterosexual, and class oppression. It is their particular task to further the development of integrated analysis and practice based upon the fact that the major systems of oppression are interlocking. To this specific group of women, the NBFO is a coalition they believe in, but it did not recognize or address black lesbian feminist politics and systems of oppression within their group" (Combahee River Collective, https://combaheerivercollective.weebly.com/history.html). Ironically, Frazier, Smith, and Smith echo the earliest seedlings of intersectional black women's struggle for social justice, especially when we consider the tripartite oppression experienced by Wheatley, Stewart, and Lee—race, class, gender.

22 See 2016 Pew Research Center Fact Tank in Numbers, http://www.pewforum.org/religious-landscape-study/religious-family/atheist/#demographic-information. "Along with the rise of religiously unaffiliated Americans (many of whom believe in God), there has been a corresponding increase in the number of atheists." Based on a 2014

study, people who identify as atheist doubled (from 1.6 percent to 3 percent). Among African Americans the percentage of increase is the lowest. However, Bishop McNeill's ("Where Are All the Black Atheists?" *The Root*, October 23, 2016), which cites the 2016 study (http://www.pewforum.org/religious-landscape-study/), points to a rising trend among African Americans as well as active work being done to increase the numbers. McNeill highlights the establishment of secular student organizations at HBCUs and the well-known "efforts led by Mandisa Thomas and Black Nonbelievers Inc." (https://www.theroot.com/where-are-all-the-black-atheists-1790857368). Conversely, the Baylor University 2006 "American Piety in the 21st Century: New Insights to the Depth and Complexity of Religion in the US" challenges data about the rise in nonbelievers or "nones." Such research relies on somewhat skewed questions that ask respondents to "select their religions family or denomination from a list. This has become increasingly problematic over the years as more and more Americans are losing a strong denominational identity. The rising number of non-denominational congregations as well as congregations that minimize their denominational ties compound the problem. The declining importance of denomination, however, does not mean that religion itself is on the wane. Rather, Americans may simply be more likely to connect with religion at the local level" (https://www.baylor.edu/content/services/document.php/33304.pdf).

23 Rosetta R. Haynes's approach departs from these trends and articulates the "radical" nature of such works: "Radical spiritual motherhood is a self-styled identity that draws upon and validates their unique experiences as black women called to do God's work" (4).

24 Her elegy "On the Death of General David Wooster" (July 1778) reveals a similarly direct and overt critique of Christian hypocrisy: "But how, presumptuous shall we hope to find / Divine acceptance with th' Almighty mind / While yet (O deed Ungenerous!) they disgrace / And hold in bondage Afric's blameless race?" (lines 27–30).

25 I use these terms to denote the significance of their simultaneous struggle against both ideological and physical oppressions, that is, to consider how cultural conditioning operates (then and now) in tandem with state-sanctioned physical violence exerted as a means of nearly total control of the citizens and their humanity. ISA

(ideological state apparatus) refers to the use of institutions such as religion and education to disseminate propaganda and culturally condition citizens toward the acceptance and ultimate internalization of the nation's values as their own, and RSA (repressive state apparatus) refers to the means by which such ideologies or values are reinforced through mechanisms of the state such as the police or the military. Ideological state apparatus is "a term developed by the Marxist theorist Louis Althusser to denote institutions such as education, the churches, family, media, trade unions, and law, which were formally outside state control, but which served to transmit the values of the state, to interpellate those individuals affected by them, and to maintain order in a society, above all to reproduce capitalist relations of production. In contemporary capitalist societies education has replaced the Church as the principal ideological state apparatus. Among Marxists, the term is contrasted with the so-called 'repressive state apparatus' of the armed forces and police, and is allotted a major role in securing compliance within developed capitalist societies." "A Dictionary of Sociology," *Encyclopedia.com*, January 26, 2019, https://www.encyclopedia.com/social-sciences/dictionaries-thesauruses-pictures-and-press-releases/ideological-state-apparatus.

Chapter 1

1 Several recent works, among many others, provide ample consideration of the ways Wheatley matters, then and now, as inspiration in the historical recovery of Black women's lives, poetic, political, and spiritual reverberations, and echoes of earlier and present times. David Waldstreicher explicates the poet's "afterlives" in *The Odyssey of Phillis Wheatley*. "In the twenty-first century, she has been reclaimed by Black poets who at times find enough material to imagine a different future as well as revised sense of the past" (343). This revised sense of the past allows us to look differently at nineteenth-, twentieth-, and twenty-first century movements for racial equity, justice, and Black aesthetics. He writes, "Wheatley's afterlives continued to follow political trends in both antislavery and antiblack direction[s]" (345) from the antebellum period through the Civil War, Reconstruction, the Harlem Renaissance, the Black Arts Movement, Black Lives

Matter, and beyond. In the parallels between her world and ours and the layovers in between, we continue to reimagine and find useful the maps she left for contemporary artivists and others. In their edited volume of poetry, *Wheatley at 250: Black Women Poets Re-Imagine the Verse of Phillis Wheatley Peters*, Danielle Legros Georges and Artress Bethany White turn to the promise and significance of Wheatley, thus shattering some of the myths about the poet's influence well beyond her time, and also allowing us to envision strategies for overcoming corresponding oppressions through the extension of creative voices that interpret her poetry for a new generation. "An acclaimed writer and political actor in her lifetime, Wheatley would not live to see herself as an inspiration for an immense number of scholarly, literary and creative texts. . . . Many, however call her and claim her as *sister* and *ancestor*" (xx). And, of course, perhaps one of the most significant works of poetic scholarship that binds the centuries of Wheatleyan works is that of the eminent writer, poet, and scholar Honorée Jeffers, who found a path to Wheatley through her intensive years of research and her poetic artistry that not only honored the legacy of Phillis Wheatley but took time to say her full name—"Phillis Wheatley Peters." Jeffers's correct recording of a fuller picture of the eighteenth-century poet's life opens our historical lens throughout the centuries.

2 Wheatley charges her readers, "Remember, Christians, Negroes black as Cain / May be refined, and join the angelic train" (lines 7–9). She goes on to reveal the problem of "race" as a determining factor in the dehumanization of people: "Some view our sable race with scornful eye— / 'Their color is a diabolic dye.'" (lines 5–6).

3 In "To the Right Honourable William, Earl of Dartmouth," Wheatley pronounces the value of her own life and laments the tragic consequences of the transatlantic slave trade and its crimes against humanity: "I, young in life, by seeming cruel fate / Was snatched from Afric's fancied happy seat: / . . . from a father seized his babe beloved" (lines 25–29).

In "On Imagination" Wheatley described imagination as she "whose silken fetters all the senses bind, / And soft captivity involves the mind" (lines 12–13). This capturing of her senses allowed her to "grapst the mighty whole [of the universe and] / . . . with new worlds amaze the unbounded soul" (21–22). This powerful "force" (line 13) was inspired by both the secular and the sacred; the calling of the work of the Word unbound her soul.

4 In Katherine Clay Bassard's *Spiritual Interrogations*, she addresses the paradoxical nature of the concept of survival as it intersects with the enslavement of African people. That is, "the survival of African peoples who crossed on the Middle Passage, a survival mandated by the enslavers, became not an 'event' to be celebrated but, in the dialectic imposed by this discourse, yet another mark of African inferiority and thus 'proof' of their enslavability" (36).

Tara Bynum unpacks or, perhaps more aptly, releases a heretofore understudied view of Wheatley that speaks to the contemporary quests for "Black Girl and Black Boy Joy" as embodied in the eighteenth-century poet. Thus Bynum rejects the overconsumption of Black suffering as the only signifier of Black authenticity, instead inviting us to consider, as I see it, a repoliticization of the politics of the enslaved Black Christian's faith as imparting not only an ethereal but also a material and quantifiable existence inhabited with joy. As Bynum suggests, "Wheatley must and does create meaning on her own terms, and these terms are not necessarily consistent or obviously racialized" (56). As such, Wheatley's work invites us as modern readers to unravel not only the political/personal conundrum within a historical context of what it means to own oneself—whether literally, literarily, symbolically, or spiritually—but also to consider how freedom came long before the "legal" document, which could not usurp the divinely sanctioned one. To be sure, Wheatley's concern for physical "legal" freedom of her African people is clear. However, her words also work to invite us into a kind of freedom that was fully liberatory.

5 Cassander Smith argues that "Wheatley employs spiritual rhetoric to build a persona of respectability. In her charge to Harvard students in her poem 'To the University of Cambridge in New-England,' she embraces stereotypes about the absence of virtue in Black Africans to derive spiritual authority and exhibit what Antonio Bly has called 'sass.' She is able to 'rebuke without necessarily appearing rebuking' in her censure of students. Also, there is a certain tension in the poem as the speaker marks both her similarity with and difference from her audience" (98).

6 John Charles Shields's 1978 University of Tennessee doctoral dissertation *Phillis Wheatley's Poetics of Ascent*, the groundbreaking work represented in Shields's 2011 *New Essays on Phillis Wheatley* (including essays by Babacar M'Baye, Phillip M. Richards, Eric D. Lamore, and Tome O. McCulley) and Vincent Caretta's 2011 *Phillis Wheatley: Biography of a Genius in Bondage* are evidence of the extensive range of scholarly work that includes the poet's attention to slavery. Keith Byerman's 2019 "Talking Back: Phillis Wheatley, Race, and Religion" "contend[s] . . . it is through her verses and other writings on spiritual matters that we can see her engagement, implicitly and explicitly, with issues of race. Like the creators of the spirituals and many of the slave narratives, she uses her faith as an alternative source of sustenance, identity, and authority in a society that refused to acknowledge her fundamental humanity" (1). His is among more recent scholarship that engages with what I've referred to in this study as the repoliticization of the spiritual.

7 On March 2, 1807, statute II, chapter 22 provided "an act to prohibit the importation of slaves into any port or place within the jurisdiction of the United States" (https://www.history.com/this-day-in-history/march-2/congress-abolishes-the-african-slave-trade). More than a half century after the trade ended, on December 6, 1865, the Thirteenth Amendment was ratified, legally abolishing slavery, although the practice perhaps continued even later if one considers those Native American tribes not within U.S. territory that abolished slavery in June 1866.

The phrase the "audacity of hope" was first publically shared in Barack Obama's 2004 speech and later repeated in his 2007 book *The Audacity of Hope: Thoughts on Reclaiming the American Dream*. The dream that Obama hoped to reclaim was ironically the very one that Wheatley hoped to implant, during an era when America was yet a British colony.

8 For a more in-depth analysis of Wheatley's "Niobe" poem in this context of the repoliticization of the spiritual, see Langley 57–96.

9 Some examples are on the *USA Today* site: https://www.usatoday.com/story/news/nation/2019/08/13/devon-bailey-shooting-colorado-family-investigation-police-shooting/2003519001/?utm_source=dlvr.it&utm_medium=twitter.

10 These lyrics are from the iconic Billie Holiday song "Strange Fruit." Song writer Abel Meeropol is said to have been inspired by a

photograph he saw of a lynching. Holiday, like Wheatley, brings a passion and emotion to the words that resonate through and to those who have shared experiences of such terror and horrors as slavery and lynching in America.

11 With regard to the symbolic power of images, Justin Hansford observed of Michael Brown's body: "It was symbolic. His body was laid out for display, and that was meant to intimidate and to show the community that this could be you next if you are in any way unsubmissive to our state violence and intimidation. And that outraged people. People came out in their thousands, by word of mouth, because they decided on their own that enough was enough." Conversely, Mamie Till, the mother of Emmet Till, purposely requested an open casket because she wanted to display the injustice and horror of state violence and intimidation—to show the world the cruel and barbaric nature of racism in America, the lengths to which hearts had, in Wheatley's terms, been "steel'd and by no misery moved."

12 Wheatley, described as a "poor naked child . . . of slender frame and evidently suffering from change of climate," was selected for purchase by Susanna Wheatley "because of 'the humble and modest demeanor and the interesting features of the little stranger'" (Caretta 14).

13 Significantly, Tara Bynum observes, "Wheatley writes letters (and about twenty-three or so are still extant) to many well-known and lesser-known men and women: namely, the Countess of Huntingdon, popular Newport minister Rev. Samuel Hopkins, John Thornton, and her friend Obour Tanner" (46).

14 Meredith Scroggin's March 28, 2016, online *Odyssey* piece describes this twenty-first-century social activist as having a somewhat Wheatleyesque demeanor: "Garza held herself as soft-spoken, passionate, but not loud, not preachy, and the ultimate message she promoted was one of love" (https://www.theodysseyonline.com/lives-matter-others).

15 Ironically, Patrisse Cullors's book *When They Call You a Terrorist: A Black Lives Matter Memoir* is described as a "poetic memoir" that underscores the legacy and the powerful import of multi-mixed-genre literature extending from Wheatley through contemporary writers (https://patrissecullors.com/about/).

16 Ayọ Tometi, one of three co-founders of Black Lives Matter, is "currently at the helm of the country's leading black organization

for immigrant rights, the Black Alliance for Just Immigration (BAJI). Founded in 2006, BAJI is a national organization that educates and advocates to further immigrant rights and racial justice together with African-American, Afro-Latino, African and Caribbean immigrant communities. As the executive director at BAJI, Tometi collaborates with staff and communities in Los Angeles, Phoenix, New York, Oakland, Washington, DC and communities throughout the southern states. The organization's most recent campaign helped win family reunification visas for Haitians displaced by the 2010 earthquake. BAJI is an award-winning institution with recognition by leading institutions across the country. A transnational feminist, Tometi supports and helps shape the strategic work of Pan African Network in Defense of Migrant Rights, and the Black Immigration Network international and national formations respectively, dedicated to people of African descent" (https://www.ted.com/speakers/opal_tometi).

17 "Black Lives Matter Profile: Opal Tometi," July 1, 2016, http://www.blacklivesmatterexposed.com/black-lives-matter-profile-opal-tometi/ (URL unavailable).

18 Locating a related model of Wheatley's mapping of recovery, Reginald A. Wilburn argues that "Wheatley's *Poems* inaugurated [a] tradition . . . [that] now provides contemporary readers a foretaste of the subversive rhetorical strategies available to early African American writers seeking fugitive routes of racial uplift by remastering the English language" (93).

19 I am indebted to Katherine Clay Bassard's inaugural and groundbreaking contribution to the analysis of this poem and in particular its relation to Wheatley's "diaspora subjectivity" and how she maps a recovery of her multiple selves ("Diaspora Subjectivity and Transatlantic Crossings: Phillis Wheatley's Poetics of Recovery," in *Spiritual Interrogations*, 28–57). Bassard's work in this area has enabled analysis such as mine through opening the lenses of so many interpretations and vistas from which to interpret Wheatley's words, and particularly how the spiritual was always political.

20 Admitting such "literary conventional, material, and economic answers [as] the popularity of the funeral poems in the 'elegy making age' of colonial America . . . [her] need for patronage from white benefactors . . . increased 'demand' for her elegiac verse" in response

to the question of why "Wheatley returned to [the elegiac] form so often," Bassard argues for other, equally compelling reasons why Wheatley "'invests' so heavily in [this] form" (59). That is, "*Poems* . . . bears . . . traces of the poet's active struggle with the discourses of Puritan theology and literary convention" (*Spiritual Interrogations* 58). Necessarily, this "struggle . . . demands the 're-accentuation' of the elegiac genre . . . [b]y inscribing . . . her own African American female subjectivity" (58).

21 I concur with Joanna Brooks's observation that Wheatley "was able to demonstrate her own capacity for emotional work, contesting racist eighteenth-century notions of African Americans as a people constitutionally incapable of ascertaining certain forms of a feeling—a people whose 'griefs,' as Thomas Jefferson writes, were 'transient,' a people who were categorically 'impassive' or 'dispirited'" ("Our Phillis, Ourselves" 15).

22 Brooks reads Wheatley's "'To a Lady and Her Children, on the Death of Her Son and Their Brother," which "describes familial separation in terms of ocean passage," as one of many "elegies [that] consistently mobilize images . . . deeply evocative of her own experience of enslavement, such as familial separations, bereaved parents, and ocean transits" as a means to "capitalize on this discourse of light and ascent" ("Our Phillis, Ourselves" 15) as displacement through sentimentality of Black women's experiences with White women's tears. She argues that Wheatley's elegies "indulge feelings of self-consciousness, self-regard, and willful passivity . . . [that] allowed white women to evade taking responsibility for their economic privilege—which capitalized on the unfreedom of enslaved men and women" (8).

23 Brooks posits an alternative to Henry Louis Gates Jr.'s well-known "iconic image of Wheatley as an enslaved woman poet subjected to a compulsory examination by eighteen elite white men as the price of her authorization." Instead, Brooks argues that Wheatley "made her groundbreaking career . . . by cultivating an intricate network of relationships among white women. She used elegies that mobilized her own grief and utilized her own canny understanding of the inner lives of white women to build a network of white female supporters; white women, for their part, used Wheatley to perform the emotional

labor of condolence and sympathy for them" ("Our Phillis, Ourselves" 7–8). She also explains that "Wheatley was deeply-connected within white women's coteries of manuscript circulation in New England and Philadelphia. Networks of white and black women also acted as sales agents for Wheatley's published poems in New England" (9).

24 Brooks highlights that Obour Tanner and Wheatley worked together on the promotion and distribution of Wheatley's first book, as did other networks of Black women ("Our Phillis, Ourselves" 8–10).

25 Dani McClain, "As a Black Mother, My Parenting Is Always Political," *The Nation*, March 21, 2019, https://www.thenation.com/article/archive/black-motherhood-family-parenting-dani-mcclain/.

26 Joycelyn Moody argues that early Black women writers "blend the discourses of black nationalism and Christianity to prophesy, in the first person, the annihilation of racists and negrophobes" (29).

27 "Wheatley understands that her life is not without contradiction and paradox. What if we, her twenty-first-century readers, believe her? She can and does love freedom, and she says she cares deeply for Susanna Wheatley. She can mourn her parents and praise her faith. What Reid-Pharr identifies as idiosyncratic is actually a greater concern for something other than a cohesive racial identity" (Bynum 56).

28 In "Remembering Phillis Wheatley," Chernoh Sesay Jr. notes that "Wheatley became a controversial figure among critics that viewed her legacy as insignificant for thinking about modes of twentieth-century racial identity and political activism." However, Sesay's assertions consider how "views of Wheatley [that] have changed [over time] reveal important patterns and changes in how African Americans have unearthed, remembered, rejected, constructed, and forgotten ideas, events, and people of the past."

29 See Wilburn who makes a convincing case for Wheatley as a subversive model of activism: "In an extension of this practice" of speaking in tongues and translating its coded language, "inflecting it with Miltonic resonances[,] aids her politically poetic vocation as a late eighteen century freedom writer" (64). Addressing the transgressive nature of nineteenth-century spirituals by Black women, Rosetta R. Haynes argues, "By shaping remembered experience into a *language of liberation*, [early Black women writers] not only assert the validity of their individual acts of self-empowerment but also gesture toward a broader

cultural transformation that becomes possible as readers seriously engage the *social and political implications* of these acts" (4; my emphasis).

30 See David Waldstreicher's convincing historical arguments on this issue in "Ancients, Moderns, and Africans: Phillis Wheatley and the Politics of Empire and Slavery in the American Revolution." He explains: "Closer attention to Somerset's contemporary Phillis Wheatley suggests a Somerset/Wheatleyan moment in 1772–73: a landmark in the struggle against slavery and a moment of crisis for the American patriots. Wheatley, as much as Somerset or Mansfield or Thomas Jefferson for that matter, exacerbated and made manifest the double meaning, and risks, of the classical and republican revival in the context of slavery. She did this, in part, by re-creating herself through the Greek and Roman classics—as a neoclassical poet—and by making the relationship of the patriots' dilemma to the ancient and modern politics of slavery a key theme of her very public project. She accomplished something politically that perhaps no man could" (709–710). In "The Wheatleyan Moment," Waldstreicher observes that Wheatley's Dartmouth poem "is about understanding that freedom and its opposites are simultaneously material, political, and spiritual, local, national, and human" (526).

See also Avijit Ghosh's blog interview with Ashwani Kumar, "Poetry Is Unannounced Civil Disobedience" (*Times of India*, July 28, 2017, https://timesofindia.indiatimes.com/blogs/Addictions/poetry-is-unannounced-civil-disobedience/). In response to the question of whether "teaching political science, writing poetry . . . is . . . a paradox," Kumar says that he "find[s] none." Instead, he maintains, "Poetry is unannounced civil disobedience or Satyagraha. It is exceptional moment of uprising against the 'power of anyone' . . . speaking truth to the power that is. So, politics is a specific way of poetic life—the power of baring, beginning, and begetting possibilities."

31 With regard to Wheatley and the legacy of the power of literature, religion, and politics, Bassard offers a particularly poignant point: "While on the one hand, it is easy to characterize African American conversion to Christianity as part of an acculturation process that denied them their own cultural distinct subjectivity, it is also easy to see why so many African Americans seized upon this discourse, especially

after the First and Second Great Awakenings made such language so widely acceptable. For individuals socially 'cursed' with a racialized and othered subjectivity, conversion represented one of the few discourses, and certainly the most prominent, holding the promise of a radical change in subjectivity. If one could move 'from sinner to saint,' she/he could also move 'from slave to free,' 'from bondage to freedom.' Thus, conversion functions in early black women's literature both as an event and as process for the revisioning of community" (*Spiritual Interrogations* 23).

32 See Jacqueline Grant's *White Women's Christ and Black Women's Jesus*. In analyzing "the concluding stanzas of 'Thoughts on the WORKS of PROVIDENCE,'" Tara Bynum asserts that "Wheatley understands fully 'the *human* requirement to discern and declare God as Creator and God of love.' Reason's gesture or 'hug' evokes 'an embracing of the yearning for mutuality' and proper discernment" (59). I agree with Bynum that probing the depths of this poet's recovery of reason leads not away from but rather toward humanity.

33 In her February 19, 2015, article "The Quest for Social Justice Goes Mobile," Melissa Jun Rowley notes: "From protests demanding democracy and justice to the rise in citizen journalism and documentation of police encounters, the year 2014 has been a year of mobilized action—mobile being the operative word. In light of civil unrest in politically charged places including Ferguson, Missouri, New York City, Hong Kong, and Mexico, a new genre of platforms and apps designed to bring underreported acts of injustice to the forefront are making their way into the hands of demonstrators across the globe" (https://www.fastcompany.com/3041445/the-quest-for-social-justice-goes-mobile).

34 In Mukhtar Ali Isani's "The Contemporaneous Reception of Phillis Wheatley: Newspaper and Magazine Notices During the Years of Fame, 1765–1774," he provides crucial evidence, culled from late eighteenth-century press reports, that contradicts claims about the significance of Wheatley to colonial America. While the "fame of Phillis Wheatley is often measured in terms of references in the writings of such eminent figures as George Washington, Thomas Jefferson and Benjamin Franklin . . . these are only a part of the evidence. Recognition among the common populace, as evident in

the newspapers and magazines of the time . . . show[s] the reach and the recognition of the poet" (260). This is an important contribution to our understanding of how media can both empower and oppress or impact any expression of the autonomy and agency of its subject—especially a Black woman of letters. As Isani concludes, the "limited space of the colonial newspaper gives significance even to the usual scanty notices of the time. Interest in the unusual colors most American notices, but one can also read a measure of national pride. British reviews, thanks to the country's magazine experience, have greater literary content and are also noteworthy as social documents, for Wheatley is recognized against the background of the British anti-slavery debate and as illustration of the fact that genius is not limited by the accident of a poet's geographic origin. Wheatley was indeed famous in her time—at least in the initial half of her short two-decade poetic career" (266).

35 B. B. Thatcher "borrowed heavily" from the infamous and discredited Margaretta Odell's biography. "Though Thatcher's Memoir is highly derivative, it does incorporate Wheatley's poems into the text in ways that Odell's [arguably discredited] Memoir does not, providing a limited critique of Wheatley's verse and drawing moral lessons from her life" (https://docsouth.unc.edu/neh/thatcher/summary.html). Benjamin Bussey Thatcher was a Bostonian anti-slavery advocate and author who wrote a memoir of Phillis Wheatley. For more information about Thatcher, see https://lawlit.net/lp-2001/thatcher.htm. See also Bassard's *Spiritual Interrogations* for a more extensive discussion of Odell's biography.

36 See "Capturing the Captivity: African Americans Among the Puritans," chapter 2 of Rafia Zafar's *We Wear the Mask*, for a more extensive explanation of this term I borrow here. Zafar observes that "'captivated' blacks like Briton Hammon and John Marrant told the story of their encounters with frightening, godless attackers, torture, and death . . . designed to engage the reader in the narrator's own experience of captivity and/or conversion" (41).

37 Shields's chapter here underscores the colonial British American reaction to the perceived power of imagination (especially for the masses). Shields points to William Duff's "decidedly negative position toward imagination . . . that 'there is . . . great danger of being betrayed into

error, from the unrestrained indulgence of imagination on religious subjects'" (*Phillis Wheatley and the Romantics* 31).

38 Here I borrow from Ida B. Wells Barnett's well-known and often cited phrase from *Southern Horrors: Lynch Law in All Its Phases*. "Nobody in this section of the country believes the old thread-bare lie that Negro men rape white women. If Southern white men are not careful, they will overreach themselves and public sentiment will have a reaction; a conclusion will then be reached which will be very damaging to the moral reputation of their women" (1).

39 Following the work of contemporary Wheatley scholars like Tara Bynum, I concur that eighteenth-century enslaved Christian Black women did indeed experience joy.

40 Wheatley's "transforming scriptures" provide a model for a return or recovery of Black women from those "natal ties" that have been chosen or prescribed for them to ones that they chose for themselves. Wheatley maps a path for a contemporary return of self to self through the very institutions that seem designed to enslave or steal African people from their own identities. "Her profundity and political effectiveness derived not just from her classicism but from its studied inflection of her Africanism—and her womanhood" (Waldtereicher, "Ancients, Moderns, and Africans" 711). As such, the young poet embodies and articulates truths that extend Wheatley's WordsWork and make significant connections between eighteenth-, nineteenth-, twentieth-, and twentieth-first-century political activists, artists, poets, preachers, political writers, readers, and thinkers.

41 In "Phillis Wheatley: The Consensual Blackness of Early African American Writing," Phillip Richards observes that "Wheatley's task of creating social consensus inevitably made her aware of the political implications of her religious language" (265). If, as Richards suggests, "Blacks" like Wheatley "exploit[ed] [existing] ambiguities" and the "oppositional stance . . . [represented in their use of] political languages . . . [appeared] 'oppositional' only to the extent that Whig and Puritan political languages created opposition voices in the broader American polity" (265), Wheatley's repoliticization of the spiritual to advocate for social justice may well prove instructive for contemporary black Christian activists, especially for those who struggle with simultaneously maintaining their faith in the context of social inequities they feel compelled to address.

42 Joanna Brooks's identification and introduction of Wheatley's words among those "African-Americans and Native Americans" whose "literary traditions . . . established a platform for . . . critical interventions into early national formulations of race" (*American Lazarus* 3) underscores the existing saturation of political discourse available for Wheatley's mapping of the repoliticization of religion for then and future generations.

43 While more recent scholarship has tended to move away from dismissing Wheatley's works based on their less than critical analysis of the poet's life and works as necessarily conforming to eighteenth-century generic, historical, and cultural norms (for example, from Thomas Jefferson to Amiri Baraka), there perhaps remain fragments of condescending gestures, especially when it comes to religion—with the most notable exceptions being Bassard and Moody, whose methods and theoretical approaches this study attempts to humbly follow toward this wave of Wheatley scholarship.

44 "TIME'S UP was born out of the need to turn pain into action. In the fall of 2017—as revelations of widespread abuse and misbehavior at the hands of powerful men sparked a global reckoning . . . to prevent abuse and ensure equity for working women . . . female farmworkers from Alianza Nacional de Campesinas provided powerful inspiration with their open letter, which pushed . . . beyond Hollywood . . . to other industries and geographies, representing women of all kinds across race, religion, and economic backgrounds . . . seizing this unprecedented moment and transforming it into meaningful and institutionalized change across culture, companies and laws" (https://www.timesupnow.com/history; URL unavailable).

Chapter 2

1 The scriptural reference is "Come now, and let us *reason* together, saith the Lord: though your sins be as *scarlet*, they shall be as white as snow; though they be red like crimson, they shall be as wool" (Isaiah 1:18, KJV).

2 The issue of colonization was complicated: "Colonization and the abolition of slavery were the two major, and often opposing, positions that Blacks took as solutions to slavery and disenfranchisement. At

one end of the spectrum were the Africans who espoused the armed overthrow of the slave system; at the other end were those who advocated colonization, the emigration of Blacks to areas, especially Africa, outside the United States. Each side had African-American spokespersons who were well-known either locally, nationally, or internationally" (Forbes 211).

3 Richardson appears to be the first scholar to directly name Stewart as the first Black woman political writer.

4 Power-Greene identifies Stewart as one of the "voices of [black] women [that] are noticeably faint" alongside "only a handful of female voices, such as . . . Sarah Mapps Douglass, and Mary Ann Shad Cary" (7). Within this group Stewart is recognized as "a rare exception, lecturing to male audiences and writing letters to the editors of abolitionist newspapers. In the late 1820s and early 1830s black women rarely entered the public arena to challenge slavery, racial prejudice, and colonization because of the 'double burden' of race and sex. . . . Stewart boldly stepped out of the private sphere to express her views when and where she could, from Massachusetts to New York" (56). In "Black Women's Anti-Colonizationist Political Thought" Adam McNeil offers additional voices: "Throughout the antebellum era, Black activist women like Maria Stewart, Sarah Forten, Charlotte Forten, and Harriet Tubman analyzed the weakness of the colonizationist argument."

5 Power-Greene underscores the difference between Black emigration and colonization, of which anti-colonizationists like Stewart were all too aware. Significantly, "many black Americans who embraced emigrationism rejected colonization to Liberia because they believed colonization ideology undermined black Americans' ability to attain citizenship for those who remained. Emigrationism was more than colonization minus white control. The key issue was black agency" (7). Bruce Dorsey characterizes this difference along similar lines: "Black emigration plans unveil the complexity of African American strategies for antislavery, citizenship rights, black nationalism, and familial and community survival" (78). Dorsey's further probing of "why sizeable numbers of white women were peculiarly absent among colonizationists" (78) is important to my argument about early Black women's repoliticization of the spiritual, as he argues that "gender conventions also shaped

the strategies and techniques of colonization reformers, suggesting a more telling reason why white middle-class men greatly outnumbered white women colonizationists. From its inception, colonizationists framed their reform activity within a definitively masculine public arena, giving colonization a gendered that is, masculine character. *Despite its posture as a religious and benevolent organization, the colonization society maintained a political cast to its operations*" (81; my emphasis). Ironically, the February 27, 1833 "Address: Delivered at the African Masonic Hall" provides at least one example of a political narrative of Black masculinity that supports Dorsey's claim that "Northern black men knew they had to fashion a competing vision of manhood to counter the vision of masculinity espoused by white colonizationists. Black activists correctly perceived the conflation of sex, black manhood, and political rights that reared its head in racist anti-abolitionist publications" and buttressed "'amalgamation' threats (subtle or blatant) [which] represented a sexualization of politics designed to maintain political and social inequality" (88).

6 The "term . . . 'religio-political' . . . [may be used] to refer to the complex ways in which this-worldly relations of power, domination and social control are inevitably intertwined with appeals to otherworldly, transcendent or supra-human sources of authority. . . . Even in the contemporary United States—ostensibly founded on a 'clear wall of separation between Church and State,' and yet still committed to the ideals of 'in God we trust' and 'one nation under God'—it is not difficult to see complex intersections between the secular and the spiritual in the construction of a collective national identity" (https://www.encyclopedia.com/environment/encyclopedias-almanacs-transcripts-and-maps/politics-and-religion-overview). See Chidester, *Patterns of Power* for further exploration and understanding of this term. Here, I cite Encyclopedia.com for a brief definition with a short overview: https://www.encyclopedia.com/environment/encyclopedias-almanacs-transcripts-and-maps/politics-and-religion-overview. Recent laws, for example in the state of Tennessee, provide a clear example of the complicated nature of the religio-political. For example, see also Tennessee Code Title 4, State Government § 4-1-407.

7 Citing "anthropologist Paul Radin," Marilyn Richardson refers to this as "a new individuation [and] integration whereby she gave herself

over to a secular ministry of political and religious witness" (Stewart, *Maria W. Stewart* 8). Richardson further observes that "from the start [Stewart's] religious vision and her socio-political agenda were intrinsically bound together, defined by one another" (9).

8 Recall that WordsWork refers to *work* done by these early Black Christian women to layer and infuse the power of the *Word* in ways that addressed the secular and felt needs of a community of Black people, enslaved, freed, and marginalized, for whom religion was hardly an opiate and sought to sanction their God-given and hard-earned human and civil/civic rights. Born out of the influences of such early radical figures of the late eighteenth and early nineteenth centuries as David Walker, Prince Hall, and some of her contemporaries like Mary Prince, Elizabeth Lovejoy Lewis, Jarena Lee, and others, Stewart's linguistic prowess and her expressive voice evinced an intimate acquaintance with and appreciation for the weight of language and the potency of her voice, especially when layered or sampled through divine power and authority. Thus, Stewart's WordsWork served to effect a re-membering and re-collection of that which was lost (*Sankofa*), both in her critique of contemporary apathy and her invocation of African diasporic culturally mediated meanings, which she comingled and interlaced with strict scriptural referents. Thus, "when Stewart inserts biblical verses into her writing, they are not just stylistic flourishes; they are the heart and soul of her message" (Valerie Cooper, qtd. in Waters, *Maria Stewart* 47).

9 Marilyn Richardson observes that "more than an outstanding medical facility, the hospital was at the end of the war, a virtual refugee camp for former slaves and their families . . . as well an industrial school functioning into the 1870s" (Stewart, *Maria W. Stewart* 85).

10 WordsWork is executed through their literary labors, which evince a religio-political aesthetic through their artivism that not only remixes through repoliticization the holy writ, but also recovers, "fetches," and indeed snatches back what was lost from the original source—the Word as God and a god for all people, including Africans and African-descended Black folks.

Alcenet observes: "Today's BLM activists know that Black American lives have existed in a precarious state and under the assault of white supremacy, just as they were during Stewart's time. Like

Stewart, today's generation has returned to a more confrontational style in defending Black humanity."

11 Christina Henderson quotes Peter P. Hinks, *To Awaken My Afflicted Brethren: David Walker and the Problem of Antebellum Slave Resistance* (Pennsylvania State UP, 1997).

12 Sulzener follows Bassard, Moody, and others when she "contend[s] that [Stewart's] most subversive ideas find expression through religious texts and themes," extending the analyses by focusing "specifically [on] those that predict the apocalypse" (1). In this way, she reads Stewart as rhetorically empowered through the apocalyptic, and as such calls her the "foremother of black women's apocalyptic expression" (1).

13 This idea of the simultaneity of sacred with secular speaks to Bassard's observations about "Stewart's use of the prayer genre embedded in the political essay" (*Transforming Scriptures* 64) as well as Willie J. Harrell Jr.'s position that "Stewart's message chimed with echoes of jeremiadic discourse: her critique of social justice; her mourning for her people; and her optimism for a future where democracy in America was selected on a nationalized basis" (314), which captures the sense of what I am suggesting here.

14 This phrase is taken from the title of W.E.B. Du Bois's book *Souls of Black Folk*, an inaugural work that introduces, among other important concepts, the theory of the double consciousness—an acknowledgment of the multiple levels upon which "race" in America has operated within the psyche of African Americans.

15 Kristin Waters observes that Stewart's "speeches and essays, many delivered in the form of the jeremiad, [are] deeply reliant on the exhortation to her audiences to undergo a revolution of spirit and political resolve to counter oppression" (*Maria Stewart* 34).

16 Here Stewart's reference to the lack of compassion and empathy that White women have for their Black "sisters" mirrors Wheatley's reference to the "steel'd . . . soul" of the White slaveholding society of men and women who remained indifferent to the separation of children from their parents, and Lee's recounting of Bishop Richard Allen's lack of empathy for a fellow Black Christian's desire to freely follow God's call to preach. Allen seems to have forgotten his very reason for leaving the White Methodist Church and forming the AME in his chilly response, which is eerily like that of the White women whom

Stewart exposes in her 1832 "Lecture Delivered at Franklin Hall": "But as to women preaching, he [Allen] said that our Discipline knew nothing at all about it that it did not call for women preachers" (Lee 12).

17 Black women were referred to as "girls" or "auntie," never Miss or Mrs., during the slavery and Jim Crow eras.

18 In Joycelyn Moody's words, "Early black holy women autobiographers document their refusal to be silenced or silent. From describing their sacred visions of the resurrected Christ to detailing their secular protests against white supremacy nineteenth-century African American women's life writing claims the right to reconstruct personal and national history from an unorthodox vantage point" (x).

19 Martha S. Jones point to the trajectory of the "the woman question debate . . . in the realm of education . . . in religious circles . . . politics . . . [and] women's leadership in antislavery and other political matters" as well as the belief, current by the end of the 1830s, that "public women were out of bounds" (27). Despite the "emerging opposition . . . that claimed more expansive roles for women in religious and political circles . . . black women" like Stewart "did not stand in precisely the same shoes as their white counterparts. They were the special targets of public disdain as expressed through popular culture" (27).

20 This particular word is of significance because of the dual connotation of emptiness and freedom from responsibility or motive, that which has no useful purpose and yet at the same time can yield dangerous consequences—despite its seeming innocuousness. The power and malevolence of this term is clearly identified in a biblical context as unfruitful, vain, and associated with wastefulness. In a contemporary context, the idea of empty or barren words that carry little or no power (for example, "thoughts and prayers") or actions that are really more like a state of idling than actual creation of progress (such as allies on Facebook or other social media, or pundits who espouse liberal ideals without real substance).

21 Valerie C. Cooper's *Words, Like Fire: Maria Stewart, the Bible, and the Rights of African Americans* analyzes the "deeply theological" and "political" nature of Stewart's words, pointing out that "understanding Stewart's theology deepens and enriches one's understanding of her political thought" (12). Indeed, Cooper argues that there is little to

"differentiate [Stewart's] political or civic speech from preaching . . . as she freely uses the Bible to frame political arguments" (17). At the same time, Cooper claims Stewart as a voice of "ecclesial authority," as a "preacher" alongside "other evangelical preachers of her time . . . like Jarena Lee" (18). "Related to double-consciousness is the notion of 'masking,' in which the radical spiritual mothers sometimes engage as a self-protective device in the presence of those possessing greater power, especially whites, to preserve their own sense of power" (Rosetta Haynes 65).

22 Ethiopianism is a religious and literary tradition that emerged in the late eighteenth century among Africans in British colonies.

23 "Stewart vigorously argues that in at least some areas—political thought, religious preaching, and social activism—gender distinctions are not just misplaced but are contrary to God's wishes for the world" (Waters, *Maria W. Stewart* 42).

24 Kristin Waters identifies David Walker as "another major source of intellectual fodder for her ready mind" in addition to Stewart's late husband James, who was "a transformative source of knowledge for [Stewart's] intellectual and political understanding" (*Maria W. Stewart* 82). Both Stewart and Jarena Lee share a history of a mentor relationship with a male Black activist.

25 Stewart's erudition is evident in her 1832 lecture at the African American Female Intelligence Society, as is her advocacy on behalf of education, to say nothing of her masterful rhetorical writing style, despite having no formal education and her early history as a domestic servant. To be sure, the well-read Stewart was at the very least an autodidact, whose precise and rigorous analyses, secular and sacred, recommend her to a community of "collegiate" nineteenth-century Black women like Anna Julia Cooper.

26 Dionte Williams of St. John's University provides a clear explanation and recounting of the history and use of this phrase: "The quote ['reclaiming my time'] came to be during a committee hearing at the White House where Representative Maxine Waters confronted the United States Secretary of the Treasury, Steve Mnuchin, over his nonresponsive and evasive behavior regarding a letter about Donald Trump's ties to Russian banks. Mnuchin appeared to stall Waters, which prompted [her] to give her latest quote. Protocol in the House

of Representatives allows for one to reclaim his/her time when one representative is being elusive. Waters kept repeating the chant/ phrase 'reclaiming my time' to get Mnuchin to answer the question" and to restore order to the committee meeting. "'Reclaiming my time' has since become a call to action for one to self-reflect on their own worth and time to configure the matters that are important" (*Odyssey Online*, August 22, 2017, https://www.theodysseyonline.com/reclaiming-time).

27 Stewart's *Meditations* demonstrate conventional meanings of the word: "profound spiritual or religious reflection or contemplation . . . [and] continuous application of the mind to the contemplation of a particular religious text, truth, mystery, or object . . . which is designed to guide the reader or hearer in meditation . . . a discursive treatment of or series of reflections upon a subject. . . . A discourse, written or spoken, in which a subject (usually religious) is treated in a meditative manner" (*OED Online*, June 2019, www.oed.com/view/Entry/115756).

Carla L. Peterson observes alignment between the metaphysical and physical aspects of Stewart's work, pointing to her "contemplation of that which lies beyond earthly life, the desire for death, awe in fact of an unknown future, fear of damnation, and devotion to, and trust in God" that accompanied a political sermonizing (61). Additionally, Peterson analyzes Stewart's *Meditations* as the perspective of one who has "adopted the person of Jeremiah, shaping her text into a kind of a jeremiad, a genre that . . . provided the mover structure of her more politically oriented writings and speeches . . . particularly pronounced . . . when Jeremiah's speech is reproduced as her own without quotation marks . . . [engaging in] 'voice merging,' a discursive technique that . . . reli[es] on the words of other well-known speakers . . . to create a more authoritative identity" (62–63). For the purposes of my reading of the *Meditations* as well as the connections I make between these early women's works and contemporary Black women's social justice advocacy work, Peterson's concept of these merging voices, which permit a move from merely restating the problem to offering solutions—"the movement from mean to ends, from sin to redemption, from the present condition of black degradation to a future state of social equality" (66)—matters significantly.

It is also instructive to consider Stewart's work as part of a stream of philosophical thought that includes (but is not limited to) White European philosophers and thinkers such as Michel de Montaigne, René Descartes, and Friedrich Nietzsche.

Importantly, while my reading of "methinks" moves in a different but connected way to Bassard's, I am indebted here to her very cogent capture of the dialogic power of the "interrogative nature" of Stewart's invocation of "methought" and its "conferral of personhood denied by larger social constructions of African American and female subjectivity" (*Spiritual Interrogations* 3–4).

28 I am thankful to Pascale Perraudin for conversations with her about the significance of the experiential with the meditative writing and philosophical.

29 In the introduction to *Religion and the Pure Principles of Morality, the Sure Foundation on Which We Must Build*, Stewart opens by invoking muses drawn from "the meditations of [Stewart's] heart as far as [Stewart's] imagination led" (4). It is also significant that in the introduction to the *Meditations*, Stewart announces that her "soul became filled with holy meditation and *sublime* ideas" (*Productions of Mrs. Maria W. Stewart* 23).

30 Matthew 5:4, Matthew 9:22. Jesus's promise and fulfillment to comfort and care for the "lowly."

31 Eva Tetterborn notes: "Beyond an assessment of what it means to mourn or to be melancholic according to traditional western classifications, it is crucial to explore the extent to which antebellum African Americans were allowed access to such emotional expressions and how antebellum realities have left an imprint on twentieth-century African American literature. When we theorize the emotional economy of slavery, we can see how twentieth-century African American literature has portrayed literary black melancholia as a productive and effective form of resistance to racist oppression. African American literature often uses black melancholia to comment on the antebellum status of the African American slave or on the contemporary status of the African American self" (103).

See also *The Black Aesthetic Unbound*. In this book I argue: "Mourning/Mooring signifies a range of figurative and literal expression used to describe the dilemma posed by inescapable cycles of conflict and accord. As a symbol, the metaphor of mourning/mooring captures the phenomenon of an imagined but nonetheless real state of lost African consciousness. Further, mourning/mooring suggests the deep sense of loss that pervades African consciousness in its attempts to reconnect with African ways of knowing, or the traditional systems of knowledge based on African worldviews that cohere and transform over time and space. Indeed, from displaced African to disenfranchised and marginalized Afro-British American, the Black writers in this study underscore the point that their New World survival depends on successfully utilizing and adhering to nearly every aspect of their mourned African and non-African worldviews—fragmented or not—as these shards provide valuable tools with which to endure" (18).

32 While tenets of Afrofuturism strictly speaking imagine power through a "post-apocalyptic" lens that inures an afterworld of black empowerment, I argue for Stewart as engaging ante- and postbellum eras as simultaneously Afrofuturistic and apocalyptic, in a similar vein to Brittany Sulzener's analyses: "Stewart combines her future looking, apocalyptic orientation with a call for social reform. Her apocalyptic discourse plumbs the tension between apocalypse, the remade post-apocalyptic world she conceptualizes, and the present world in which she offers instructions for social reform that has the potential to remake the nation. America, according to Stewart, should not be memorialized, reified, or celebrated as the pinnacle of democracy. Rather, it must be destroyed entirely or so transformed that the new creation surfacing from the chaos bears little resemblance to the everyday apocalyptic of black women's lives in the nineteenth century" (6).

33 In her biographical sketch that prefaces her *Meditations* we learn "her husband had been a gentleman of wealth, and left her amply provided for; but the executors literally robbed and cheated her out of every cent; so she was left entirely alone in the world—without mother, father, sister, or brother—in fact, not a living relative in the world to care for her, and with so much amiability and piety of character that she would have suffered wrong rather than defend her rights" (3).

34 In "Revisiting Justice in the First Four Beatitudes in Matthew (5:3–6) and the Story of the Canaanite Woman (Mt 15:21–28)," Rukundwa and Van Aardeand observe: "It is quite probable that after seeing the devastated condition of the crowds, which neither the Roman regime nor the religious leaders were responding to, Jesus was forced to act and to create a space for them to speak" (929). Rukundwa and Van Aardeand highlight the obvious, that the original meaning of this scripture was political at its origins, and I've been trying to assert that Stewart's use of it repoliticizes it within specific historical antebellum Black nationalist contexts, which remain relevant and useful as tools to challenge contemporary alt right/nationalist movements that rely on biblical scripture to defend anti-Black violence and justify oppression and violence against underrepresented and oppressed peoples, specifically Black and Brown women's bodies—across the spectrum.

35 Barbara Baert highlights the generally accepted view of the provocative nature of the woman's actions: "The story of the haemorrhaging woman or Haemorrhoissa (Mark 5:24–34) occupies a special place among the miracle healings described in the Bible. Unusually, the healing occurs through a touch initiated by the sick person, a woman who has been bleeding for twelve years. In the exegetic literature, it is commonly argued that her touching of Christ was beyond the bounds of propriety. Moreover, it is considered to be a charged gesture, as Jesus senses that the woman's touch has sucked power from him" (11).

Of particular relevance to this scripture for considering how Stewart's meditation might provide a map for symbolic and literal recovery of Black women is the significance that Demasure accords touch: "At the beginning of the narrative, the woman is nameless, which reduces her identity to her illness, but after she is healed Jesus calls her 'daughter,' which implies that a personal relationship has been established. This changes her identity dramatically. Touch is subsequently placed within the framework of a personal relationship, which comes through her faithful touch. The text states that the woman felt that she was healed and that Jesus, the healer himself, is not untouched in the process; he felt that the power has gone forth from him. However, it is noteworthy that Jesus has not become impure by her touch" (75). Demasure's analysis of meaning in the scriptural connotation of touch addresses some of the implications for repoliticization of the Word. That is, touch can be diversely interpreted and with very different consequences: "Touch brings forth a discourse on power, on closeness and distance, on both the respect of boundaries and the transgression thereof. Philosophy seems to indicate that touch is gendered and belongs to women. However, it is dangerous to think this way because this discourse can easily lead to discrimination. (Female) touch would only provide knowledge that is less important than the knowledge that (male) sight and word can bring. In fact, the *noli me tangere* has brought about the interdiction for women to touch sacred objects, to bring communion to sick people, and to preach and baptize. . . . This discrimination *cannot* rely on the biblical texts; the women in the stories have *not been punished for seeking to touch*" (80; my emphasis). See also Baert, Kusters, and Sidgwick. E.

36 Although Bassard's analysis of Frances Harper's biblical poems intends to show that she "exceeds the desire to appropriate the bible for political ends" (*Transforming Scriptures* 45), Bassard's attention to Harper's "undoing of racial hermeneutics," the "transgress[ion] [of] boundaries of gender" (45) provides instructive and intertextual connections between Harper's "The Syrophoenician Woman" and "Saved by Faith" (45). See also Myers.

37 Matthew 9:22: "But Jesus turned him about, and when he saw her, he said, Daughter, be of good comfort; thy faith hath made thee whole. And the woman was made whole from that hour."

38 Numerous scholars, following Evelyn Brooks Higginbotham's inaugural work, *Righteous Discontent*, have complicated a historically and politically oversimplified view of nineteenth-century Black women's writing of respectability. See Cooper, *Beyond Respectability*; April R. Haynes; Stover; and White. Allissa V. Richardson also provides yet another, more contemporary, lens on dissemblance from the perspective of twenty-first-century activists, with surprising diversity on a number of critical entry points. Recently, Brittany Sulzener argues that while Stewart's messages to Black women are "in line with domestic and uplift ideologies . . . [she] complicates this reading by suggesting the importance of black women outside their homes. Stewart figures a new community led by black women as business owners, investors, and activists, but suggests that this vision cannot be realized through an affect of meekness and submission" (4).

39 Genesis 37:25. See also Samuel Sewall's *The Selling of Joseph* as a potential cultural and literary influence for Stewart.

40 "There is a balm in Gilead / To make the wounded whole; / There is a balm in Gilead / To heal the sin sick soul."

41 Reference to Anna Julia Cooper's words in her 1886 essay "Womanhood: A Vital Element in the Regeneration and Progress of a Race" (63).

42 From co-founder of the United Farm Workers Delores Huerta's response to the defeatist attitudes of Latino leaders, who doubted they could defeat the powerful grower lobbyist, "¡Sí, Se Puede!" to Barack Obama's use of the English translation in his 2008 campaign slogan "Yes, We Can!" to the 2019 rallying cry of immigrant reform protestors, Stewart's words signal a refusal to be conquered even as they adamantly speak truth to power.

43 Importantly, Evans punctuates the point that "Black women theorizing their social position is not a new phenomenon. As early as Phillis Wheatley (1770s), Maria Stewart (1830s), and Frances Harper (1850s), activists have publicly reflected on the meaning and experience of their social standpoints as black women" (10). For an extended analysis and complication of the implications of Collins's standpoint theory for contemporary social justice movements, see Harnois.

Chapter 3

1 Richard Allen (1760–1831) was the founder of the African Methodist Episcopal Church. Ironically, he was the first Black minister ordained in the Methodist Episcopal Church, and it was he, Absalom Jones, and several other Black members of Methodist Church who founded the first Black Protestant denomination in Philadelphia because of the discrimination that Black people experienced in the White church. This would be significant given Allen's initial objections to Lee's preaching based on her gender. See Newman for details about the founding of AME Church and Richard Allen's role.

Robert J. Patterson highlights the irony of Allen's patriarchal response to Lee's calling: "Not only was Allen [Lee's] friend, but he also had founded the AMEC to defy racism and therefore seemed to possess an enlightened perspective about how society had perverted the Bible to support disenfranchisement. Allen, perhaps as a great-grandfather to contemporary black liberation theologians, did not enact a similar hermeneutics of suspicion against the Bible as it pertained to sexism and gender equality" (65).

2 Frederick Knight has found that Lee died in poverty in Philadelphia in the winter of 1864.

3 Lee's memoir was originally published in 1836. That version was revised in 1849.

Margaret Washington underscores the significance of women like Lee in early activism who "became mainsprings in the ultimate success of organized antebellum reform" (417). Importantly, they were "quietly promoting reform through education, temperance, benevolence, literary and church societies, and underground work [and] had an antislavery society fifteen years before Salem" (422). "Since bondage prevented free will, perfectionists opposed slavery. Other manifestations of universal holiness and goodness included combatting all evil, unclean, inhumane behavior including alcoholism, war, imprisonment, tobacco, prostitution, opium addiction, gluttony, capital punishment, and other 'transgressions'" (422). "Women, to save their own souls, condemned slavery and supported elevating Africans Americans, and in 1835 established the Ladies New-York City Anti-Slavery Society with these goals in mind" (422).

4 Citing Jane Donawerth, Bethany Mannon explains that "preachers like Jarena Lee . . . base their rhetorical work in biblical interpretation" (146). Necessarily, "the language of women's rights enters rhetorical theory" in religious contexts rather than textbooks (146). Relatedly, Robert J. Patterson argues that nineteenth-century Black women writers like Lee, using womanist theology, engaged in what he terms "a triple-twined re-appropriation of language, literary convention, and biblical metaphor" (58). Thus, "black women not only inserted themselves in African American (male), women's (white), and American (white male) literary histories. They also conceptualized black women's civil rights in ways that displaced the centrality of the black male subject in African American political and cultural histories" (58).

Sarah Bessey joins these traditions of evangelical women's preaching, faith-based activism, and spiritual autobiography. In *Out of*

Sorts: Making Peace with an Evolving Faith, she affirms that "most of our theology is formed by autobiography" (2). Moreover, modern women's practices indicate a reappearance of the nineteenth-century evangelicalism that Gerson describes as "a faith assured of its social position, confident in its divine calling, welcoming of progress, and hopeful about the future" (5). And perhaps, much like Lee, Stewart, and Wheatley, they engage the political through the spiritual: "The Holy Spirit awakening is exactly that: staying woke. An empowering for a purpose. Awakenings aren't just for our personal benefit but for the benefit of the entire people of God and for the reconciliation and redemption of the world" (172–173).

5 Burrow argues that "what is striking about Lee's statement is how she points out what can happen if care is not taken to insure that the by-laws of the church government and discipline are in harmony with the best in the Christian faith. She is suggesting that sexism may not only be a matter of attitude, but a structural problem as well. This means, of course, that not only would there be a need for converting individuals, but of radically altering church doctrines, creeds, by-laws, etc., if sexism is to be eliminated" (320).

6 Such nineteenth-century early pro-Africentric models are echoed in the mid- to late twentieth-century Black Power Movement, when Black people regularly greeted one with the appellation "brother" or "sister" as a way to rewrite a narrative of pathology within which African American families were constructed.

7 Women were allowed to hold Bible study and women's church meetings as well as exhort, but they were not allowed to preach. Exhorting was an element of preaching that was used to call the people to the convictions of their faith. "Methodists drew a technical distinction between exhorting and preaching. . . . In theory, exhorting consisted of simply telling one's testimony of conversion or relating life experiences in the faith, with the goal of imploring one's listeners toward greater holiness and fuller service. Preaching and exhorting were often used together, so that a preacher's sermon might be followed by an exhortation from someone else. While exhorters could be . . . any Methodist or recognized adherent, man or woman . . . only licensed preachers were supposed to exercise the privilege of taking a text" (Wigger 29).

8 "Holiness was an essential mark of Methodist Theology" (Watson 18). "Most divisions prior to the formation of the FMC were related one way or another to Methodism's original sin of complicity regarding slavery and its own institutional racism" (6). Watson observes that the significance of "holiness" or "seeking sanctification" "often occurred in corporate contexts, particularly in the communal contexts of class meetings, quarterly meetings, and camp meetings. And even when the pursuit of holiness occurred somewhat privately it was almost always prompted by a conversation with another Methodist" (38–39). "Holiness was not merely an abstract doctrine, but was important precisely because it was about the kind of life that is possible in Christ and should be pursued until experienced" (29).

9 I draw upon Rosetta Haynes here, who so aptly observes of the tension between God's call and humanity's attempt to disrupt it, "not only do [women like Lee] perform for God, for whom they must ultimately demonstrate their effectiveness at fulfilling the *calling for which they were chosen*, but they must also perform for those who are critical of them as women daring to transgress the gender boundaries that cut them off from the male" (51). I would add that this "performance" for those other than God took the form of what I refer to as "calling the call." One example can be seen in Haynes's description of "Lee's performance," which executes a preemptive challenge to her authority to preach. "Identifying herself with the reluctant prophet Jonah, Lee further builds her credibility with her audience, whom she thoroughly convinces of her power and authority: 'During the exhortation, God made manifest his power in a manner sufficient to show the world that I was called to labour according to my ability, and the grace given unto me, in the vineyard of the good husbandman'" (44). By asserting that her exhortation is "sufficient to show the world" that her call to preach the gospel is authentic, Lee eloquently claims divine sanction for the public nature of her ministry. She is essentially declaring that "all the world's a stage" for her powerful spiritual performances and that "God Himself has ably groomed His protégé" (52). Further, "as an indicator of their preaching power, the radical spiritual mothers frequently describe the impact they have upon their audiences" (52). Moreover, "the extent to which the radical spiritual mothers can captivate,

inspire, and elicit such responses from their listeners is a gauge by which they can measure their effectiveness as instruments of God. Though they attribute their power to God, and their identities as preaching women are authenticated by Him, their subjectivities are nonetheless partly constituted through their relationship with their audiences; engaged in a dynamic reciprocity, the radical spiritual mothers not only aid their listeners by helping to bring about repentance, conversion, and sanctification, but they are in turn aided through their audiences' corroboration of their power, authority, and identities as authentic spiritual leaders" (53).

10 "Black women must do theology out of their tri-dimensional experience of racism/sexism/classism. To ignore any aspect of this experience is to deny the holistic and integrated reality of Black womanhood. When Black women say that God is on the side of the oppressed, we mean that God is in solidarity with the struggles of those on the underside of humanity, those whose lives are bent and broken from the many levels of assault perpetrated against them" (Grant, "Womanist Theology" 201).

"Black women, because of oppression determined by race and their subjugation as women, make up a disproportionately high percentage of the poor and working classes. However, the fact that Black women are a subjugated group even within the Black community and the White women's community does not meant that they are alone in their oppression within those communities. In the women's community poor White women are discriminated against, and in the Black community, poor Black men are marginalized. This suggests that classism, as well as racism and sexism, has a life of its own. Consequently, simply addressing racism and sexism is inadequate to bring about total liberation. Even though there are dimensions of class which are not directly related to race or sex, classism impacts Black women in a peculiar way which results in the fact that they are most often on the bottom of the social and economic ladder. For Black women doing theology, to ignore classism would mean that their theology is no different from any other bourgeois theology. It would be meaningless to the majority of Black women, who are themselves poor. This means that addressing only issues relevant to middle-class women or Blacks will simply not do. The daily struggles of poor Black women must serve as the gauge for the verification of the claims of womanist theology" (201–202).

"Though Black women's relationship with God preceded their introduction to the Bible, this Bible gave some content to their God-consciousness. The source for Black women's understanding of God has been twofold: first, God's revelation directly to them, and secondly, God's revelation as witnessed in the Bible and as read and heard in the context of their experience" (202).

Grant points to Lee as an example of a Black woman who was "able to appropriate certain themes of the Bible which spoke directly to [her] reality. . . . [She] constantly emphasized the theme of 'Life and Liberty' in her sermons which were always biblically based" (203).

11 "'It's not just men who perpetuate patriarchy,' said [the Reverend Neichelle] Guidry, a 33-year-old black female pastor who currently serves as the Dean of the Chapel at Spelman College. 'You have women who don't believe women should be ordained. Don't believe women should preach. Don't believe women should wear that dress in the pulpit'" (Ryder).

12 Lee's thirty-nine references to "family" in this 1849 full version of *Religious Experience and Journal of Mrs. Jarena Lee, Giving an Account of Her Call to Preach the Gospel* invite a critical examination of the construction of family and intimate relations from her perspective. The families to whom she refers are at once diverse (in terms of race, religion, class, culture, and caste) and provide a range of versions, from religious converts to doctors to murderers (for example, "Sharp killed all his family, except his oldest," 47). These human families provide another way to think about the way we expect narrators to depict family and perhaps invite a probing of what family might mean within the context of slavery in the British colonies during the era of Lee's itinerant preaching.

13 David Proper's excellent biography of poet and activist Lucy Terry—*Lucy Terry Prince—Singer of History*—points to an anecdotal incident (albeit unsubstantiated by archival evidence) in which Terry argued "before the trustees, quoting abundantly text after text from the scriptures in support of her claims for [the] reception" of her son to Williams College. Jupiter Hammon's essay calling for literacy so that enslaved persons can read the Bible and be better Christians is one

covert expression of the political need for literacy within a religious context. For more information about literacy and the education of Black children during the colonial era, see Bly, "In Pursuit of Letters."

14 Lee's reference to Black people getting a "white man to teach them" appears elsewhere in the narrative. Before coming to Ammonsburg, she notes that "slaves [in Niagara] that came [to hear her preach] felt their freedom, began to see the necessity of education, and hired a white man to teach them to read and write among themselves, and have Sabbath schools" (49).

15 Importantly, zero tolerance refers to the way that "Black youth have been dramatically disproportionately suspended and expelled from school since the explosion of so-called zero tolerance policies modeled on the racist 'war on drugs'" (Jones and Hagopian 37–38).

16 In Kathleen McIntosh and Kate Bagley's *Women's Studies in Religion*, they observe in Lee's text a womanist theology that departs (albeit not entirely) from problematic structures of nineteenth-century Christian symbolism of marginalizing oppressed peoples: This type of work was able to "move away from a traditional oppressive Christology with respect to women, to an equalitarian Christology. This kind of equalitarian Christology was operative in Jarena Lee's argument for the right of women to preach" (61) in the passage I cite above. Notably, "while contemporary womanist theology has challenged the space between God's plan and individuals' wills, early African American women writers and activists [like Lee] often foregrounded their rights to be God's agent of truth, power, and social change by claiming their Christian birthright" (61).

17 Rosetta Haynes reads the power of motherhood as she "theorize[s] the concept of radical spiritual motherhood as an empowering subjectivity constructed by nineteenth-century African American" women spiritual autobiographers that is used "to apply to a particular pattern of behavior that draws upon and transforms the conventional roles that were assigned to women" (48). Radical spiritual motherhood allowed women like Lee "to reconceptualize power from a protofeminist perspective in the midst of a rigidly patriarchal culture," thus, "investing these writers with a particular consciousness that informed their use of religion as a tool for critique and transformation" (48). "Radical spiritual motherhood is an expansive conception

of maternity that extends the scope of the biological family to regard all humans as potential recipients of maternal care, both spiritual and material. This care may include spiritual sustenance such as that provided through preaching and prayer or material support such as that given to the poor and the sick" (48).

18 "Beginning in 1818, Lee traveled thousands of miles, preaching a socio-religious liberation theology, and by confronting gender prejudice, a woman's rights theology" (Hartigan-O'Connor and. Materson 422). As one of the spiritual leaders of "an activist denomination, African Methodism [Lee worked with others as they] endorsed abolition, temperance, and the Free Produce Society; convened the first National Black Convention and exposed the American Colonization Society as perpetrators of black degradation through 'demon rum.'" Regrettably, "after Allen's 1831 death, male pressure forced her off the circuit. In response, Lee joined black women spreading socioreligious tenets independently" (422).

19 Both in the 1836 and 1849 versions of her narrative and journal it is clear that Lee "uses a personal conversion story, detailing both Lee's divine call to ministry and the ways she served God through public speech, to argue for women's preaching" (Mannon 7).

20 Significantly, Lee's womanist theologizing engages with more contemporary challenges to a "male image of the divine," highlighting the "equalitarian Christology . . . operative in . . . Lee's argument for the right of women to preach," and by extension "universal salvation" for all people regardless of race as well (Grant, "Womanist Theology" 219). Lee exposes an "ontological issue at stake" that theoretically negates "maleness" and by extension "whiteness" as valid symbols of Christ (219). Hence, "the significance of Christ is not his maleness" or whiteness, but rather his humanity (220). Grant articulates the connection between eighteenth-, nineteenth-, and twenty-first-century politicization of religions: "For Lee, this meant that women could preach; for Sojourner, it meant that women could possibly save the world; for me, it means today, this Christ, found in the experience of Black women, is a Black woman" (220).

In *Black Women Writing Autobiography*, Joanne M. Braxton analyzes the implications of religion for the nineteenth-century Black woman narrators of the slave narrative, and especially the spiritual autobiography. She suggests that for Black women like Lee, writing is a form of "personal" and "political" "power." This "power with God [that] is expressed in dreams, premonitions, and visions," as Braxton defines it, invites critical considerations about the implications of Lee's repoliticization of religion to impact social justice for "others" (enslaved and free Black men and women), but also to regain ownership of her narrative and her life, and significantly her simultaneous dedication to her faith and calling. "These narratives of vision and power [are] an important 'type' among early spiritual autobiographies" (50).

21 Similarly, Bassard argues that "Lee's stunning authority over her own texts—'written' . . . published . . . and distributed by herself—belies her social position as a poor black woman living in the first half of the nineteenth century" (*Spiritual Interrogations* 87). Part of the problem for scholars had to do with their reliance on "Andrew's editorial decision" to reprint Lee's 1836 (somewhat abbreviated) memoir, to the exclusion of what Bassard argues is a far more substantive edition—the 1849 *Journal* (89).

22 Several points from Caruba's article are worth noting here: "Both the university and the church have important ties to the country's issues with race relations. The Prairie View A&M campus was built upon land that used to be a plantation employing slaves." "'This is our legacy. This is who we are,' said Rev. Linda Connor, an AME itinerant elder based in Austin and organizer of the service. 'The AME church was born out of fighting for justice.'"

23 Specifically, prophetic reading "explores how the idea of prophesying is used to challenge prominent interpretations of the Bible that framed blacks and women in subservient and inferior positions" (Haywood 32). Prophetic works refer to the social activism of early Black preachers like Lee and others.

24 Bassard observes, for example, "in the process of 'giving an account of her call to preach the gospel,' Lee's spiritual 'call' from God is embedded with narratives of race, gender, and class in the psychosocial production of subjectivity" (*Spiritual Interrogations* 92). Importantly, "Lee is [not only] writing at the height of the Second Great Awakening . . . she is writing, as well . . . [during a time when] the African American church was the primary institutional vehicle . . . serving not only as

spiritual center but as schoolhouse, [and] meeting place for political gatherings" (93). "Lee constructs her text on the basis of the African American cultural forms of preaching and the spirituals that themselves deconstruct the opposition between worldly, and otherworldly, political and spiritual" (93).

25 Similarly, Rita Roberts explores the significance of this religious movement and its widespread political consequences for Black people, especially trailblazing women like Lee.

26 I emphasize the words *plant*, *water*, and *increase* to signify my scriptural sampling of 1 Corinthians 3:6–23 to draw a parallel between the significance of the intergenerational value of these early Black Christian women writers as inaugural elements in the development of social justice movements that were undergirded by the power of God as a "master builder" who lays a foundation upon which a community of equally imperfect and flawed workers continue to build toward the ultimate goal of salvation. This scripture highlights the diversity of influencers and contributions, each of which fulfills a necessary step in the process: "I have planted, Apollos watered; but God gave the increase / So then neither is he that planteth any thing, neither he that watereth; but God gave the increase / . . . / For we are labourers together with God" (verses 6–9). The works of Lee, Wheatley, and Stewart demonstrated and emulated the power of community and faith toward building a better world for oppressed people—especially Black women.

Chapter 4

1 It is worth noting that while Harper's reinterpretation of biblical texts is outside the scope of my study here, Katherine Bassard has written extensively on the subject. For in-depth analysis, see her *Transforming Scriptures* and *Spiritual Interrogations*—definitive and groundbreaking studies that make the work of this book possible.

2 While I recognize that *braiding* like *WordsWork*, is a term that could quite handily serve as a motif throughout this text—or even, perhaps, has such a complicated history in cultural and literary studies that it might constitute a scholarly work in its entirety—I employ it only briefly here. Explicitly, my employment of the term here is as a

descriptor that can be used to articulate yet another layer of aestheticization of Black women's works. A more exhaustive analysis of "braiding" is outside the scope of this present study. Elsewhere, I have drawn upon symbols of traditions and customs as markers to precisely articulate Black cultural nuances within an aesthetic frame of reference. Notably, in *The Black Aesthetic Unbound*, the term *lappa* is employed to connect the diversity and multiplicity within as a link between continental and diasporic Africa, pointing to the "simultaneity of the oral and written in signifying, in the intersectionality and overlap of the symbolic and the material in the *lappa*, in the identification of the interpretive with the prophetic . . . and in the literal and figurative sojourning of the African women and men not only to themselves . . . but also to their mother's and father's houses" (50). Likewise, WordsWork "entails a complex braiding of multiple and fractured knowledge and interpretive strategies" taking early Black writers like Wheatley and others to and through spaces and "place[s] of rupture, metaphorically, figuratively, physically, psychically, and most of all cautiously" (23).

3 Rosetta Haynes locates two key aspects of liberation theology present in Black women's spiritual autobiography: "humanization . . . possessing the power and opportunity to help shape the world in which we live" and "conscientization," which is "a coming to critical consciousness of one's ability to participate in shaping the world . . . 'a continuing process of new actions (however small) and new reflections and learning'" (Russell, qtd. in Haynes 7).

4 These words are taken from the refrain of Tyler Perry's speech at the 2019 BET Awards, where he was awarded the Ultimate Icon Award.

5 Elsewhere I take up the concept of fabrics within a West African context to connect multiple ways of understanding how Black aesthetics are unbound through language. Advancing a "strategic method for interpretation," I argue for "*palava* [as a] vernacular theory based on a woman-centric vision of literature [that] is governed by the language of the commonplace as signified by the *lappa*, which is a piece of cloth used primarily by women" (Langley 47). Citing "Ogunyemi's description of the fabric . . . [*lappa* is a] simple two or three yards of [versatile] fabric . . . used as a dress, a blanket, a pillow, a curtain or screen, a mattress or sling, a wall decoration, or . . . cushion [to] to

protect the load it carries" (47). WordsWork is similarly adaptive and multifaceted.

6 Stewart's words quote Romans 7:19–25, where Paul grapples with the desire to do good, despite his carnality, and ultimately concludes that the power of Christ will empower him to overcome human impulses and temptation in favor of godly goodness.

7 Levernier validates claims of Wheatley's consciousness of social justice through religion with his convincingly supported argument that she "would have learned much more than mere catechism. From the sermons and tracts that she heard and read, she would have received direct exposure to the latest philosophical and theological thinking on human rights and social contracts. From the clergy she would have also learned that slavery was in essence incompatible with both Christianity and democracy." Drawing upon data from Harry Ploski's 1976 *The Negro Almanac*, which addresses Wheatley's witnessing of "the irony inherent in the actions of American patriots who proclaimed a deep hatred of political oppression and an enduring love for liberty while they themselves held approximately one half of a million Africans in bondage" (33), Levernier's conclusions signal a similar irony inherent and echoed in contemporary twenty-first-century "American patriots" whose actions are diametrically opposed to their words. Bynum evokes a similar argument related to Wheatley's socio-religio-political awareness: "Wheatley prays in the language of a self-affirming spiritual agency in order to minister a *liberatory and love based theology* that evidences Frances Smith Foster's assertion that for Black women, 'the *work of the word* was as much an outreach program as it was a self-creating process'" (79; my emphasis). Truly, WordsWork was a necessary and powerful tool in the repoliticization of the spiritual for the political.

8 Cassander Smith's key argument regarding Wheatley that she uses "assimilation as a core strategy" (78) to attain respectability in transgressive rather than passive or conventional ways is instructive in two ways related to my own arguments. First, Wheatley's use of conventional or normative constructs and tenets is a method to assert her autonomy over oppressive structures like religion. Second, like the politics of respectability, the politics of religion is put at the service of those most victimized and dehumanized by its systemic institutions.

Thus, Wheatley's use of "strategies include poetic and spiritual imitation" (79).

9 "The double knowledge of both self and other creates subjective positions that are useful for analyzing white behavior, especially when powerful others suffer from the one-ness of epistemic ignorance" (Waters, *Maria Stewart* 11).

10 Farah Jasmine Griffin challenges the radical and transgressive appropriation of the term *mercy*, especially as it relates to Wheatley's "On Being Brought from Africa to America." Griffin maintains that although Wheatley "may be said to initiate a Black prophetic tradition in the Americas, speaking truth to power and issuing an admonition . . . in order to be granted a hearing, she must accept the absurd terms presented to her: Africa is pagan, slavery is an act of *mercy*." For Griffin, such is a "major dilemma of the Black artist and intellectual in the West; in order to be heard by those who oppress you, you must first accept the false premise that justifies your oppression. The enslaved understand that their masters assume slavery is justified. At best, the masters think they are acting mercifully; they do not believe themselves to be acting unjustly. They are in the position to grant mercy to their slaves, when, in fact, what the slaves deserve is justice" (20). My reading of Wheatley's "mercy" does precisely the opposite, in that it challenges the very notion that God's mercy has delivered the "pagan" African from "benightedness." The "mercy"—that is, forgiveness bestowed by God—is contingent upon a confession and turning away from sin. Thus, whatever the masters may "think," they who would continue to sin with impunity would neither be in a position to receive mercy nor, as they are human, not God, are they in a position to grant mercy. Recall that those who either reject or stand in the way of others' faith cannot receive mercy. The physical and spiritual atrocities recalled suggest the "suppression of the deadely serpent in it's egg," as Wheatley advises elsewhere. While it may be true to some extent that "humans who have the power to punish," such as slave owners and oppressors who clearly appear to have benefited from such limited capability, Wheatley's WordsWork identifies the power they do not have (29).

11 I loosely rephrase the term "speaking to the empire" in the manner used by Bill Ashcroft, Gareth Griffiths, and Helen Tiffin in their 1989

text, *The Empire Writes Back: Theory and Practice in Post-Colonial Literatures*. In it they consider the way that postcolonial subjects speak or converse primarily with their colonial masters. Here, I argue that while Wheatley speaks to multiple audiences, her primary dialogue is not with the master—or the empire. She also, of equal importance, speaks to concerns and needs beyond that of the oppressor. I argue she speaks through the empire's language in coded ways—using the Word to repoliticize and recover the value of what was lost through slavery and colonization of African and African-descended people.

12 The scriptural reference is to "I am come that they might have life, and that they might have it more abundantly" (John 10:10, KJV).

Chapter 5

1 See Haywood's *Prophesying Daughters* for more detailed analysis of visions and voices that served as confirmations of God's calling upon her life (2–3).

2 Citing Marilyn Richardson, Kristin Waters emphasizes the "two-ness that may become three-ness, a triple-consciousness, an intersectional view that stems both from the race/class/gender oppression experiences by the observer, but also from the vantage points of insights seized from the triply oppressive standpoint" (*Maria Stewart* 11).

3 Lucia Hodgson's observations about the failure of scholars and critics to acknowledge Wheatley as a child are particularly relevant here: "Neither Brooks nor Erkkila considers Wheatley's youth in relation to her rhetorical tactics. Yet in the 1760s and 1770s Wheatley was referred to *and referred to herself* as a 'girl'" (665–666). Hodgson's primary concern here is with how "the scholarly emphasis on Wheatley's womanhood strengthens the case for her agency, but simultaneously elides the strategies that made that agency possible" (666), how "Wheatley's literary child persona . . . [could] speak to her social superiors about family, religion, and politics while mitigating the threat associated with her wronged and enslaved African body" (664). However, I extend Hodgson's thesis to demonstrate a through line of not only the "scholarly adultification" of Wheatley, but also the continuing continuum of cultural "adultification" of young Black girls. Try as she might to insert and announce herself as a girl—in

both her references to her own childhood and her works that address children—the world continues to refer to the eighteenth-century poet as a woman, and as I have observed, I use the terms interchangeably but do so even as I reject such adultification of Black girls.

4 "Beyond a lack of attention to the literary record Wheatley produced about childhood, Wheatley's own childhood has also remained obscure, approached but never fully excavated in biographical writings" (Owens 729). Additionally, Owens observes that the poet's "personal correspondence reveals that, by the age of roughly twenty, Wheatley not only grasped childhood's racial limits, but also the pliancy of its terms" (734).

5 I refer here, of course, to Bassard's construction of Wheatley's elegiac mode as a form of autobiography, pointing to "Bahktin's theorizing that there is 'no clear-cut, essentially necessary dividing line between autobiography and biography' . . . [arguing that] Wheatley's appropriation of an Other's speech from an Other realm was her own metaphorical rendering of her culturally displaced subjectivity" (*Spiritual Interrogations* 83). I also want to extend Bassard's claims about the "value of biography as elegiac (auto) biography . . . a vehicle for [Wheatley's] poetic and prosaic self-expression" and the attendant "religious articulation grounded in social change" (84) to a consideration of the poetic and prosaic assertions and articulations of self in *Blackgirl* as a twenty-first-century connection.

6 "Catholicism was a place, a way for me to gauge how to exist in the world. Inside of this trauma, there was hope" (Burke, qtd. in Segura). While Burke explains that she is no longer Catholic, she remains a Christian, and it is clear in this article and others that faith figures prominently in the work she does—from her 1997 nonprofit organization Just B to her 2007 founding of the Me Too movement to her current advocacy, which extends beyond Me Too.

7 While freethinking is not the focus of this study, I've included this category of Black women here in order to acknowledge their contributions to the spectrum of resistance that links the political with the religious through their a-religious stance. While strictly speaking much work on Black women and spirituality has focused on traditional religious beliefs or practices in such major world religions as Judaism, Islam, and Christianity, the voices of those who deny or

refuse to accept traditional or conventional ways of understanding religion and perhaps its antithesis are important to this discourse. Analise Fonza argues that "black women atheists should be at the table with women who struggle for reproductive rights and with those who fight for religious rights. . . . They too struggle for human rights and in particular for the rights of women to choose not to believe in a god or supernatural ideas" (186). Thus, Fonza maintains that "Black atheist women must be a part of these dialogues and debates on matters related to gender, religion, and human rights" (186). Scholars like Christopher Cameron outline a history of African American secularism from the slavery era through Jim Crow, the Harlem Renaissance, the civil rights and Black Power eras, and contemporary social justice movements. One prevailing argument is that the politics of respectability is deeply embedded in the embracing of conservative values among Black people through traditionally sacred forms of spirituality. Last but not least, my observation here regarding the experiences of Black women outside of the normative frameworks of religion and faith supports tenets of naming, flexibility, and the concept of the coexistence of spiritual and secular worlds that Black women inhabit, despite predominating experiences through Christianity, especially Protestantism, that are privileged in much of the literature by Black women of the eighteenth and nineteenth centuries.

8 Bey maintains: "What theological 'no-bodying' does is deprive a person of the humanity that structures our very being-in-the-world. Our subjectivity is gained, in large part, by our being-in-the-world as embodied humans, so for a theology to abstract us and in many ways devalue our embodiment consequently devalues the core of our subjectivity" (3).

9 In her critique of womanist theology, Monica A. Coleman lists some of the many possibilities in what she terms an already existing "third wave" of "this theological movement" known as womanist theology: "We can identify ourselves as male and female, Christian, Muslim, pagan, new-thought, Buddhist, and Ifa. We can call ourselves academics and activists and ministers, priests, nuns, and iyalorishas [referring to Yoruba Ifa priestesses]. . . . We will be straight, lesbian, and bisexual, faithful and humanist. . . . Some of us may be southerners, Christians,

and members of the NAACP. Others of us may be northerners, Dutch, South Africans, Black Nationalists, or Greens." Those who may confront such issues as "bisexuality, colorism and standards of beauty, eating disorders and obesity, class realities . . . mental health, progressive Christianity, paganism, indigenous spirituality, and participation in other world religions—like Baha'i and Buddhism" (95). Indeed, womanist theology, Alice Walker's term *womanist*, and concepts of Black feminism can be seen in Coleman's catalogue of possibilities as those that are representative of some of the possibilities for Black women in their naming of their spirituality on their own terms.

10 Katherine Clay Bassard, Cedrick May, Joycelyn Moody, and Jennifer Rycenga (among others) have analyzed the intertextual fluidity of spirituality within the politicized voices of Black women like Wheatley. Indeed, these scholars have gone beyond merely suggesting the simultaneously spiritual, political, and personal dimensions of these author's productions. They have shifted our lenses toward a more critical understanding of early Black women's deployment of faith-based knowledge as vital elements in their spiritual mission truths. In short, these scholars have provided us with the necessary tools and lenses through their theories and methodologies to give proper justice to more rigorous and in-depth probing of their words for meaning that matters to and for (from my perspective) Black women. They permit us to derive meaning such that early Black Christian women's writing may direct us to where and when they enter discourses of gender, class, race, sexuality, and social justice.

In particular, attending to their manipulation of the genre of African American written prayers, Bassard articulates the significance of understanding the diversity within Black spiritual writing. Black people were "never a monolithic group of Bible readers, but have, from their first encounters with the text, evidenced a range of Bible-reading practices" (*Transforming Scriptures* 2). It is important to read Black women's religious works as both spiritual and political, particularly the earliest texts, because of what they reveal about the "biblical intertextuality" imbedded in authors' use of signifying scriptures (for example, "the trope of the talking mule") to advance anti-slavery, women's rights, and social equality among free Black and White America.

11 These words are meant to signify on several fronts First, there is the biblical reference from Esther 4:14, KJV: "For if thou altogether holdest thy peace at this time, then shall there enlargement and deliverance arise to the Jews from another place; but thou and thy father's house shall be destroyed: and who knoweth whether thou art come to the kingdom for such a time as this?" Second, there is the reference to each woman positioning herself as the one speaks truth to power precisely at the most crucial time and with regard to the most critical issues facing her people: Wheatley's instructive reminder in "To the University of Cambridge in New-England" when she emphasizes her position as Black instructor to White privileged men: "An Ethiop tells you 'tis your greatest foe" (line 28); Lee's questioning of patriarchal authority: "Why not the woman? seeing he died for her also" (*Religious Experience and Journal* 11); and Stewart's "Who shall go forward and take off the reproach that is cast upon the people of color? Shall it be a woman?" (*Maria W. Stewart* 20). Third and finally, the title of the short autobiographical sketch by the Reverend Debora K. Blanks, AME minister and chaplain, whose sermon "Tell God Where It Hurts" connects words that absolutely matter and reframe political contexts from nineteenth- to twentieth-century oppressive injustices (qtd. in Larue 55).

12 As such, Black women can be interpreted as instruments of the divine who enrich and replenish lands contaminated by race, class, and gender inequity by turning the soil and planting seeds for equality, social justice and, most important, freedom for their sisters and brothers in bondage. Significantly, Bassard notes that "black women's consistent turn to scripture for literary material is an attempt to position themselves as inheritors of the prophetic mantle" (*Transforming Scriptures* 12).

13 From Margaretta Odell's biography, which observes that Wheatley "does not seem to have preserved any remembrance of the place of her nativity, or of her parents, excepting the simple circumstance that her mother poured out water before the sun at his rising—in reference, no doubt, to an ancient African custom."

14 Evie Shockley hypothesizes about the "aptness of this metaphor of Middle Passage" (794), pointing to how African American "poems argue that the Middle Passage was a rupture that has been and continues to be inscribed in multiple discourses informing and shaping

the subject position of African Americans, even into the first decade of the twenty-first century. Any healing to be found in these poems will be produced not through a textually manufactured wholeness, but through a reckoning with the discursive evidence of that rupture" (795).

15 Citing Christen A. Smith, Rosetta Haynes notes: "Liberation theology essentially is an attempt to reconceptualize the Christian faith from the perspective of the poor and oppressed. At heart, it contends that the Christian gospel, the 'good news,' is that God is working—and that God's people should therefore be working—in history to combat and eradicate all forms of oppression and domination, whether social, cultural, political, economic, or spiritual" (7).

16 "Maya Angelou: Of Religion and Rainbows," *Los Angeles Times*, May 17, 1992, https://www.latimes.com/archives/la-xpm-1992-05-17-tv-76-story.html#:~:text=I%20spent%20some%20time%20with,want%20to%20be%20a%20Christian.

17 This interview about Reverend Yolanda Norton's Beyoncé Mass was posted on CBC Radio's *Tapestry* as part of the full program "Spiritual Healing Beyonce Style" on June 15, 2018. Additionally, "Flaws and All" is the title of a Beyoncé song to which Reverend Norton refers, describing it as essential because she interprets Beyoncé's lyrics through the lens of the spiritual—however, the question remains open regarding to whom Beyoncé might be referring—God, her husband, her fans. For Norton, the question is settled.

18 "I will praise thee; for I am fearfully and wonderfully made: marvellous are thy works; and that my soul knoweth right well" (Psalm 139:14, KJV). This scripture not only raises the issue of the value of all human beings, but also asserts that the power gifted therein authorizes resistance.

Conclusion

1 It is worth noting that while "English women's reproductive work took place solely in the domestic economy, African women's reproductive work could, indeed, embody the developing discourses of extraction and forced labor at the heart of England's national design for the colonies. By the eighteenth century, English writers rarely employed

black women's breasts or behavior for anything but concrete evidence of barbarism in Africa" (Morgan 187–188).

2 This refashioning of White women's identity in eighteenth-century America was constructed as a model of education and a normalizing foundation for the American family unit, and marriage was supposed to have tamed the natural impulse to sexual proclivity. Their roles had shifted to that of teachers, stabilizers, and respectable women who were granted limited and relative power based on their legal and social status as wives and mothers. This is not to say that married White women (*femme covert*) were entirely free, as they too were considered, legally speaking, to be under the control of their husbands, based on *coverture* laws. Single White women (*femme soles*) led significantly freer lives because they could enter into legal contracts, own real property, sue in courts, live where they wanted, and work in most occupations, though they too had limitations on the type of work and education they could attain. Moreover, class cannot be overlooked in our consideration of White women's ascending social status. Linda Kerber observes that "Welter's 'cult of true womanhood' was interpreted by Lerner as a vehicle by which middle-class women elevated their own status. 'It is no accident,' Lerner wrote in 1969, 'that the slogan "woman's place is in the home" took on a certain aggressiveness and shrillness precisely at the time when increasing numbers of poorer women left their homes to become factory workers'" (12).

3 Carter G. Woodson's 1925 *Free Negro Heads of Families in the United States in 1830 Together with a Brief Treatment of the Free Negro* exposes another dimension of seventeenth- and eighteenth-century White womanhood that complicates any oversimplified binary with regard to the position of White women in early colonial America. White women of the servant and poorer classes (some of whom were on a par with enslaved Black women) experienced similar retaliatory juridical measures with regard to their progeny. However, such statutes were soon abandoned. For example, a 1681 Maryland law "enacted: That whatsoever free-born women shall intermarry with any slave, shall serve the master of such slave during the life of her husband; and that all the issues of such free-born women, so married, shall be slaves as their fathers were" (vii) was repealed and reduced to the

penalty of a "fine on the master or mistress and on the person joining the parties in marriage" (viii). It is worth noting that the language constructed "divers free-born *English*, or white women [as] always [fulfilling] the satisfaction of their lascivious and lustful desires" (vii). As a result, White women who "co-mingled" with Black men, whether "by the instigation, procurement or connivance of their masters, mistresses, or dames" (viii), were considered for all intents and purposes as de facto Black women. Eventually the law was repealed, as Woodson observes, "to prevent masters from prostituting white women to an economic purpose" (viii). Of course, there were other penalties exacted for the "prevention of that abominable mixture, and the spurious issue" (x), such as fines, imprisonment, indenture, and extension of periods of indenture for White violators and their mulatto children.

4 One indication of the relative power that some White women exercised over Black women can be seen in such seemingly "incidental" facts as John Wheatley's purchase of the young Phillis as a companion for his wife, Harriet Jacob's narration of the oppressive interventions and dominance of Dr. Flint's wife over her life, and of course Frederick Douglass, Olaudah Equiano, and other early Black writers' chronicling of the relative power White women wielded over enslaved people owned by the White men to whom they were married (who owned them). In "Shades of White: Gender, Race, and Slavery in the Caribbean" Cecily Jones explains that "colonial slavery was not exclusively perpetrated by men. European women were also deeply implicated within its structures, both 'at home' and 'out there' in the colonies. Wealthy women made profitable investments in the apparatus of slavery, financing shipbuilding and associated slave trade industries, including the insurance and banking houses that underwrote slavery. Many, of course, owned slaves themselves. Women of the poorer classes also found opportunities for economic and social advancement in the colonies. They farmed small plots of land, ran taverns and shops, and imported consumer goods and labourers for road and bridge building works. They also worked as domestics on plantations and as itinerant traders. Colonialism created opportunities for socioeconomic advance for white women, particularly the unmarried and widowed."

Notably, during the late eighteenth century in colonial America White women often inherited property in the form of human chattel (Dornan). However, while they inherited slaves, they were often not permitted under the life estate statute to free their slaves upon death. "Life estate is an estate whose duration is limited to the life of the party holding it, or to that of some other person. Life interest is a claim or interest in real or personal property, not amounting to ownership, and limited by a term of life, either the lifetime of the person in whom the right is vested or that of another" (*Black's Law Dictionary*, 5th ed., 1979, 833).

See also Cecily Jones, *Engendering Whiteness*. As early as 1993 Hilary McD. Beckles addresses the dearth of scholarly attention to the significance of White women's roles in the enterprise of slavery. "White Women and Slavery in the Caribbean" attends to the gap in studies that overlook the "significance of ideological, social and economic inputs from white women . . . the planter's wife as a socio-economic agent . . . [especially] the white woman as owner of slaves, agricultural lands, and other forms of property" (66–67).

For the most recent scholarship, see Stephanie E. Jones-Rogers's groundbreaking book *They Were Her Property: White Women as Slave Owners in the American South*. As some scholars have observed, it is difficult to ascertain with certainty the extent of White women's slave ownership, or even to gather sufficient statistics. This is due, in part, for poorer classes of White women, to illiteracy and the lack of written documentation. Of course, given that only approximately one-third of White people even owned slaves, the numbers for women would necessarily have been minimal. What is significant is that the race-based system of free labor (chattel slavery) created a gap in power between White and Black women in the antebellum era.

Perhaps a minor point but nonetheless relevant is that a small number of free Black women owned slaves and managed plantations during the nineteenth century. "In the rural Lower South, a few free women of color entered the planter class. Most of them were directly related to whites, of French or Spanish and African heritage (creoles of color) or had at one time cohabited . . . with a white planter. Usually, they had either inherited their land or been given a start by a white benefactor. Yet it took financial ability and business acumen to expand their holdings" (Schweninger 18).

5 "In mid-17th-century Virginia, for instance, statutes stipulated that adult women of color were to be taxed, like all men. However, adult white women were not taxed at all, with attempts to tax indentured white women proving unenforceable. These laws created some of the earliest statutory distinctions among free Virginia women and made race a 'cornerstone' of womanhood. When confusion over the status of free black women arose a couple of decades later, a new law declared that, despite their freedom, they should not 'be admitted to a full fruition of the exemptions and impunities' of English women. The taxes levied on women of color reflected the assumption that, unlike their white counterparts, free women of color were suitable for physically burdensome agricultural labor and occupied a debased position across colonial America. Further non-gender-specific legal disabilities followed in the early eighteenth century, when all free people of color were debarred from serving as witnesses in trials, except for those of slaves" (Snyder).

6 In Genesis 22:13 God asks Abraham to sacrifice his son: "Take now thy son, thine only son Isaac, whom thou lovest, and get thee into the land of Moriah; and offer him there for a burnt offering upon one of the mountains which I will tell thee of." However, just as Abraham is about to comply, the patriarch sees a ram in the bush and sacrifices it instead. "And Abraham lifted up his eyes, and looked, and behold behind him a ram caught in a thicket by his horns: and Abraham went and took the ram and offered the animal up for a burnt offering in the stead of his son" (22:13).

7 I share the view of Bynum in her recovering of Wheatley's joy. That is, I have tried in this study to attend to an "interiority that twenty-first-century readers don't often read onto or into enslaved [indentured or nominally free Black] women" (60) as a way to provide a transitional cross-generational link between the eighteenth and twenty-first centuries.

Works Cited

Alcenat, Westenley. "New Age Activism: Maria W. Stewart and Black Lives Matter." *Black Perspectives*, July 24, 2017, 1–5, https://www.aaihs.org/new-age-activism-maria-w-stewart-and-black-lives-matter.

Amenyedzi, Seyram B., Yosi Apollo Maton, and Marceline L. Yele. *Sankofa: Liberation Theologies of West African Women*. U of Bamberg P, 2023.

Amoloku, OlaOmi M. *The Mammy, the Breeder, and the Race Woman: Storytelling as Subversion in Selected Novels by Contemporary Black Women Writers*. 2019. Middle Tennessee State University, MA thesis.

Andrews, William. *Sisters of the Spirit: Three Black Women's Autobiographies of the Nineteenth Century*. Indiana UP, 1986.

Angelou, Maya. "Still I Rise." *The Complete Collected Poems of Maya Angelou*. Random House, 1994.

Ashcroft, Bill, Gareth Griffiths, and Helen Tiffin. *The Empire Writes Back: Theory and Practice in Post-Colonial Literatures*. 2nd ed. Routledge, 2002.

Badu, Erykah. "On and On." *Baduizm*, 1997.

Baert, Barbara. "Who Touched Me and My Clothes? The Healing of the Woman with the Hemorrhage (Mark 5:24b–34parr) in Medieval Visual Culture." *Annual of the Antwerp Royal Museum*, 2011, 9–51.

Baert, B., Kusters, L., and E. Sidgwick. "An Issue of Blood: The Healing of the Woman with the Hemorrhage (Mark 5:24b–34; Luke 8:42b–48; Matthew 9:19–22) in Early Medieval Visual Culture." *Journal of Religion and Health*, vol. 51, no. 3, 2012, 663–681.

Barnett, Ida B. Wells. *Southern Horrors and Other Writings: The Anti-Lynching Campaign of Ida B. Wells, 1892–1900*. Edited by Jacqueline Jones Royster. Bedford/St. Martin's Press, 1997.

Bassard, Katherine Clay. *Spiritual Interrogations: Culture, Gender, and Community in Early African American Women's Writing*. Princeton UP, 1999.

———. *Transforming Scriptures: African American Women Writers and the Bible*. U of Georgia P, 2010.

Beckles, Hilary McD. "White Women and Slavery in the Caribbean." *History Workshop Journal*, no. 36, Colonial and Post-Colonial History, Autumn 1993, 66–82.

Berlin, Ira. "American Slavery in History and Memory and the Search for Social Justice." *Journal of American History*, vol. 90, no. 4, March 2004, 1251–1268.

———. *Many Thousands Gone: The First Two Centuries of Slavery in North America*. Belknap Press of Harvard UP, 1998.

Bessey, Sarah. *Out of Sorts: Making Peace with an Evolving Faith*. Howard Books, 2015.

Bey, Marquis. "She Had a Name That God Didn't Give Her: Thinking the Body Through Atheistic Black Radical Feminism." *Journal of Feminist Scholarship*, vol. 9, Fall 2018, 1–17, https://digitalcommons.uri.edu/jfs/vol9/iss9/2.

Beyoncé. "Bigger." *The Lion King: The Gift*. Parkwood Entertainment, 2019.

———. "Flaws and All." *B'Day Deluxe Edition*. Parkwood Entertainment, 2007.

Black Lives Matter. "Herstory," July 17, 2017, https://blacklivesmatter.com/about/herstory.

———. "Shifting Culture Through the Joy Experience," March 4, 2024, https://blacklivesmatter.com/shifting-culture-through-the-joy-experience/.

Bly, Antonio. "In Pursuit of Letters: A History of the Bray Schools for Enslaved Children in Colonial Virginia." *History of Education Quarterly*, vol. 51, no. 4, November 2011, 429–459.

———. "'ON *Death's* Domain Intent I Fix My Eyes': Text, Context, and Subtext in Wheatley's Elegies." *Early American Literature*, vol. 53, no. 2, 2018, 317–341.

Boyd, Melba Joyce. *Discarded Legacy: Politics and Poetics in the Life of Frances E. W. Harper, 1825–1911*. Detroit: Wayne State University Press, 1994.

Braxton, Joanne. "Autobiography and African American Women's Literature." *The Cambridge Companion to African American Women's Literature*, edited by Angelyn Mitchell and Danille K. Taylor, Cambridge UP, 2010, 128–149.

———. *Black Women Writing Autobiography: A Tradition Within a Tradition*. Temple UP, 1989.

Brooks, Joanna. *American Lazarus: Religion and the Rise of African-American and Native American Literatures*. Oxford UP, 2003.

———. "Our Phillis, Ourselves." *American Literature*, vol. 82, no. 1, March 2010, 1–28.

Brown, Kathleen M. *Good Wives, Nasty Wenches, and Anxious Patriarchs*. U of North Carolina P, 1996.

Brown, Vincent. "Social Death and Political Life in the Study of Slavery." *American Historical Review*, vol.114, 2009, 1231–1249.

Burke, Tarana. *BBC Newsbeat*, July 9, 2020.

Burnley, Lawrence. "The Movement for Black Lives Has Always Been Spiritual." *Yes Magazine*, June 19, 2020, https://www.yesmagazine.org/opinion/2020/06/19/black-lives-movement-spiritual.

Burrow, Rufus Jr. "Sexism in the Black Community and in the Black Church." *Journal of the Interdenominational Theological Center*, vol. 13, no. 2, 2018, 317–332.

Byerman, Keith. "Talking Back: Phillis Wheatley, Race, and Religion." *Religions*, vol. 10, no. 6, June 25, 2019, 1–8, https://doi.org/10.3390/rel10060401.

Bynum, Tara. *Reading Pleasures: Everyday Black Living in Early America*. U of Illinois P, 2023.

Caretta, Vincent. *Phillis Wheatley: Biography of a Genius in Bondage*. Cambridge UP, 2011.

Carter, J. Kameron. *Race: A Theological Account*. Oxford UP, 2008.

Caruba, Lauren. "Hundreds Attend Waller County Prayer Vigil for Sandra Bland." *Houston Chronicle*, July 26, 2015, https://www.houstonchronicle.com/news/houston-texas/houston/article/Hundreds-attend-Waller-County-prayer-vigil-for-6406926.php.

Chansky, Ricia Anne, editor. *Auto/Biography in the Americas: Relational Lives*. Routledge, 2016.

Chatelain, Marcia, and Kaavya Asoka. "Women and Black Lives Matter: An Interview with Marcia Chatelain." *Dissent Magazine*, Summer 2015, https://www.dissentmagazine.org/article/women-black-lives-matter-interview-marcia-chatelain.

Chepp, Valerie. "Activating Politics with Poetry and Spoken Word." *Contexts*, vol. 15, no. 4, 2016, 42–47.

Chidester, David. *Patterns of Power: Religion and Politics in American Culture*. Prentiss Hall, 1988.

Cobb, W. Montague. "A Short History of Freedmen's Hospital." *Journal of the National Medical Association*, vol. 54, no. 3, 1962, 271–287.

Coleman, Monica A. "Must I Be a Womanist?" *Journal of Feminist Studies in Religion*, vol. 22, no. 1, Spring 2006, 85–96.

Collier-Thomas, Bettye. *Daughters of Thunder: Black Women Preachers and Their Sermons*. Jossey Bass, 1997.

——. *Jesus, Jobs, and Justice: African American Women and Religion*. Alfred A. Knopf, 2010.

Collins, Patricia Hill, and Sirma Bilge. *Intersectionality*. Polity Press, 2016.

Cone, James H. *Black Theology and Black Power: 50th Anniversary Edition*. Orbis Books, 2018.

Cooper, Anna Julia. "Womanhood: A Vital Element in the Regeneration and Progress of a Race." *The Voice of Anna Julia Cooper: Including a Voice from the South and Other Important Essays, Papers, and Letters*, edited by Charles Lemert and Esme Bhan. Rowman and Littlefield, 1998.

Cooper, Brittney C. *Beyond Respectability: The Intellectual Thoughts of Race Women*. U of Illinois P, 2017.

——. *Crunk Feminist Collection*. Feminist Press, 1997.

——. *Eloquent Rage: A Black Feminist Discovers Her Superpower*. St. Martin's *Press*, 2018.

Cooper, Valerie C. *Words, Like Fire: Maria Stewart, the Bible, and the Rights of African Americans*. U of Virginia P, 2011.

Crenshaw, Kimberlé W., Andrea J. Ritchie, Rachel Anspach, Rachel Gilmer, and Luke Harris. "Say Her Name: Resisting Police Brutality Against Black Women," 2015, https://scholarship.law.columbia.edu/faculty_scholarship/3226.

Crunkadelic. "There Is a *Balm* in Wakanda; or, Why Black Joy Matters." The Crunk Feminist Collective, February 22, 2018, http://www.crunkfeministcollective.com/2018/02/22/there-is-a-balm-in-wakanda-or-why-black-joy-matters/.

Cullors, Patrisse. https://www.patrissecullors.com/.

Cullors, Patrisse, and asha bandele. *When They Call You a Terrorist: A Black Lives Matter Memoir*. St. Martin's Griffin, 2020.

Dangarembga, Tsitsi. *Black and Female: Essays*. Graywolf Press, 2023.

Dangerfield, Celnisha L. "Lauryn Hill as Lyricist and Womanist." *Understanding African American Rhetoric: Classical Origins to Contemporary Innovations*, edited by Ronald L. Jackson II and Elaine B. Richardson, Routledge, 2003, 209–222.

Davis, Angela Y. *Freedom Is a Constant Struggle: Ferguson, Palestine, and the Foundations of a Movement*. Haymarket Books, 2016.

Davis, Camea. "Sampling Poetry, Pedagogy, and Protest to Build Methodology: Critical Poetic Inquiry as Culturally Relevant Method." *Qualitative Inquiry*, vol. 27, no. 1, 2021, 114–124.

Demasure, Karlijn. "Healing and the Forbidden Touch: A Reflection on Selected Scripture Stories." *Touch in the Helping Professions*, edited by Martin Rovers, Judith Malette, and Manal Guirguis-Younger. U of Ottawa P, 2017, 69–82.

Dery, Mark. "Black to the Future: Interviews with Samuel R. Delany, Greg Tate, and Tricia Rose." *Flame Wars: The Discourse of Cyberculture*, edited by Mark Dery. Duke UP, 1994, 179–222.

Donawerth, Jane. *Conversational Rhetoric: The Rise and Fall of a Women's Tradition, 1600–1900*. Southern Illinois UP, 2012.

Dornan, Igne. "Masterful Women: Colonial Women Slaveholders in the Urban Low Country." *Journal of American Studies*, vol. 39, no. 3, December 2005, 383–402.

Dorsey, Bruce. "A Gendered History of African Colonization in the Antebellum United States." *Journal of Social History*, vol. 34, no. 1, Autumn 2000, 77–103.

Douglass-Chin, Richard J. *Preacher Woman Sings the Blues: The Autobiographies of Nineteenth-Century African American Evangelists*. U of Missouri P, 2001.

Dunbar, Paul Laurence. *When Malindy Sings*. Musson, 1903.

Escher, Constance K. *She Calls Herself Betsey Stockton: The Illustrated Odyssey of a Princeton Slave*. Kindle ed., Wipf and Stock, 2022.

Evans, Stephanie Y. *Black Women in the Ivory Tower, 1850–1954: An Intellectual History* UP of Florida, 2007.

Everett, D. Anthony. "Changing the World Race Relations. Why Black Lives Matter: A Spiritual View." *Rethink Church: Race Relations, Standing Together for a World Free of Racism*, http://www.rethinkchurch.org/articles/race-relations/why-black-lives-matter-a-spiritual-view.

Fessler, Leah. "How the Leader of Black Lives Matter Defines 'Power.'" Quartz, September 16, 2018, https://qz.com/1391762/black-lives-matter-co-founder-alicia-garzas-definition-of-power/.

Fielder, Brigitte. Presentation at the Society of Early Americanists, Eugene, Oregon, March 1, 2019.

Fonji, Libianca *People*. Apple Music, December 6, 2022.

Fonza, Annalise. "Black Women, Atheist Activism, and Human Rights: Why We Just Cannot Seem to Keep It to Ourselves!" *CrossCurrents*, vol. 63, no. 2, 2013, 185–197. Project MUSE, https://dx.doi.org/10.1353/cro.2013.a783305.

Forbes, Ella. "African-American Resistance to Colonization." *Journal of Black Studies*, vol. 21, no. 2, December 1990, 210–223.

Fox, Regis M. *Resistance Reimagined: Black Women's Critical Thought as Survival.* UP of Florida, 2018.

Frame, Marsha Wiggins, Carmen Braun Williams, and Evelyn L. Green. "Balm in Gilead: Spiritual Dimensions in Counseling African American Women." *Journal of Multicultural Counseling and Development*, vol. 27, October 1999, 182–192.

Francis, Sherese. "The M(n)stry: Phillis Wheatley and Fugitive Imagination." July 22, 2017, https://futuristicallyancient.com/2017/07/22/the-mnstry-phillis-wheatley-and-the-imagination-of-the-enslaved/.

Gandhi, Mohandas. *Autobiography; or, The Story of My Experiments with Truth.* 1927; reprint, Navajivan, 1940.

Garrison, William Lloyd. Preface to *Poems on Miscellaneous Subjects*, by Frances Harper. J. B. Yerrinton and Son, 1854.

Gerson, Michael. "Trump and the Evangelical Temptation." *Atlantic*, April 2018.

Giddings, Paula J. *When and Where I Enter: The Impact of Black Women on Race and Sex in America.* Harper Collins e-Books, 2009.

Gorman, Amanda. *The Hill We Climb: An Inaugural Poem for the Country.* Viking, 2021.

———. "Hymn for the Hurting," May 31, 2022, https://sacompassion.net/poem-hymn-for-the-hurting-by-amanda-gorman/.

Grammer, Elizabeth Elkin. *Some Wild Visions: Autobiographies by Female Itinerant Evangelists in Nineteenth-Century America.* Oxford UP, 2002.

Grant, Jacqueline. *White Women's Christ and Black Women's Jesus: Feminist Christology and Womanist Response*, AAR Academic Series. Scholars Press, 1989.

———. "Womanist Theology: Black Women's Experience as a Source for Doing Theology, with Special Reference to Christology." *Journal of the Interdenominational Theological Center*, vol. 13, no. 2, Spring 1986, 195–212.

Green, TeResa. "A Gendered Spirit: Race, Class, and Sex in the African American Church." *Race, Gender, and Class in American Politics*, vol. 10, no. 1, 2003, 115–128.

Greene-Hayes, Ahmad. "Black Religious Studies, Misogynoir, and the Matter of Breonna Taylor's Death." *Religions*, vol. 12, no. 8, 2021, 1–11.

Greene-Hayes, Ahmad, and Joy James. "Cracking the Codes of Black Power Struggles: Hacking, Hacked, and Black Lives Matter." *The Black Scholar*, vol. 47, no. 3, 2017, 68–78.

Griffin, Farah Jasmine. *Read Until You Understand: The Profound Wisdom of Black Life and Literature*. Norton, 2021.

Halliday, Aria S. *The Black Girlhood Studies Collection*. Women's Press, 2019.

Hardesty, Jared Ross. *Unfreedom: Slavery and Dependence in Eighteenth-Century Boston*. New York UP, 2016.

Harnois, Catherine E. "Race, Gender, and the Black Women's Standpoint." *Sociological Forum*, vol. 25, no. 1, March 2010, 68–85.

Harper, Frances. *A Brighter Coming Day: A Frances Ellen Watkins Harper Reader*. Feminist Press, 1993.

Harrell, Willie J. Jr. "A Call to Political and Social Activism: The Jeremiadic Discourse of Maria Miller Stewart, 1831–1833." *Journal of International Women's Studies*, vol. 9, no. 3, May 2008, 300–319.

Harris, Elisabeth McClanahan. "Conversion and Counter-Memory: Jarena Lee, Maria Stewart, and the Spiritual Motherhood of Mary Magdalene." *Nineteenth-Century American Women Writers and Theologies of the Afterlife*, edited by Elisabeth McClanahan Harris and Emily Hamilton-Honey, Routledge, 2021, 96–110.

Harris, Travis. "Comparing Refocusing and Redefining Hip Hop: An Analysis of Lecrae's Contribution to Hip Hop." *Journal of Hip Hop Studies*, vol. 1, no. 1, Spring 2014, 14–37.

Hartvik, Allen. "Catherine Ferguson: Black Founder of a Sunday School." *Negro History Bulletin*, vol. 59, nos. 1–3, 1996, 5–7, https://aardoc.sites.amherst.edu/Ferguson_1.html.

Hassan, Riffat. "Islamic Hagar and Her Family." *Hagar, Sarah, and Their Children*, edited by Phyllis Trible and Lefty M. Russell. Westminster Knox Press, 2006, 149–167.

Haynes, April R. *Riotous Flesh: Women, Physiology, and the Solitary Vice in Nineteenth-Century America*. U of Chicago P, 2015.

Haynes, Rosetta, R. *Radical Spiritual Motherhood: Autobiography and Empowerment in Nineteenth-Century African American Women*. Louisiana State Press, 2011.

Haywood, Chanta M. *Prophesying Daughters: Black Women Preachers and the Word, 1823–1913*. U of Missouri P, 2003.

Henderson, Christina. "Sympathetic Violence: Maria Stewart's Antebellum Vision of African American Resistance." *MELUS*, vol. 38, no. 4, Winter 2013, 52–75.

Henderson, Mae Gwendolyn. "Speaking in Tongues: Dialogics, Dialectics, and the Black Woman Writer's Literary Tradition." *African American Literary Theory: A Reader*, edited by Winston Napier, New York UP, 2000, 348–368.

Higginbotham, Evelyn Brooks. *Righteous Discontent: The Women's Movement in the Black Baptist Church, 1882–1920*. Harvard UP, 1994.

Hill, Lauryn. "Everything Is Everything." *The Miseducation of Lauryn Hill*. Ruffhouse, 1998.

——. "Final Hour." *The Miseducation of Lauryn Hill*. Ruffhouse, 1998.

——. "Zion." *The Miseducation of Lauryn Hill*. Ruffhouse, 1998.

Hodgson, Lucia. "Infant Muse: Phillis Wheatley and the Revolutionary Rhetoric of Childhood." *Early American Literature*, vol. 49, no. 3, 2014, 663–682.

hooks, bell. *Feminist Theory: From Margin to Center*. South End Press, 1984.

Isani, Mukhtar Ali. "The Contemporaneous Reception of Phillis Wheatley: Newspaper and Magazine Notices During the Years of Fame, 1765–1774." *The Journal of Negro History*, vol. 85, no. 4, Fall 2000, 260–273.

Jeffers, Honorée Fanonne. *The Age of Phillis*, Wesleyan Poetry Series. E-book, Wesleyan UP, 2022.

Jefferson, Thomas. "Query XIV." *Notes on the State of Virginia*. E-book, Digireads.com, 2010.

Jones, Cecily. *Engendering Whiteness: White Women and Colonialism in Barbados and North Carolina, 1627–1865*. Manchester UP, 2007.

——. "Shades of White: Gender, Race, and Slavery in the Caribbean." *Open Democracy*, June 25, 2015, https://www.opendemocracy.net/beyondslavery/cecily-jones/women-and-slavery-in-caribbean-whiteness-and-gilded-cage.

Jones, Denisha, and Jesse Hagopian. *Black Lives Matter at School: An Uprising for Educational Justice*. Haymarket Books, 2020.

Jones, Feminista. *Reclaiming Our Space: How Black Feminists Are Changing the World from the Tweets to the Streets*. Beacon Press, 2019.

Jones, Martha S. *All Bound Up Together: The Woman Question in African American Public Culture, 1830–1900*. U of North Carolina P, 2007.

Jones-Rogers, Stephanie E. *They Were Her Property: White Women as Slave Owners in the American South*. Yale UP, 2019.

Jordan, June. "The Difficult Miracle of Black Poetry in America; or, Something Like a Sonnet for Phillis Wheatley." *The Massachusetts Review*, vol. 27, no. 2, Summer 1986, 252–262.

Jordan, Winthrop. *White over Black: American Attitudes Toward the Negro, 1550–1812*. U of North Carolina P, 2012.

Jørgensen, Anne Mette. "Sankofa and Modern Authenticity in Ghanaian Film and Television." *Same and Other: Negotiating African Identity in Cultural Production*, edited by M. E. Baaz and M. Palmberg. Nordic Africa Institute, 2001, 119–141.

Julion, Wrenetha A. "Black Mothers Are Dying: The Toll of Racism on Maternal Health." *Stat*, January 11, 2018, https://www.statnews.com/2018/01/11/racism-maternal-health-erica-garner/.

Karenga, Maulana. "Black Men and Women Rising: Resurrection After Social Death" *Los Angeles Sentinel*, April 17, 2014.

Kerber, Linda. "Separate Spheres." *Journal of American History*, vol. 75, no. 1, June 1988, 9–39.

Knight, Frederick. "The Many Names for Jarena Lee." *The Pennsylvania Magazine of History and Biography*, vol. 141, no. 1, January 2017, 59–68.

Langley, April. *The Black Aesthetic Unbound: Theorizing the Dilemma of Eighteenth-Century African American Literature*. Ohio State UP, 2008.

Larue, Cleophus G., editor. *This Is My Story: Testimonies and Sermons of Black Women in Ministry*. Westminster John Knox Press 2004.

Lee, Jarena. *Religious Experience and Journal of Mrs. Jarena Lee, Giving an Account of Her Call to Preach the Gospel*. Published for the author, 1849.

Legros Georges, Danielle, and Artress Bethany White, editors. *Wheatley at 250: Black Women Poets Re-Imagine the Verse of Phillis Wheatley Peters*. Pangyrus, 2023.

Levernier, James A. "Phillis Wheatley and the New England Clergy." *Early American Literature*, vol. 26, no. 1, 1991, 21–38.

Lizza, Erica. "Race, Religion, and Black Lives Matter." Berkeley Center for Religion, Peace & World Affairs, April 23, 2018, https://berkleycenter.georgetown.edu/features/race-religion-and-black-lives-matter.

Lorde, Audre. "Winds of Orisha." *The Collected Poems of Audre Lorde*. Norton, 1997, 150–153.

Lucky, Crystal J. Introduction to *A Mysterious Life and Calling: From Slavery to Ministry in South Carolina*, by Charlotte S. Riley, edited by Crystal J. Lucky. U of Wisconsin P, 2016.

Mannon, Bethany. "Xvangelical: The Rhetorical Work of Personal Narratives in Contemporary Religious Discourse." *Rhetorical Society Quarterly*, vol. 49, no. 2, 2019, 1–21. DOI: 10.1080/02773945.2018.1547418.

May, Cedrick. *Evangelism and Resistance in the Black Atlantic, 1760–1835*. U of Georgia P, 2008.

McClain, Dani. "As a Black Mother, My Parenting Is Always Political." *The Nation*, March 21, 2019, 1–17, https://www.thenation.com/article/archive/black-motherhood-family-parenting-dani-mcclain/.

McIntosh, Kathleen, and Kate Bagley, editors. *Women's Studies in Religion: A Multicultural Reader*. Routledge, 2006.

McNeil, Adam. "Black Women's Anti-Colonizationist Political Thought." *Black Perspectives*, February 22, 2019, 1–4, https://www.aaihs.org/black-womens-anti-colonizationist-political-thought/#fnref-50884-1.

Mehlinger, L. R. "The Attitude of the Free Negro Toward African Colonization." *The Journal of Negro History*, vol. 1, no. 3, June 1916, 276–301.

Mercedes. "the cries of our sons." hello—poetry, September 2018, https://hellopoetry.com/tag/blacklivesmatter/.

Milligan, Jazz A. *Historical Sisters: Black Feminist Actions Across History and Literary Studies*. 2022. City University of New York, master's thesis.

Mitchell, Joseph. *The Missionary Pioneer; or, A Brief Memoir of the Life, Labours, and Death of John Stewart, [Man of Colour] Founder, Under God of the Mission Among the Wyandotts at Upper Sandusky, Ohio*. J. C. Totten, 1827.

Moody, Joycelyn. *Sentimental Confessions: Spiritual Narratives of Nineteenth-Century African American Women*. U of Georgia P, 2001.

Morgan, Jennifer L. "'Some Could Suckle over Their Shoulder': Male Travelers, Female Bodies, and the Gendering of Racial Ideology, 1500–1770." *The William and Mary Quarterly*, vol. 54, no. 1, January 1997, 167–192.

Moses, Wilson Jeremiah, editor. *Classical Black Nationalism: From the American Revolution to Marcus Garvey*. New York UP, 1996.

Myers, Ched. *Binding the Strong Man: A Political Reading of Mark's Story of Jesus*. Orbis Books, 2008.

Newman, Richard S. *Freedom's Prophet: Bishop Richard Allen, the AME Church, and the Black Founding Fathers*. New York UP, 2008.

Nordyke, Kimberly, and Allison Crist. "BET Awards: Tyler Perry Delivers Powerful, Uplifting Speech to Sadig Ovatio." *The Hollywood Reporter*, June 23, 2019, https://www.hollywoodreporter.com/news/general-news/tyler-perry-delivers-powerful-uplifting-speech-at-bet-awards-1220521/.

Norman, Anna. "Protest in the Black Lives Matter Movement: An Interview with Activist and Lawyer Justin Hansford." *Open Democracy*, October 2, 2017.

Norton, Yolanda. "'God Delivered': Minister Describes the Healing Power of the Beyoncé Mass." *Tapestry*, CBC Radio, June 15, 2018, https://www.cbc

.ca/radio/tapestry/spiritual-healing-beyonc%C3%A9-style-1.4705154/god-delivered-minister-describes-the-healing-power-of-the-beyonc%C3%A9-mass-1.4705157.

Odell, Margaretta Matilda. *Memoir and Poems of Phillis Wheatley, a Native African and a Slave. Dedicated to the Friends of the Africans*, 1834, Documenting the American South, https://docsouth.unc.edu/neh/wheatley/wheatley.html.

O'Neale, Sondra. "A Slave's Subtle War: Phillis Wheatley's Use of Biblical Myth and Symbol." *Early American Literature*, vol. 21, no. 2, Fall 1986, 144–165.

Owens, Camille S. "'I, Young in Life': Phillis Wheatley and the Invention of American Childhood." *Early American Literature*, vol. 57, no. 3, 2022, 727–749.

Pace, Joel. "Afterthoughts: Romanticism, the Black Atlantic, and Self-Mapping." *Studies in Romanticism*, vol. 56, no. 1, Spring 2017, 113–126.

Patterson, Orlando. *Slavery and Social Death: A Comparative Study*. Harvard UP, 1982.

Patterson, Robert J. "A Triple-Twined Re-appropriation: Womanist Theology and Gendered Racial Protest in the Writings of Jarena Lee, Frances E. W. Harper, and Harriet Jacobs." *Religion & Literature*, vol. 45, no. 2, Summer 2013, 55–82.

Perchard, Tom. "Hip Hop Samples Jazz: Dynamics of Cultural Memory and Musical Tradition in the African American 1990s." *American Music*, vol. 29, no. 3, Fall 2011, 277–307.

Perry, Samuel L., and Andrew L. Whitehead. "Christian America in Black and White: Racial Identity, Religious-National Group Boundaries, and Explanations for Racial Inequality." *Sociology of Religion*, vol. 80, no. 3, 2018, 1–22.

Peterson, Carla L. *"Doers of the Word": African-American Women Speakers and Writers in the North (1830–1880)*. Oxford UP, 1995.

Power-Greene, Ousmane K. *Against Wind and Tide: The African American Struggle Against the Colonization Movement*. New York UP, 2014.

Rael, Patrick. "Black Theodicy: African Americans and Nationalism in the Antebellum North." *North Star*, vol. 3, no. 2, Spring 2000, 1–24.

Ravikumar, Vandana. "De'Von Bailey Was Shot in the Back and Killed by Police, His Family Says. They're Rallying for 'Justice.'" *USA Today*, August 13, 2019, https://www.usatoday.com/story/news/nation/2019/08/13/devon-bailey-shooting-colorado-family-investigation-police-shooting/2003519001/?utm_source=dlvr.it&utm_medium=twitter.

Richards, Phillip M. "Phillis Wheatley and Literary Americanization." *American Quarterly*, vol. 44, no. 2, June 1992, 163–191.

——. "Phillis Wheatley: The Consensual Blackness of Early African American Writing." *New Essays on Phillis Wheatley*, edited by John C. Shields and Eric D. Lamore, U of Tennessee P, 2011, 247–270.

Richardson, Allissa V. "Dismantling Respectability: The Rise of New Womanist Communication Models in the Era of Black Lives Matter." *Journal of Communication*, vol. 69, 2019, 193–213.

Richardson, Marilyn. Foreword to William Andrews, *Sisters of the Spirit: Three Black Women's Autobiographies of the Nineteenth Century*. Indiana UP, 1986.

——. Introduction to Maria Stewart, *Maria W. Stewart, America's First Black Woman Political Writer: Essays and Speeches*, edited by Marilyn Richardson. Indiana UP, 1987, 3–27.

Ritchie, Andrea J. *Invisible No More: Police Violence Against Black Women and Women of Color*. Beacon Press, 2017.

Roberson, Susan. "Maria Stewart and Rhetoric of Mobility." *Journal of International Women's Studies*, vol. 4, no. 3, May 2003, 56–61.

Roberts, Rita. *Evangelicalism and the Politics of Reform in Northern Black Thought, 1776–1863*. Louisiana State UP, 2010.

Roberts, Wendy Raphael. *Awakening Verse: The Poetics of Early American Evangelicalism*. Oxford UP, 2020.

Rukundwa, Lazare S., and Andries G. Van Aarde. "Revisiting Justice in the First Four Beatitudes in Matthew (5:3–6) and the Story of the Canaanite Woman (Mt 15:21–28): A Postcolonial Reading." *HTS: Theological Studies*, vol. 61, no. 3, 2005.

Rycenga, Jennifer. "Maria Stewart, Black Abolitionist, and the Idea of Freedom." *Frontline Feminisms: Women, War, and Resistance*, edited by Marguerite R. Waller and Jennifer Rycenga. Routledge, 2001.

Ryder, Gina. "This Female Black Preacher Wants to Dismantle Religious Patriarchy." *Vice*, June 13, 2018, https://www.vice.com/en_us/article/nekn7g/this-female-black-preacher-wants-to-dismantle-religious-patriarchy.

Sancho, Ignatius. *Letters of the Late Ignatius Sancho, an African. To Which Are Prefixed Memoirs of His Life*. J. Nichols, 1784.

Schlesinger, Arthur M. *The Disuniting of America: Reflections on a Multicultural Society*. Routledge, 1996.

Schweninger, Loren. "Property Owning Free African-American Women in the South, 1800–1870." *Journal of Women's History*, vol. 1, no. 3, Winter 1990.

Segura, Olga M. "Founder Tarana Burke: 'Jesus Was the First Activist I Knew.'" *Sojourners Magazine*, September 24, 2018, 1–3.

Sesay, Chernoh, Jr. "Remembering Phillis Wheatley." *Black Perspectives*, June 26, 2016, https://www.aaihs.org/remembering-phillis-wheatley/.

Sewall, Samuel. *The Selling of Joseph: A Memorial*. Bartholomew Green and John Allen, 1700, http://www.masshist.org/objects/query3.cfm?queryID=57.

Shields, John Charles. *Phillis Wheatley and the Romantics*. U of Tennessee P, 2010.

———. *Phillis Wheatley's Poetics of Ascent*. 1978. University of Tennessee, PhD dissertation.

———. "Phillis Wheatley's Subversion of Classical Stylistics," *Style*, vol. 27, no. 2, Summer 1993, 252–270.

Shields, John Charles, and Eric D. Lamore, editors. *New Essays on Phillis Wheatley*. U of Tennessee P, 2011.

Shockley, Evie. "Going Overboard: African American Poetic Innovation and the Middle Passage." *Contemporary Literature*, vol. 52, no. 4, Winter 2011, 791–817.

Smith, Cassander. *Race and Respectability in an Early Black Atlantic*. Louisiana State Press, 2023.

Smith, Christen A. "Facing the Dragon: Black Mothering, Sequelae, and Gendered Necropolitics in the Americas." *Transforming Anthropology*, vol. 24, no. 1 2016, 31–48.

Smith, Merril D. *Women's Roles in Eighteenth-Century America*. Greenwood Press, 2010.

Snyder Terri L. "Women, Race, and the Law in Early America." *Oxford Research Encyclopedia of American History*, September 2015, DOI: 10.1093/acrefore/9780199329175.013.12.

Soyinka, Wole. "This Past Must Address Its Present," Nobel Lecture, December 8, 1986, https://www.nobelprize.org/prizes/literature/1986/soyinka/lecture/.

Stewart, Maria W. "An Address Delivered at the African Masonic Hall in Boston, Feb. 27, 1833." *The Liberator*, April 27, 1833, 68. America's Historical Newspapers, October 25, 2010.

———. "An Address: Delivered Before the Afric-American Female Intelligence Society of Boston." *The Liberator*, April 28, 1832, 66–67. America's Historical Newspapers, October 25, 2010.

———. "The First Stage of Life Written by Maria W. Stewart, 1803–1879." *Repository of Religion and Literature and of Science and Art*, April 1861, 84–86; July 1861, 140–141; October 1861, 187–188.

——. *Maria W. Stewart, America's First Black Woman Political Writer: Essays and Speeches*. Edited by Marilyn Richardson. Indiana UP, 1987.

——. *Meditations from the Pen of Mrs. Maria W. Stewart*, 1879. A Celebration of Women Writers, https://digital.library.upenn.edu/women/stewart-maria/meditations/meditations.html.

——. *Productions of Mrs. Maria W. Stewart Presented to the First African Baptist Church & Society*. Friends of Freedom and Virtue, 1835, http://digilib.nypl.org/dynaweb/digs/wwm9722/@Generic__BookView. Reprinted in *Spiritual Narratives*, compiled by Sue E. Houchins, Oxford UP, 1988, 1–84.

——. *Religion and the Pure Principles of Morality, the Sure Foundation on Which We Must Build*. 1831. Reprinted in Maria Stewart, *Maria W. Stewart, America's First Black Woman Political Writer: Essays and Speeches*, edited by Marilyn Richardson, 28–42. Indiana UP, 1987.

——. "Why Sit Ye Here and Die?" "Lecture Delivered at the Franklin Hall, Boston, September 21, 1832." Reprinted in Maria Stewart, *Maria W. Stewart, America's First Black Woman Political Writer: Essays and Speeches*, edited by Marilyn Richardson, 45–49. Indiana UP, 1987.

Stover, Johnnie M. *Rhetoric and Resistance in Black Women's Autobiography*. UP of Florida, 2003.

Strout, Carolyn, Sam Park, Dan Lyon, and Monica Rohr. "How Nikole Hannah-Jones' 1619 Project Ignited the Critical Race Theory Backlash." *Chalkbeat*, July 19, 2021, https://tn.chalkbeat.org/2021/7/19/22578764/nikole-hannah-jones-1619-project-ignited-the-critical-race-theory-backlash.

Sulzener, Brittany. "Night of Death, Morning of Rebirth: Maria W. Stewart's Apocalyptic Futures." *Nineteenth-Century Contexts*, 2019. DOI: 10.1080/08905495.2019.1669371.

Taylor, Clarence. *Black Religious Intellectuals: The Fight for Equality from Jim Crow to the 21st Century*. Routledge, 2002.

Ted. "Opal Tometi: Human Rights Activist." https://www.ted.com/speakers/opal_tometi.

Temple, Christel N. "The Emergence of Sankofa Practice in the United States: A Modern History," *Journal of Black Studies*, vol. 41, no. 1, September 2010, 127–150.

Tetterborn, Eva. "Melancholia as Resistance in Contemporary African American Literature." *MELUS*, vol. 31, no. 3, Fall 2006, 101–121.

Thatcher, B. B. *Memoir of Phillis Wheatley, a Native African and a Slave*. Geo W. Light, Lyceum Press, 1834, https://docsouth.unc.edu/neh/thatcher/summary.html.

Truth, Sojourner. "Address to the Equal Rights Association," May 9, 1867. Iowa State University, Archives of Women's Political Communication, https://awpc.cattcenter.iastate.edu/2017/03/21/address-to-the-first-annual-meeting-of-the-american-equal-rights-association-may-9-1867/.

Waldstreicher, David. "Ancients, Moderns, and Africans: Phillis Wheatley and the Politics of Empire and Slavery in the American Revolution." *Journal of the Early Republic*, vol. 37, no. 4, Winter 2017, 701–733.

——. *The Odyssey of Phillis Wheatley*. Macmillan, 2023.

——. "The Wheatleyan Moment." *Early American Studies*, vol. 9, no. 3, 2011, 522–551.

Washington, Margaret. "Religion, Reform, and Antislavery." *The Oxford Handbook of American Women's and Gender History*, edited by Ellen Hartigan-O'Connor and Lisa G. Materson Oxford UP, 2018, 417–442.

Waters, Kristin. "Crying out for Liberty: Maria W. Stewart and David Walker's Black Revolutionary Liberalism." *Philosophia Africana*, vol. 15, no. 1, Winter 2013, 35–60.

——. *Maria W. Stewart and the Roots of Black Political Thought*. UP of Mississippi, 2021.

Waters, Kristin, and Carol B. Conaway, editors. *Black Women's Intellectual Traditions: Speaking Their Minds*. U of Vermont P, 2007.

Watson, Kevin M. *Old or New School Methodism? The Fragmentation of a Theological Tradition*. Oxford UP, 2019.

Wheatley, Phillis. *Complete Writings*. Penguin, 2001.

White, E. Frances. *Dark Continent of Our Bodies: Black Feminism and Politics of Respectability*. Temple UP, 2001.

Wigger, John H. *Taking Heaven by Storm: Methodism and the Rise of Popular Christianity in America*. U of Illinois P, 2001.

Wilburn, Reginald A. *Preaching the Gospel of Black Revolt: Appropriating Milton in Early African American Literature*. Duquesne UP, 2014.

Wimbush, Vincent L. *Scripturalizing the Sacred: The Written as Political*. Routledge, 2015.

Woods, Curtis Anthony. *The Literary Reception of the Spirituality of Phillis Wheatley (1753–1784): An Afrosensitive Reading*. 2018. Southern Baptist Theological Seminary, PhD dissertation.

Woodson, Carter G. *Free Negro Heads of Families in the United States in 1830 Together with a Brief Treatment of the Free Negro*. Association for the Study of Negro Life and History, 1925.

Wright, Nazera Sadiq. "Maria W. Stewart's 'The First Stage of Life': Black Girlhood in the 'Repository of Religion and Literature, and of Science and Art.'" *MELUS*, vol. 40, no. 3, Fall 2015, 150–175.

Zackodnik, Teresa. *Press, Platform, Pulpit: Black Feminist Publics in the Era of Reform*. U of Tennessee P, 2011.

Zafar, Rafia. *We Wear the Mask: African Americans Write American Literature, 1760–1870*. Columbia UP, 1997.

Zyad, Hari. "My Gender Is Black." *Afropunk*, July 12, 2017, https://afropunk.com/2017/07/my-gender-is-black/.

Index